GOD'S PICTURE OF *you*

THE STORY OF YOUR HEALING & WHOLENESS

BRIAN D. FARLEY

First Paperback Edition

Published by Freiling Publishing, a division of Freiling Agency, LLC.

P.O. Box 1264,
Warrenton, VA 20188

www.FreilingPublishing.com

ISBN 978-1-950948-52-9

Printed in the United States of America

CONTENTS

Part 3: God Sees You Complete

ACKNOWLEDGMENTS

Without the loving support of my incredible, beautiful, godly wife, Heather Farley, this book could not have been written, she has been my closest friend, co-laborer, greatest supporter, exercise trainer and confidant for 28 years and I cannot thank her enough for all she does for me.

My sons, Aaron (Hannah) and Andrew bring great joy to me. They are wonderful young men, who we are very proud of. We are also so grateful to Hannah, who does her best to keep Aaron straight. Without these boys, I would not have known the adult perspective on Chuck E. Cheese.

My parents have always been fantastic supporters of their one and only child. My dad has proofread many pages of this and other books and papers. My mom loves me and cheers me on when only a mother would. My parents spoiled me in a good way with love and Transformers, and today, I am a very grateful adult son. I have learned generosity and hard work from my dad. I have learned to care for people from my mom. I have learned love from both of them.

Each person who has ever supported our ministry as a church member or financial ministry partner as we have had the privilege to travel the United States has been a massive blessing to us as well. This book would not have been written without you.

I am also thankful to many ministerial colleagues, supportive bishops who have allowed me to itinerate in their territories, pastors who have given us the privilege to speak in their churches and friends who have served on the council of Brian Farley Ministries Incorporated. In these categories, special thanks go to Bishops: Doug Beacham, Garry Bryant, Talmadge Gardner, Tommy McGhee, Mike Gray, Tim Lamb, David Moore, Danny Nelson, Greg Amos, Manuel Pate, Ray Willis and Assistant Bishop Doug Bartlett.

While we cannot thank everyone by name who has made this book possible, ministerially speaking, we are grateful for more than 200 churches and hundreds of individual donors to Brian Farley Ministries.

Most of all, I am thankful to the Lord Jesus Christ for His salvation provided on the cross of Calvary, the creation, provision and protection of Father God and the continually infilling, leading and guiding of the precious Holy Spirit. Jesus is alive and well. He still heals, performs miracles and we proclaim His death until He comes again.

I also wish to thank the reader of this book. Without you, this book would have no purpose. May the Lord Jesus bless all who read this book. May you know Jesus is alive and loves you! May His healing power, grace, and LIFE flow through your body, spirit, soul and mind as you read or listen to the words of this book.

INTRODUCTION

Have you ever wondered if God really has a plan for your life? Have you ever doubted His existence and thought about going with the modern, false narrative that He is just an old, outdated fairy tale? Maybe the Bible is full of neat stories embellished over time? Was that church you were dragged to as a child just a silly waste of time that your parents thought might help you get your act together morally?

This book is being completed as the author is one week away from his 46th birthday, so about half the people on the planet have lived longer. The other half have lived less. The author does not claim to be a genius, know it all, or expert on many subject matters. I cannot intelligently discuss quantum mechanics or advanced mathematics and do not claim to be a master of ancient literature or history. However, there are some subjects that I know something about. Not because I read about them in someone else's book or studied them in an Ivy League college, but because I have seen them with my very own eyes.

I was reared in a home that taught me from a young age to fear God. I was taught that we served a miracle-working God, and I heard a few stories in my own family of small to mid-size miracles. As an older child, I had the privilege to sit under the powerful preaching of R.W. Shambach at Pace Assembly of God and remember his powerful, first-hand stories of miracles in crusades of A.A. Allen and later in his own meetings. I can still recall the stories of a baby growing limbs, blind eyes opened and deaf ears hearing. As a child, they filled my heart with fascination and wonder. I believed them with my whole heart. I did not know that in less than two decades from those church services I attended, listening intently on the pews of Olive Road Church of God in Pensacola, Florida and Pace Assembly, just a few miles away, that I would one day see God do healing miracles in my own life and ministry.

The purposes of this book include reminding people that God has a personal and good plan for your life, Jesus died on a cross to forgive you and save you from the consequences of your sins, Jesus is a healing Savior who still performs incredible and scientifically undoable miracles and all the stuff in your life (if you will trust Jesus) will work out for your good.

While this book hopes to tell you of salvation and God's overall plan for your life, the center of the book focuses much on miracles or healing. There are several key themes about Christian healing that may help you and your circumstances as you apply them to your own life. While faith, divine healing and other miracles are wonderful, you must never forget the purpose of miracles. The purpose of Christian miracles is to bring credit and glory to Jesus...

> *Fellow Israelites, listen to this: Jesus of Nazareth was a man accredited by God to you by miracles, wonders and signs, which God did among you through him, as you yourselves know.*
>
> Acts 2:22 New International Version

> *People of Israel, listen! God publicly endorsed Jesus the Nazarene by doing powerful miracles, wonders, and signs through him, as you well know.*
>
> Acts 2:22 New Living Translation

The point of Christian miracles is to "accredit" or "publicly endorse" Jesus by God the Father. The point of miracles is to direct people to the One who holds the power of the healing or miracle. If someone is miraculously healed by Jesus, but neglects to acknowledge Him, then the greater point of the miracle was lost. The true and living God does not primarily heal people so they might live a few more years or decades, He primarily heals people so they might find eternal and lasting peace and life in trusting in Jesus.

It is my prayer that as you read this book, you may encounter the miraculous, have your faith built, but most of all...that you may have lasting and eternal life and peace as you trust Jesus as your Lord and Savior.

PART I

GOD SEES YOU SAVED

PRE-BOOK QUESTION

What if an angel appeared to you?

Disclaimer: This question is not for theological purposes. It is not intended to teach any deep theology about angels, demons, and their power(s), but only to connect some thoughts in people's minds…

Imagine with me, if you can, that you are a parent of a young child. Imagine that an angel or some other powerful celestial being came to you one day and said, "You have a choice. I have the power to give your child an incurable cancer or not. The doctors will be able to do very little in the way of treating this child if I allow your child to get the cancer. The doctors will have no chemotherapy or radiation that is effective against the cancer. The doctors will be certain that the child will die within six months of discovering the cancer. Almost all the other children who have ever had this cancer died within six months. Now you have the choice of whether or not your child will receive the cancer. If you say yes, they will get the cancer. If you say no, they will not get the cancer."

If that were you, do you immediately know what your answer would be? I think most of us would say that we certainly know our answer would be "NO! Certainly do not give my child cancer!"

This question is just to get you thinking, we will come back and look at the question again later. For now, continue reading this book.

CHAPTER 1

Instant Pictures, Movies *and* Masterpieces...

THE WAY GOD CAN FIX THINGS IN OUR LIVES

Taking Instant Pictures

In today's digital world, we are accustomed to instant and easy photographs taken on devices tethered to us at all times. Our devices make it simple to snap a picture and then almost as easily clean it up with filters, photo editing software and some devices can even correct bad focus. However, when I was a child, this was not the case. In the 1970s, '80s and most of the 1990s, taking a picture and getting the results in the form of a photograph that you could examine while holding it in your hand was, by today's standards, a tremendous process.

The other day in January 2020, I smiled to myself. I was in an airport in the American South where a gift and candy store was selling disposable film cameras. I'm not sure who was buying them, but even more perplexing was, if you bought this camera, once you took the pictures- where could you go to develop the film?

Not being a country boy, I have always joked that I have always known where meat and vegetables originated- the grocery store! In like manner, my children, almost cannot remember when photos came from anywhere, but their phone. We not only expect photos to come from our phones, but they are instant and good quality.

Around 1978, I remember seeing a couple of amazing things at my grandparents' house. One was a game on the black and white television called "Pong" (another story for another day) and at that same Christmas gathering, someone had a Polaroid camera. Even as a very young child, I was well accustomed to cameras as my father was a pretty serious photographer on the hobby level. He had all kinds of cameras, lenses, flashes and tripods laying around the house, but I had never seen a Polaroid. In the 1970s, '80s, and 90s, you needed to have your film developed by a lab once the pictures were taken. In the 1970s, my dad would send his film off somewhere in the mail. It seemed to take forever to get the developed photographs back. Then as the '80s arrived, we would go to a local store and it would only take a few days. Eventually, the one-hour service was developed, and you could get your film developed in just 60 minutes, you paid a premium price for this service. BUT the Polaroid, this magic little box camera took a picture, and in just a few seconds, you could see the image develop right before your eyes. The shutter button was pressed and a magic sound and action followed quickly. I can still so clearly recall the noise of the camera mechanically spitting out the undeveloped film. The sound was something like the magic sound of Optimus Prime of 1984 Generation One Transformers fame when he transformed from a robot to a truck in all his cartoon glory! Then an instant photographer ritual ensued...The ritual normally involved people blowing on the film, shaking it around or dancing with one foot in the air while it developed. I'm not sure if any of that made any difference, but all the budding instant photographers would seem to do this. In about a minute, a normally terrible quality picture would emerge. So often, these pictures were completely out of focus and dreadful by today's standards. The little package of film only contained something like maybe ten pictures or so, in my experience...often only two to four of those ten would be decent pictures. Many times, two or three would be completely terrible, basically trash, and the other two or three would be mediocre quality at best.

The thing was, nobody seemingly cared about the bad pictures, nobody cared about the very expensive cost of the film, what they remembered was the two to four gloriously cool, instant and technologically marvelous wonders of the pictures that came out well. I don't think my dad ever had an instant camera...to him; it would have been a terrible insult. The quality of the picture was of utmost importance to him. Our house was adorned with my dad's original photography. His pictures included time-lapse car lights on the highway at night, my family, nature scenes of our beautiful nearby Florida beaches, Carolina mountains and the neatest one I can remember of my brother and I. I am an only child, so my dad double-exposed a picture of me on both sides of a table eating, silly today, and super easy, but the coolest thing you can imagine as a three-year-old in 1977. The difference in what was possible with an instant camera and my dad's super expensive Nikons was hard to put into words, but as they say, "*A picture is worth a thousand words.*"

The Nikon pictures, or if you are a Canon person (Nikons and Canons don't mix like Chevy and Fords) the Canon pictures- took time to produce, but it could make something beautiful, clear and exposed just right. The Polaroid was no doubt faster and, in many ways, a unique camera, but it was for all intents and purposes according to late '70s standards a very basic camera when it came to the actual camera part of the device. All the Polaroid magic was in the instant film cartridge. Which, did I mention, had its own magic battery in it to make that cool film transformer eject sound? For all the magic of the film, the battery, the sound, the almost instantaneous image, the camera itself was fixed focus, had almost no other controls and sometimes didn't even have a flash. This lack of actual photographic technology severely limited the Polaroid by 1970s photography standards. My dad's pictures normally turned out good and often looked really great. The camera could be controlled in so many ways that every aspect of the picture could be improved just before taking it. The focus would be good, the amount of light needed or not needed, the speed of the shutter, and so many other things I don't even fully understand since I never really got involved in photography. That's the other part of picture taking 30-40 years ago, back then especially, WHO took the picture was as important, if not more important, than what camera it was taken with.

Now, I am sure that a great and persuasive argument could be made in 2020, that who takes the picture is still more important than what the picture was taken with. I understand that even today, professional photographers can make a world of difference when having a portrait made or purchasing professional commercial photography. Just last year, when selling a piece of property, I paid $400 more for a realtor who used a professional photographer to take the regular pictures and also take many drone shots from high above since it was a beautiful piece of waterfront property. The property sold within 30 minutes of being listed, and I think the professional shots may have played into the decision. There is definitely value in professional photographers even in 2020 and probably for decades to come, but in the 1970s it was different. As a three-year-old, if you had given me one of my dad's Nikons or a similar Canon, I wouldn't have been able to do much with the machine. The bulk of the camera alone would have hindered my baby hands from picking it up. If I could have got it (with an often-attached foot long zoom lens) up to my eye, I wouldn't have known what to do with it. The array of knobs, buttons and "thing-a-ma-jiggers" on a 1977 pro SLR camera was overwhelming. Entire classes were taken, not to teach you to become an intermediate or expert photographer, but just to teach you how to take a half-way decent picture. My dad, as a serious camera hobbyist and others who were career professional photographers could quickly adjust all those settings and snap a picture in just a moment. Later, as I became a teen, my dad tried to interest me in professional photography, but after a short phase, I was not that interested. One of the main reasons I lost interest was I did not quickly master the complex settings and found the process super tedious, even in the late '80s and early '90s. The skill it takes to take a good picture is much less now. If you can pay $500 for a smartphone, you can take a decent picture. While the 2020s photographer still makes a large difference, the 1970s cameras' photographers made all the difference. A great camera in a great photographer's hands can take a masterpiece.

In one way, the Polaroid and the Nikon were similar, though. They were both unforgiving. Once the shutter button was pressed, that picture was taken. In that moment of time, the film was seared with the image and likeness of whatever laid before the lenses' point of view. In the 70s and 80s, there was no going back to delete the picture and immediately take it again. You might have 10, 12 or 36 or so chances on the film cartridge, disc or roll, but you were stuck. That image is what would be produced either instantly, in one hour or in several days in the mail from some far-off place.

Today, God has an intended picture of your life and mine. Unlike cameras of the 2020s, this picture is not instant and it cannot be taken by a novice photographer. As the master creator, He is, God's designs for your life are far greater than we can imagine. Every life was created ultimately for His glory and when the picture is framed by Him and for His purposes, it will also, put the subject of the picture in the very best light possible. Glamour Shots of the 1980s and Instagram/Snapchat filters of the teens and twenties can make a very flawed subject appear marvelously beautiful, if only for a fleeting instant. A life fully surrendered to God will produce the best picture of that subject, and it will make this life a blessing to everyone involved in the process, God, you and the others that your life will bless.

God's picture of you is also different than both the early Nikons and the 1970s Polaroids. His picture of you is forgiving. Just as Photoshop, Gimp and many other photo editors can repair red-eye, clean up fuzz, fix a bad focus, correct colors, and turn a regular picture into a stunning portrait...God can take a badly damaged or stewarded life and make it into something wonderful.

Making movies

Like both the Nikon and Polaroid, the image of your life, if taken right now is static. It is made in the image and likeness of God; however, with God, He thinks in terms of the end from the beginning. God really sees the completed work of your life much more like a movie than a still picture. The movie we call "the picture of you," in God's eyes, also isn't something shot for America's Funniest Home videos, dumb pranks on YouTube or ten-second videos of cats and dogs on Facebook. "God's Picture of You" that is the film of your lifetime, isn't a ten-second carelessly shot meme. It is more along the lines of movie cinematic masterpieces like *Lord of the Rings, The Color Purple, Rocky, The Shawshank Redemption, Back to the Future, Braveheart, Roots, Titanic, Forest Gump, The Empire Strikes Back, Avatar, The Lion King, Minority Report, The Fugitive* or *The Passion of the Christ.* The point is not about what film is best, but these films, even though one may not always agree with the message or language sometimes used, these films are often considered masterpieces. They were not thrown together in a moment. A talented writer or team of brilliant writers spent months, and in some cases years, developing the stories. Visual effects artists toiled for countless hours, making sure lights, sound and special effects were all exactly right. Often a world-renown composer and orchestra wrote and played intricate musical scores, which set the tone for the drama on screen. Sometimes, the stories were all true or based on the truth of often terrible circumstances and evils overcome by those involved in the events. Other times pure fantasy on the screen was depicted by gifted actors and actresses so the audiences suspended their unbelief, even if for only an hour or two. Time, energy, blood, sweat, tears and millions of dollars were invested by masters to produce incredible experiences.

God's Picture of You

The picture or film of you, that God has in mind for your life is greater than anything Steven Spielberg could ever think of, and it is certainly more appealing than you or I could imagine. Unlike the best writers and producers of Hollywood, God is not limited. His creativity, energy, money and resources are limitless and His desire to be in fellowship and express His love to a lost and dying world is unmatched. The only thing needed to begin to unlock God's picture of your very best life is your full surrender to His plan. He wants creative control. He wants full custody of His children. He can be trusted with incredible results for those who will give Him the keys. This is the main overarching point of this book; you are God's masterpiece...

> *"For we are God's masterpiece. He has created us anew in Christ Jesus, so we can do the good things he planned for us long ago."*
>
> EPHESIANS 2:10 NEW LIVING TRANSLATION

If you are ready, God is ready to transform your life into something beautiful. He sees an empty frame and can fill it with His beauty and majesty. You were thought of before the earth was formed, and His plan for you is incredible. Maybe you are saying, "That's nice, but I have already really messed up my life. It is so bad, God could not redeem my life at this point." The old, famous show, "*The Joy of Painting*" with Bob Ross demonstrated this point dramatically. Bob was famous for painting live on public television and was known for painting "happy little trees." He also was well-loved for what he did with his mistakes. Bob endeared himself to many people because when a mistake was made, he would incorporate it into the painting and explain that it was not meant to be that way, but he demonstrated that he could take a missed brush stroke and convert it into a happy little tree, blade of grass, the top of a wave in the ocean or whatever the case may be. God does the very same thing with our mistakes, once we give our lives to Him...

> *So I went down to the potter's house, and there he was working at his wheel. And the vessel he was making of clay was spoiled in the potter's hand, and he reworked it into another vessel, as it seemed good to the potter to do.*
>
> JEREMIAH 18:3,4 ENGLISH STANDARD VERSION

As a potter can take and reform a vessel when it gets off track, God does the very same thing with His children. Whatever has taken place in our life that was meant to destroy us, if it is submitted and surrendered to the Holy Spirit, it can then be used to further the Kingdom and the process of forming the image of Christ in our character.

Whatever you are experiencing right now, if it is dedicated to God, it can and will be redeemed for His glory and it will work out for your good.

Thoughts and Questions to Discuss:

1. Have you ever wished God would hurry up with what He is doing in your life?
2. Would you prefer someone doing work for you to do a fast job or a quality job?
3. Can you think of a time when God "photo-shopped" a mistake for you?
4. What makes a good movie? When you are at someone's funeral, what made a good life?
5. Do you think God is trustworthy?
6. Has there ever been a time when you wished you would have been more patient and let God complete a work He was doing when you jumped ahead of His plan due to impatience?
7. In a decade from now, what will you be glad that you slowly trusted God for today?

Brian Farley and some of his double-exposed “siblings”, circa 1977.

Mountain Stream landscape by Dale Farley
from Brian's childhood home.

Lighthouse landscape by Dale Farley from Brian's childhood home.

CHAPTER 2

Mice, Mazes *and* Peanut Butter...

Seeing the End from the Beginning

A lot is said in these verses of scripture...

> *"God saved you by his grace when you believed. And you can't take credit for this; it is a gift from God. Salvation is not a reward for the good things we have done, so none of us can boast about it. For we are God's masterpiece. He has created us anew in Christ Jesus, so we can do the good things he planned for us long ago."*
>
> Ephesians 2:8-10 New Living Translation

Before we can really understand the concept of God making a masterpiece of our lives, we have to first understand that God is not limited like us and He knows the end from the beginning. Verse 10 says that, "He has created us anew in Christ Jesus, so we can do the good things he planned for us long ago." In this verse, we are reminded that God does not work in time as we do. As finite beings, we are limited to what, in Star Trek terms, is called the "space-time continuum." This science fiction term has been and continues to make interesting plotlines in science fiction stories and the serious scientific thoughts of people like Einstein and Stephen Hawking to this day. In the Twilight Zone, Back to the Future and a thousand other popular tales, people are trapped somewhere between the past, present and future. We can imagine "what if" scenarios and how one, single action can change the entire future of a person, civilization or the universe. These ideas capture the imaginations of mere mortals because we are held in the present. No matter how much we wish we could change yesterday's mistakes or jump ahead of painful conditions to a preferable future, we cannot escape the now. From God's viewpoint, though, now, yesterday and tomorrow have all already happened. He sees the end from the start of things. This is the reason the Bible can tell us ultimately what will happen in the future, God will win, He will wipe away tears and His children will live with Him forever in peace. (See the Book of Revelation). For us, though, this is hard to imagine.

In sixth grade, my school required me to enter into a science fair. For the fair, students were assigned to make an elaborate project for science class. One popular scientific thing to work with were mice. Running mice through mazes was a popular scientific experiment subject during the 1980s, so I built a maze with peanut butter at the end (I discovered peanut butter may be a better bait for mice than the classic yellow cheese). My "Can Mice Learn?" project won me first place in my grade that year. Enough of my shameless, middle school bragging...the point is, in that project, I learned some things that stuck with me for life. One, mice are kind of fun to play with. Two, mice cannibalize dead mice in their cages at an amazingly fast pace (strange, gross, but true). Three, when looking at the mouse maze from above, it was amazingly simple to see how the mouse should travel to the end and get to the peanut butter; however, for the mouse, it was exceedingly difficult the first time they attempted the maze. As most anyone could have predicted from former scientific data, the mice almost always improved their time running the maze. At the first shot, the mouse would be very confused and slow. Each time they were put in the maze, though, they ran the maze faster and faster. It's been some 35 years now, so I cannot remember all the specifics, but I remember that while each mouse learned at a different rate than their other mouse friends, each mouse would improve with practice and a couple of them became experts in short order. One mouse in particular, (I called him Herbie the Speed Demon) that had initially taken a very long time to complete the maze, after a month of running the maze, he could immediately go straight to the peanut butter with no wrong turns. He would quickly devour the great prize in store for his little whiskers.

Since the experiment was for a science fair, I could not do this, but I often wanted just to pick the mouse up and move them to the end. Some of the less intellectually talented mice made me feel sorry for them. What I learned, though, was that even the mentally slower mice would also improve greatly if I left them alone and let them run the race again and again. The slower little furry guys and gals may not have been as fast as Herbie the speed demon, a seemingly Harvard IQ educated rodent, but they also improved greatly and went to the prize much, much faster.

If I had picked them up and moved them to the end, it would have messed with my scientifically recorded data and more importantly, it would have detrimentally affected their ability to learn how to handle the maze. I can only imagine the first time a mouse was plucked out of its little, cozy mouse environment complete with food, water, shelter, an exercise wheel and plastic, mouse entertainment tubes where they could have fun and explore with their little furball friends. In one moment, the mouse (we will call Fluffer) is happy, content and as much as a small rodent can be, probably pretty content with day to day mouse life. In the next moment, this mouse is placed by itself in a harsh, large, wooden maze where possibly they could smell the aroma of peanut butter far off in the distance. From that moment, Fluffer has to be confused, overwhelmed and sometimes Fluffer even seems to almost give in to despair and sit down. From Fluffer's point of view, this is the most complicated, difficult, aggravating and discouraging thing he can imagine. From my gigantic sixth grade perspective, peering over my little Mouse Maze Kingdom, I could see the end from the beginning. If the mouse had my perspective, it would have experienced no problems whatsoever going immediately to the peanut butter, but at the same time, the mouse would have learned nothing.

Our relationship with God and the path we travel on in this life, in some ways, is not all that different from the plight of Herbie and Fluffer. We often feel that what we face today is overwhelming. From our perspective, often, life is very overwhelming. If we could only see God's perspective, though, things would be so much easier. For sixth grade me, I could not have the mouse skip the maze to get to the prize for the sake of scientific learning and, more importantly, to pass the sixth grade. With God, He could do anything, but He allows us to stay in the sometimes confusing maze of life, so we can learn. For the mice, the goal was that they would learn to run the maze and get the peanut butter in a faster time. Herbie and Fluffer, did not have the luxury of speaking to me, peering down on them, and asking me which would be the best direction to go at the next turn, or would this turn end up in another dead end. With God, we may feel like we are in a maze sometimes, but there is a great difference in us and God and the mice and me. The mice could only speak mouse (if that's a thing), and I could not speak mouse while they could not speak English. If as children of God, we stop and take time to ask God which path is best, or what job would I be best suited for, who would make the most compatible spouse for me or which house should I buy or rent...He does not often speak in English, but He will guide and direct our hearts in a still, small "voice."

The maze of life that God has us in is not to punish us or make things miserable on purpose. When life is lived so it glorifies God by trusting Him, you can be sure that it will be worth it. When we cannot see the big picture, we have to trust that not just looking over a physical maze, but looking beyond the good and bad decisions we have made and will make, the time used wisely for the Kingdom and the time squandered by selfishness can all be redeemed by the maker of time and space. As He sits perched above not only the physical universe, He also knows what will happen at the end of what we call time, and He certainly knows what will happen in the vapor of a moment of eternity that is called our life.

When Ephesians 2:10 says that, "*He has created us anew in Christ Jesus, so we can do the good things he planned for us long ago.*" The Word of God speaks of the good things He planned for us long ago. He declares that before we were even born, He knew us.

> *"I knew you before I formed you in your mother's womb. Before you were born I set you apart and appointed you as my prophet to the nations."*
>
> Jeremiah 1:5 New Living Translation

Just as God knew Jeremiah was to a be a prophet to the nations before He even formed him, Jesus knew that you and I were created for a purpose even before we were born. Many conservative, evangelical Christians believe that life begins at conception, but the purpose of our lives started even before we were formed in the womb.

God sits above time and space, and He had good things in store for us before we were born. Every turn of life, good or bad, God knows the outcome before we ever make the choice and if we will follow Him and trust Him, we will learn, grow and become accustomed to hearing His voice clearer with every step we take. When we go our own way, turn off communication with our Heavenly Father and ignore the promptings of the Holy Spirit, we quickly veer into the pit of self-reliance, and in short order, we will come to the end of ourselves. On the other hand, when we trust God, we will find that His plans for us are better than ours and we can rest in the fact that He will bring us to a good end.

Thoughts and Questions to Discuss:

1. According to Ephesians 2, who saves us?
2. According to Ephesians 2, how are we saved?
3. According to Ephesians 2, why does God save us?
4. According to Jeremiah 1, when did God know us?
5. Can you see the future?
6. Do you think God can see the future? If so, can He be trusted with your future?
7. In a decade from now, what will you be glad that you slowly trusted God for today?

Middle Schooler Brian Farley in Pensacola
Christian School Science Fair, circa 1986.

CHAPTER 3

Flipping Houses, Dog Poop *and* 100% Profit...

WHAT ARE YOU WORTH?

Please understand one disclaimer about this chapter before we get too involved in it, according to the Bible, everyone is not saved. Unfortunately, everyone will not be saved. God gives man the free-will to determine for themselves whether or not they will submit their will to the Lordship of Jesus Christ. The Bible makes it clear that if we reject Jesus as Lord and Savior, we will not gain eternal life, but if we confess Him, we will be saved. Jesus said in John 6 that the work we have to do is to simply believe in Him...

> *Jesus answered, "The work of God is this: to believe in the one he has sent"*
>
> JOHN 6:29 NEW INTERNATIONAL VERSION

The Word explains that when we believe in Jesus, we have eternal life...

> *For God so loved the world that he gave his one and only Son, that whoever believes in him shall not perish but have eternal life.*
>
> JOHN 3:16 NEW INTERNATIONAL VERSION

But the Word also warns that if we are ashamed of Jesus in front of men, He will also, one day be ashamed of us in front of Our Heavenly Father...

> *If anyone is ashamed of me and my message, the Son of Man will be ashamed of that person when he returns in his glory and in the glory of the Father and the holy angels.*
>
> LUKE 9:26 NIV

So, even though, Jesus has accomplished the work of saving us by dying on a cross to pay the penalty for our sins, and even though this work of salvation that He accomplished is forever and for all eternity (a permanent sacrifice) not temporary as the blood of animals was in the Old Covenant... we must still accept this gift in order to receive it. God does not force Himself upon us. He keeps our free will intact. If He did not, we would not be serving a loving God. Heaven could not be heaven, if people who did not want to be there were forced to be there.

So, all of that is to say that a strong disclaimer must be made to the rest of this chapter. Universalism is not taught in the Bible. Universalism is the teaching that everyone will be saved automatically and with no act of their own choice. Why would one want to go to heaven if they had neglected, despised and ignored God their entire life? If someone had chosen selfishness and a commitment to self-gratification their entire earthly life, they would have no desire to spend eternity with a righteous God that is Lord of all. Universalism is both void of biblical evidence and logical thinking.

Having said that, ***God sees you saved***.

For those who desire to know God, seek His fellowship, know Him personally and are willing to admit that they are dependent on the Creator and Sustainer of Life...God sees you saved.

It may not currently be in our finite minds to be able to envision what God can see concerning our future condition in this life and the next, but God is a visionary God.

Long before it was popular and seemingly on every cable television show to "flip houses," I had the privilege to flip a few houses. Some of the houses we flipped we just made a few thousand dollars because we purchased them in halfway decent shape, lived in them for a couple of years and made modest improvements, mainly just cleaning, painting, and other aesthetic changes. It is interesting how much the value of real estate can increase just from the hedges being trimmed immaculately, new mulch under the bushes, super tight edging lines on the sidewalk, removing any unkempt grass over concrete and installing a couple of inexpensive, but new appliances on the inside. These types of changes are easy to imagine by anyone with attention to detail, but other house flipping situations require a lot of vision.

In early 2006, we embarked on our largest house flipping project. We were privileged to purchase a house about to go into foreclosure. It was a win-win, the person selling it was about to lose all of their investment to foreclosure and we were able to purchase it far below market value. The house had comparable real estate evaluations in the immediate area around it at almost twice the asking price. This sounds good and attractive on the surface, but there is always a reason that many pre-foreclosure homes can sometimes sell at a fraction of their value. This house was no exception.

The home had been occupied by the owner for a while, but they had moved out and turned it into a rental. The renters did not take proper care of the home. The renters had basically destroyed the home. They had knocked holes in the walls, left trash everywhere, the appliances were all trashed, there was a shed/garage building in the back packed from floor to roof with junk that could easily have qualified for the show "Hoarders." The grass, in this half-acre yard, had not been cut probably for two years (it took about 8 hours or more to cut the grass the first time because it was so thick and even matted) and the most fun was the inside clean up.

Inside, the renters had a large number of dogs and cats. The renters did not feel like cleaning up after them, so they allowed the animals to use the restroom wherever they felt like pooping. This led to a house full of dog and cat feces. The owner had been dealing with some health problems, so they were not able to remedy the situation.

Over the course of the next two months, several 40-yard dumpsters of debris were removed from this 1,100 square foot house. All the floor covering had to be removed and replaced, the appliances had to be replaced, several days of fumigation were required, repairs were needed to the air conditioning systems, much of the electrical had to be replaced and the list goes on and on. Eventually, after about 60 days of work, two to four days a week with lots of volunteer help from family and friends, lots of paid help to professional handymen and contractors, and lots of sweat equity from Heather and myself, the house was finished. The house had the same address as it did two months earlier, the foundation was the same, the walls were pretty much the same, the garage building in the back was the same... but almost everything was simultaneously different. When I first stepped into the little house, two months earlier, there is no way I would have ever considered moving into the house with my wife and then young sons. It was a house of horrors. Houses we had purchased in the past and improved (maybe 25% improvement), possibly could have been purchased by most anyone with a little vision and creativity. This house, on the other hand, was more like a 75-80% improvement. The shell was the same, but very little else. This house required a creative, visionary to really be seen for its full potential. Others may have been able to see it, but even those who quickly could see its potential would then also have to have several other qualities to see the improvement take place. For this house to be brought to the place it was two months later all of the following qualities were required: a vision for what it could be, resources to purchase it, patience to endure throughout the process, recruiting capabilities to hire and enlist the team to perform the work, the willingness to put forth the effort and time and the "stick-tu-i-tive-ness" to stick to it until it was complete.

Many people (possibly ones with better sense and less time on their hands than we did) would have ignored this house, but we saw something that we thought we could make happen and would be happy living in. Once we were finished, we moved into the little house as happy as we could be, we knew we had a good bit of equity if we needed or wanted to sell. Unexpectedly, I received a call two months after we had moved into the house. It was for a promotion and I would need to move. We took the job and put the house on the market. The house sold in less than two hours from the time it was listed, and it sold for twice what we paid for it, less than four months before, thankfully profiting us the most money we had ever made in such a short period of time.

We had not planned to sell the house that quickly. We knew the house had some value, but we did not expect to sell it so quickly or for the price it sold. We were very blessed and thankful for the sale. This was one of those cases where we operated a lot like God does in the lives of those who love Him.

When we first stepped foot in that house, it was as disgusting as disgusting can be, but I immediately saw the potential. If the house would have been sentient, I am not sure that it would have been able to see its own potential. Years of decay, neglect and bad choices by its occupants had hidden the value of the little house.

A lot of people are walking around with tons of potential. Many people have far more value than they can see. The bad choices, neglect and sometimes the choices of others toward these people have hidden their true value and worth. A parent will sometimes thoughtlessly say, "You will never amount too much." A cruel kid in school can say, "You are ugly." Someone will hear something ruthless about their weight, appearance, intelligence or whatever the case may be, and these words can set in their spirit, causing depression, deep-seated resentment and bitterness toward a person, group or people or just the world in general. When these things happen, it is right in line with what Satan has planned for people. Jesus said in John 10:10 in the New Living Translation that, "The thief's purpose is to steal and kill and destroy. My purpose is to give them a rich and satisfying life."

Satan has a lot of people believing his lies:

- you are not worth much
- you cannot recover from your bad choices
- people like you never escape their families
- your past is always going to hold you back
- you might as well give up

Jesus, on the other hand, says things like:

- I have come to give you life
- you are more than a conqueror
- the plans I have for you are for your good, for a hope and a future
- you mean so much to me that I died to pay for your redemption

What we listen to and who we listen to is very important. The older I get, the more I realize it is more important to control what I am listening to even than what I actually do. When you are young, it is easy to concentrate on doing a lot of good work to be successful. As I age, I am beginning to understand that I must keep listening to the right people saying the right thing much more than I must just do the right thing. Doing the right things involves keeping the right motivation. If I lose motivation, I will no longer do the right things. So, keeping the right motivation, the right beliefs, the right people speaking into my life is of utmost importance. In a day where many people get their insight, wisdom and motivation from social media feeds, news feeds and Netflix...it is of utmost importance that I am taking in the right social feeds, news feeds and anything else streamed before me. The Apostle Paul writes of this in Philippians 4:8 and 9, *"Finally, brothers, whatever is true, whatever is honorable, whatever is just, whatever is pure, whatever is lovely, whatever is commendable, if there is any excellence, if there is anything worthy of praise, think about these things. What you have learned and received and heard and seen in me—practice these things, and the God of peace will be with you."* English Standard Version

Paul writes under the inspiration of the Holy Spirit that what we are thinking about (what we are putting in our heads) is of utmost importance. He explains in verse nine to put into practice the things we are learning. When we learn violence, hate, cursing, negativity, sadness, hopelessness and despair, these are just about the only things we can expect to reproduce as we go about our daily lives. On the flip-side, when we dedicate our brains, spirits and hearts to the things of the Spirit (love, joy, peace, gentleness, patience, kindness, goodness, faithfulness, self-control), we can expect good, godly output from our lives.

> *But the fruit of the Spirit is love, joy, peace, patience, kindness, goodness, faithfulness, gentleness, self-control; against such things there is no law.*
>
> GALATIANS 5:22,23 NEW AMERICAN STANDARD BIBLE

This is why it is so important to spend time daily in the Word of God and then to be careful about what we are taking in throughout the day on our devices. When we decide we want to let the Lord make a new image, picture or movie out of our life, if we are expecting masterpiece quality results as we talked about earlier, then we will need to put in masterpiece quality ingredients. The building blocks of these ingredients are the Word of God as found in the Bible, excellent things, helpful things, encouraging things and lovely things. This is why somctimes it is necessary for the person who has decided to move forward with God as the sole architect of his or her life to purge social media feeds, re-think entertainment choices, re-prioritize things like exercise and diet, and generally pursuing wisdom instead of foolishness.

Satan always has something evil he is trying to sell us. The Spirit of God, on the other end of the spectrum, also has something good and pleasant that He has planned for us as well. Satan and the world's system speak loudly and get in your face; however, more frequently than not, the Lord is speaking in a still, small voice. Much as a gentleman will not force himself on a woman, the Holy Spirit will never force Himself on you. Satan will rape you spiritually and laugh about it. The choice is yours to listen to God or the Devil.

Thoughts and Questions to Discuss:

1. According to John 6:29, what is the main work God has called us to do?
2. Do you believe God can see your life as a part of His plan before you can do so?
3. Does your past hold you back with God?
4. Have you ever remodeled/re-furbished something? Did it take a while? Was it worth it?
5. Do you think God or Satan offers a better "life deal" in the things they say to and about us? Why?
6. Have you ever thought you had less value than you really do? If God loved you enough to die on a cross for you, what does that say about the value He puts on your life?
7. Are the things you are listening to, viewing and consuming helping you build a stronger faith life and move in the direction you want to go in life? If not, how could you change the direction of your life to grow in peace as you begin to look more like Jesus?

CHAPTER 4

Talking Birds, Bosses *and* Listening to Your Heart...

WHO ARE YOU LISTENING TO?

Who is speaking into your life?
Who are you listening to?

I heard about a man that walked into a pet store. The store had a variety of exotic birds for sale, including three beautiful parrots. The man asked the owner, "How much are the parrots?" The owner's reply was, "Well, that depends on which one you are talking about?." He said that the first one is $500, and he can talk. About that time, the bird said, "Polly want a cracker?" The man then asked, "Well, how much is the second parrot?" The owner said, "He's $5,000." The man could hardly believe his ears, so he asked, "Why, what is the difference in the first bird and the second parrot?" The second bird had a laptop computer set up with the bird in the cage, but there was no other apparent difference in the birds. The owner then explained that the second bird could not only speak, but he is also fluent in Spanish, and at night he codes in several programming languages on the computer, including HTML and JAVA.

The owner explained that the bird was at that very time writing several video games designed specifically for parrots to play. About that time, the bird pledged allegiance to the American flag in perfect Spanish. The man was very impressed and then asked, "Well, how much is the third bird?" The owner hesitated, then explained that he was not for sale. The man persisted, "Come on, everything is for sale at the right price." Then the owner answered, "Well, I suppose I would take half a million dollars for that bird." The man was shocked and said, "Be serious, he's just a parrot! What can he possibly do that makes him worth $500,000?!" The shop owner said, "Well, to tell you the truth, I am not sure what he can do. I never see him doing anything, but I do know that the other two birds say 'sir' to him and call him 'THE BOSS.'"

Who is speaking into your life? Who do you call the boss?

I'm not referring to your employment supervisor, most of us have, or at some point, have had a boss. The question is, "Who and what are you listening to for guidance, instruction, direction, encouragement and accountability?" Many people are listening to themselves; others are listening to the devil and many choose to listen and submit to the Holy Spirit and the Bible.

The first boss you can listen to is yourself. If you are listening to yourself, you are listening to a source of information that can have very negative consequences...

> *"The heart is deceitful above all things and beyond cure. Who can understand it?"*
>
> JEREMIAH 17:9 NEW INTERNATIONAL VERSION

It's very popular in our culture to be told the advice, "Just listen to your heart." There was even a popular song about the concept released by the group Roxette in 1988. In the power ballad, the pair sings that you should...

> *Listen to your heart when he's calling for you Listen to your heart there's nothing else you can do I don't know where you're going and I don't know why, But listen to your heart before you tell him goodbye.*
>
> "LISTEN TO YOUR HEART" -ROXETTE, 1988

I liked Roxette and can hear the song in my head right now, but the advice is better left to catchy pop tunes than it is to actually take to heart. Now, while you should examine your heart from time to time and possibly the boyfriend that the late Marie Fredriksson sang about should not have been dumped so quickly and easily...as a general rule, the wisdom of the prophet Jeremiah should be heeded. The heart can sometimes lead us correctly, but first, the heart must be tuned correctly. Just like a fine piano, you can play the world's finest Steinway and Sons or Yamaha Grand Piano, but if those instruments have been in the wrong environments, without special attention paid to them, they will sound terrible. When a piano sits in an empty church or school auditorium, in a matter of months at the most, it will be out of tune. The more humid the room is, the faster this degradation of sound will happen. The heart is similar.

While the Bible here is actually speaking more of what we might call the soul, the inner being of the person, is what we cannot trust. Our heart/soul/mind, all of that, can easily lead us in the wrong direction. Most every bad financial impulse purchase we make is because we get something in our hearts. Over time when we think about that new car, bigger house or whatever it is, we will convince ourselves that we cannot live without it. The heart can quickly rationalize 1,000 reasons we need to or even must purchase something that we cannot afford and that we do not need. If the heart was tuned correctly, though, this may not be the case.

Just as the master piano tuner can hear and adjust each string to the exact tightness level it needs to produce the correct tone when the hammer strikes it, our Creator can adjust our heart so it can produce a beautiful life that will bless others, please Father God, and make our lives something that we can feel good about ourselves. Only when we are "in tune" with the Father's heart can our hearts be trusted. We stay in tune by being in the Word of God and prayer daily. Romans 12 reminds us we "renew our mind" daily. When we read, study or carefully listen to the Word of God, our mind is made new. It is cleansed from the thoughts of the flesh and is made in line with the thoughts of the Spirit (the mind of Christ). If we are not surrendered to the Spirit of God guiding and leading our life, then we are in no position to "listen to our heart" because it could easily lie to us. We have a certain propensity as selfish human beings to see things our own way, do things in our own best interest and make decisions that may hurt others or even our own future in favor of gratifying the desires we have today. No, generally speaking, the heart cannot be trusted. If we are the boss of ourselves, then we are probably going to eventually regret this decision.

The second boss we can listen to is Satan himself. Now since this is a Christian-based book, we make some assumptions you are probably interested in pleasing God. However, we probably are not dedicating our life to Satan, but some certainly have and people always will. Today, Satan worship may show up under the title of atheism or agnosticism. It is convenient to say one does not believe in God, as opposed to saying they are worshipping Satan. From the beginning of time, the spirit of Satan says, "I am going to do what I want to do and nobody is going to tell me otherwise." That attitude stems from Lucifer himself when he said...

> *You said in your heart, "I will ascend to the heavens; I will raise my throne above the stars of God; I will sit enthroned on the mount of assembly, on the utmost heights of Mount Zaphon. I will ascend above the tops of the clouds; I will make myself like the Most High." But you are brought down to the realm of the dead, to the depths of the pit.*
>
> Isaiah 14:13-15 New International Version

This scripture describes how Lucifer decided that he was unhappy with living under God's authority, so he, therefore, decided he would ascend to heaven and "make myself like the Most High." This type of attitude is at the heart of Satan worship. In the early 1980s America of my childhood, there was a lot of concern about literal Satan worship running rampant in the country. Every Halloween, you would hear about children or a young lady being sacrificed to Satan somewhere. While I certainly do not doubt this because when we choose to do what we want to, we are all capable of great evil, just as we are capable of great good. I would think most "Satan worshippers" do not set up sacrifices to Him. Some may choose to actually set up altars to Lucifer or offer sacrifices, but when someone says, "No one [including God] is going to tell me what to do!" They are, at least in spirit, participating in a form of Satan worship.

Satan's lie from the very start in the garden of Eden, is that we need no one telling us how to live. Satan lied to Adam and Eve when He convinced them that God was just trying to trick them into submission to Him in Genesis. Satan convinced the first earthly rebels against God that, "God knows that your eyes will be opened as soon as you eat it, and you will be like God, knowing both good and evil." Genesis 3:5 New Living Translation

Satan is great at telling half-truths like that. He prophecies that if they ate of the fruit that "your eyes will be opened" and this was true. What was a lie, though, is that they would not die..."'You won't die!" the serpent replied to the woman.'" Genesis 3:4 New Living Translation

Immediately, when they ate the fruit two things happened: 1) "their eyes were opened" and 2) they started to die. What Satan had not explained about the consequences of sin was that when their eyes were opened, not that their eyes were opened to how God had been abusing them, holding them back or being the tyrant so many think He is. Their eyes were opened to their being naked. They had been innocent and vulnerable, but God was taking care of their every need and even watching over them psychologically as they were under His care, close fellowship and protection. He had not been withholding anything good from them, He had been protecting them and caring for them all along. Even sadder, was that the moment they ate the fruit, the close bond of fellowship was broken with their Heavenly Father and they started to die. Death was not imminent, but now, because of sin, it had entered their bodies. There is something pure and right about holiness that transmits the life, presence and peace of God. When the fellowship with God is broken, that life power does not flow very well. Thankfully, the flow has been restored through the sacrificial death of Jesus, the Son of God, when He died to redeem mankind on the Cross of Calvary. Today, we can again walk in at least a portion of that connection that Adam and Eve once had with the Father when they walked daily with Him in the garden of Eden. They knew His presence every day in an unfettered, face to face kind of way. Today, we do not know God in that same way, but we can experience His presence through the Holy Spirit because of the redemptive work Jesus accomplished on the Cross. One day,.if we have placed our faith in Jesus as our Lord and Savior, we will again walk in that continual presence of the Lord in heaven. Until then, we can experience moments of glory when we walk in surrender to the Lord.

Through that act of disobedience to God in the garden, sin and death entered the world and the human race. It is easy to see the immediate and disastrous results that Adam and Eve experienced when they sinned. Today, because we are born into sin, we do not experience the results of disobedience so drastically (because it is now our normative nature to sin), but when we sin, do not deceive yourself, Satan has taken something from us every time we are tempted and give into temptation. Each time we make Lucifer the boss, in a way, we worship Him and we hurt our potential (at least our potential in that moment) as a man or woman of God to know God intimately and be all that He has called us to be. Listening to the voice of Satan: 1) hinders our flow of the Spirit through disturbing our close fellowship with God 2) hastens the power of death and 3) proclaims Satan as our temporary master. There is a much better option we have as to who to listen to in this life.

The third boss you can listen to is the Holy Spirit. It seems almost impossible at times, when Satanic pressure and the power of the flesh rise up inside of us, but we have a choice to listen to and obey the Holy Spirit. The Holy Spirit rarely speaks in our English (or whatever your native language may be), but we can sense and feel His leading and gentle guidance in our hearts. This guidance differs from 'Listening to our heart" that is spoken of earlier in the chapter. When we "listen to our heart" it is often a highly emotional experience we feel we MUST do. These desires come from the flesh and our ongoing desire to do what we want to do. We often justify them a million ways, but most of the time, when we "listen to our heart," we are simply being selfish.

When our heart is in tune with the things of God, we will often do things that are not natural to us at all. When you see someone doing something that others recognize as self-sacrificial and "great," often the Holy Spirit is involved. The Holy Spirit teaches us self discipline. That nasty word "discipline" has the word die inside of it. Discipline is ultimately personified by Jesus when He first prayed in the garden of Gethsemane that if there was any other way for the Father's plan of redemption for mankind to be carried out that the Father would please allow that. When Father God clarified it, there would be no other plan, Jesus submitted to the torture and death on the Cross. We believe that Jesus walked in His humanity while He took on the form of the Son of Man and walked the earth for 33 and 1/2 years. Jesus was fully man and fully God simultaneously; however, he performed miracles and carried out his earthly life and ministry without using His divinity. Had He used his divinity, then He would not have been able to tell us we could do even greater things than He did while He walked the earth as a man...

> *Very truly I tell you, whoever believes in me will do the works I have been doing, and they will do even greater things than these, because I am going to the Father.*
>
> JOHN 14:12 NEW INTERNATIONAL VERSION

Jesus did all He did as a man, not as God, this means that if we are listening carefully, completely and fully to the Holy Spirit that incredible things can be accomplished for the Kingdom of God. When we live a yielded life to the Holy Spirit, our life can count for more than we can comprehend in the natural.

How do you know the difference in when you are simply "listening to your heart" and when you are listening to the Holy Spirit?

A few ways to tell if you are listening to your heart or listening to the Holy Spirit:

When "Listening to Your Heart"

1. the result of following may be selfish and mainly benefit yourself
2. the voice/leading/guidance from the heart may be overwhelming - powerfully, pressuring you to do whatever it is
3. the voice/leading/guidance often does not consider how doing whatever it is that you are going to do will affect others long term
4. the guidance may go against the clear, understandable teachings of the Bible (this will never be God, it will always either be your heart or purely Satanic in origin)
5. the guidance may seem very "spiritual," but it may not glorify Jesus, it may only glorify you or other people
6. unwise, rebellious people will often agree with what your heart is saying

When Listening to the Holy Spirit (your "listening to your heart" may be included in this occasionally, but it will be a "yielded heart" that is truly set on doing the will and work of God…)

1. the guidance will normally be gentle and more of a pulling toward than a pushing
2. the guidance will often not benefit yourself or only minimally benefit yourself, but it will usually be for the best interest of others
3. the guidance will encourage you to consider how the result of your action will benefit or be a detriment to others in the long term

4. the guidance will not go against clear, understandable teaching of Scripture. The Holy Spirit will never go against the Bible, no matter how popular this may seem even by current cultural themes
5. the guidance will ultimately glorify Jesus
6. wise, godly counselors will often agree with the guidance

The bottom line is that we all have choices about who we will listen to and follow. Taking our cues from Satan's leading and guidance will often provide immediate pleasure and gratification. Following our heart may or may not work out for us. In the end, we will never regret the choice to follow Jesus by listening and obeying the voice of the Holy Spirit. When we follow Satan, we play now and pay later, but when we follow the Lord, we pray now and rejoice later.

Thoughts and Questions to Discuss:

1. Who are "three bosses" we can listen to?
2. What is the problem with exclusively listening to our heart, according to Jeremiah 17:9?
3. Isaiah 14, gives a clue...who are we most like when we want to be independent of God?
4. Who did Jesus listen to when He walked the earth in the form of a man?
5. In John 14:12, what does Jesus say about our capabilities if we listen to the Spirit of God?
6. What type of people will sometimes agree with your heart when your heart is telling you selfish things?
7. What type of people will sometimes agree with you when listening to the Holy Spirit?

CHAPTER 5

Skee-ball, Thieving Rats *and* Trading Junk *for* Value...

WHAT DOES IT MEAN TO BE REDEEMED?

Redemption

If you run in Christian circles, it will not take very long before you hear a lot of talk about the word "redeemed" or "redemption." What does it mean to be redeemed?

Google's use of the Oxford dictionary defines redemption in several ways including...

> *re·demp·tion-*
> *1) the action of saving or being saved from sin, error, or evil.*
> *2) the action of regaining or gaining possession of something in exchange for payment, or clearing a debt.*

Redemption is an interesting word. In my circles, I have normally thought of redemption in the spiritual sense of Jesus simply forgiving my sins and the sins of all the world who will accept His payment for their sins.

Redemption can also be rightly used in the sense that many arcades use it as, where an exchange is supplied.

A few years ago, when my boys were at home, and I was leading a family of my wonderful wife and our two young boys, we would somewhat frequently visit one of America's favorite family pastimes...Chuck E. Cheese. If you are unfamiliar with Chuck E. Cheese, Chuck is a large rat who runs a pizza restaurant chain. Chuck E. Cheese, is a place specially designed to simultaneously perform three impressive tasks: 1) entertain young children by distracting them with lots of video games, commercial/carnival type games and playing videos of large puppets playing music (in the old days, the big puppets were actually present for this) 2) serve very mediocre pizza and 3) take as much money as possible from poor and middle-class parents who are not aware that you should run from rats. (Chuck E. Cheese is a large rodent that residents of New York City will know to avoid because of his propensity for carrying rabies). Anyway, Chuck E. Cheese is an American ritual where families go to have birthday parties and celebrations of all kinds for their children. One of the staple attractions of a Chuck E. Cheese is the skee-ball machines.

For the uninitiated, skee-ball is a machine somewhat resembling a small bowling lane with a large curve at the top. The top curves to cause the ball to launch into the air and land in one of a few circles. Each circle has a larger point amount from the largest circle (with the lowest amount) to the smallest, inner circle with a very high amount. There are also very small additional circles on the far left and right tops of the machine, which also have very high amounts. Each game gives you five or six balls to roll. The higher you score by landing the balls in the highest point areas causes things to happen. If you produce a high enough score, the machine will produce siren sounds and lighting effects, but more importantly, as you rack up a high number of points, the machine will spit out a number of tickets. The higher the score, the more the tickets the machine will produce.

When you first enter, Chuck E. Cheese, you will decide how many tokens you want to spend in the arcade. You will trade your hard-earned money for a set of basically worthless tokens that can be spent on the video games and the other table-type games like ski-ball. As you and your children make a day of it, you can quickly spend upwards of $50-120 or more for a family of four (this is back in 2001-2009) as you pay Chuck for pizza, soda and game tokens. If you have the privilege of holding a birthday party for one of your children and 12-30 of their friends and family, you can EASILY drop hundreds and hundreds of dollars on this day with a large rat puppet. As the children "earn" more and more tickets from playing ski-ball and the other 50 games in this world of amazing fun, eventually they will want to do the most exciting thing in the world with these tickets.

There is a place in Chuck E. Cheese's and other family arcades such as these where you will take your tickets to be exchanged. Interestingly enough, the place where the tickets are exchanged for "prizes" is often called a "Redemption Center." The Redemption Center is often a large glass case with a 16-year-old worker behind it who will assist you and your children with swapping out your tickets (which just a couple of hours ago were your hard-earned cash) for these incredible prizes. The prizes are a variety of things that are usually made of plastic, in China and can be found in "high end" catalogs such as "Oriental Trading Company." Your five year old will be amazed that he "earned" enough tickets to exchange only 300 tickets for a spectacular treasure such as a plastic ring or a new school eraser or if they spent enough money and time, possibly even something that if you were to purchase it at Walmart or on Amazon, would cost you somewhere in the area of $5 to $20. Remember, the parents may have spent $500 or more if they were hosting a large birthday party. I have often prophesied of the future life of these fabulous prizes. Depending on the age of the child, they will normally bring somewhere between two and twelve minutes of happiness before they are forgotten, discarded or broken. Normally within a few months, they will be sold at a yard sale, garage sale, given to a thrift store or thrown away. Chuck provided many good memories, family and friends bonded, children were loved, large rats played musical instruments, people ate too much pizza and kids got some small joy from winning "incredible prizes."

While I am being a little facetious about the Chuck E. Cheese experience, there is a great spiritual lesson that can be extrapolated from the modern American children's arcade experience. That Redemption Center is a perfect, reversed picture of what Christ has done for us. In my experience, as a young, hard-working pastor, I would save up for weeks to provide those birthday parties, for years working at a part-time or full-time job in addition to pastoring to provide my kids an experience where hopefully they would one day say, we were loved and we had a good childhood. All that work I did to produce hard earned cash was "stolen" by that rat. All those hard-earned tickets (representing my hours of labor of love) were exchanged for something that had very little value whatsoever. The truth is, as adults, we realize, the "Redemption Center" was taking our good hard-earned money, converting it to less valuable tokens, converting those tokens to less valuable tickets, converting those tickets to possibly even less valuable prizes. The short explanation of it would be that the Rat took my hard-earned cash (that had good value) and traded it/"redeemed" it for almost worthless junk that my children would soon forget. Now that my boys are grown, I imagine if you ask them what was the best physical present their parents ever gave them, they might answer PlayStation, guitar, drum set, the computer, 55-gallon aquarium, the Xbox, a car...but I would think it is unlikely that either of my sons would talk about even the most impressive prize they won at Chuck E. Cheese.

What is amazing, is that while Chuck E. Cheese takes our valuable cash and exchanges it for something almost worthless, on the cross, Jesus took our worthless sins and exchanged them for His glorious righteousness, joy and peace of the Holy Spirit. When we go to Jesus in faith believing, He exchanges our worst sins, shame and wickedness for His complete forgiveness, care and Son-ship (or Daughter-ship!).

What have you been carrying around that is just a bunch of junk? You can exchange it at the cross and Jesus will take all of your sin, baggage, hang-ups and hiccups. He will take all that mess and exchange it for His: righteousness, peace, joy, friendship, right standing with God and divine purpose in life.

Before the world was formed, God had you in mind.

> *...he hath chosen us in him before the foundation of the world, that we should be holy and without blame before him in love.*
>
> EPHESIANS 1:4B KING JAMES VERSION

While you may not be saved (knowing Jesus in the fullness of His power and majesty, having accepted His divine sacrifice in exchange for your sins) today, long before you were born, God saw the ability for you to be saved. In His great love for humanity, God the Father made a plan to redeem mankind of the death-grip power our sins had on us. He made it possible for us to know Him, walk in His forgiveness, experience His grace (both to receive it and give it to others) and have the experience of a personal relationship with God through the power of the Holy Spirit.

God saw you saved before you ever even fully realized your need to be saved. Today if you would like to receive His loving forgiveness, grace, mercy and the peace that passes all understanding...it is not difficult to do so. The price paid for you and me on the cross of Calvary was extremely high. Jesus literally died for your sins and mine. If you will trust Him today, admit that you are a sinner and ask Him to forgive you and be the Lord of your life, you will start a process of total transformation. Instantly, upon believing in Jesus as Savior and Lord, your spirit will be saved, and then for the rest of your life, your soul (your mind, will and emotions) will be transformed daily into the image of your Savior. He will begin to fill you with His thoughts, His will and His purposes. If you would like to experience a new life of freedom, grace, fulfillment and purpose...you can start right now.

To know Jesus or in other words to "be saved" (eternally from spiritual death in punishment of sin for eternity in a terrible place called hell and to have the ability to be free from the complete enslavement of sin in this life) there is a relatively simple, but humbling, thing to do on your part. The Bible says,

> *"If you openly declare that Jesus is Lord and believe in your heart that God raised him from the dead, you will be saved. For it is by believing in your heart that you are made right with God, and it is by openly declaring your faith that you are saved. As the Scriptures tell us, "Anyone who trusts in him will never be disgraced." Jew and Gentile are the same in this respect. They have the same Lord, who gives generously to all who call on him. For "Everyone who calls on the name of the Lord will be saved.""*
>
> ROMANS 10:9-13 NEW LIVING TRANSLATION

A LOT is said and promised in these Few Scriptures, Let's break it down...

1. Openly declare that Jesus is Lord
2. Believe in your heart that God raised Him from the dead
3. You will be saved

The explanation: by believing in your heart you are "made right" with God By openly declaring you are saved.

The promise: the scripture tells us that anyone who trusts in Jesus will NEVER BE DISGRACED. Now that's pretty cool! If you are trusting Jesus, you WILL NOT be disgraced. To not be accepted by God would be disgraceful, so we are promised that by default, we will be accepted by God the Father as long as we trust in Jesus, and not only that, but if you are trusting in Jesus and step out in faith then you will not be disgraced in any way, the Lord will take care of those who trust Jesus.

The "proper race": Jews and Gentiles (Jews are Israelites and Gentiles simply means everyone else), so this means EVERYONE qualifies to be saved.

The same Lord: the same Lord generously gives to ALL who call on Him, and then it reiterates that EVERYONE who calls on the name of the Lord WILL be saved.

So, how do I become "saved"?

Or how do I become a "Christian"?

Or how do I become a "Follower of Christ"?

A lot of people desire a prayer they can pray to become a Christian, but interestingly, the Bible actually says very little or nothing about prayer when it comes to becoming a Christian. It talks about 1) declaring who Jesus is and 2) believing He was raised from the dead. When you have a realization of who Jesus is, there will be more than a prayer. You will pray, but not once, you will pray often. Probably if you realize that Jesus literally rose from the dead and defeated the power of death (the greatest enemy of all) then you will be wise to pray to Him daily, frequently and as the Apostle Paul says in the New Testament, without ceasing. It is good to have a time when you can look back and say, that was the day, this was the time, that I dedicated my life to Jesus. With that in mind, the following is a prayer you can pray, and if you mean it sincerely, you will be saved. Humbly and sincerely, pray this prayer, and if at all possible-pray it and say it out loud...

> *Dear Father God,*
>
> *I believe you sent Jesus to die on the cross for my sins.*
>
> *I believe that Jesus is Lord of all and He died and rose again three days later, defeating death, hell and the grave and paying the price for all my sin.*
>
> *Please forgive me of all my sin.*
>
> *I confess that I am a sinner and I need a Savior.*

Please wash me clean right now of my sin,
Holy Spirit please enter my spirit
and help me to live for You.

I say and proclaim that Jesus is Lord.
Thank you for saving me.
Help me to follow you all the days of my life.
In the name of Jesus Christ. Amen.

If you just sincerely prayed that prayer, and you have chosen to believe that Jesus is Lord, you have just gained eternal life. The words of the prayer are not a magic formula, but if you sincerely believe that Jesus rose from the dead, you are saved. (You see, if He rose from the dead, He is still alive and He can do ANYTHING in your life.) Any problem we have is minuscule compared to the resurrection power of Jesus.

Now it is important to proclaim or "openly declare" that Jesus is Lord. So, make a point to tell someone as soon as possible. If you can, go to a church service as soon as possible to the closest Bible-believing church. Ask the church's pastor if they believe that 1) Jesus is the only way to heaven and 2) the Bible is the perfect Word of God. If that pastor says yes to both, the church is good enough. If they say no, or make excuses, then go to another church. Find a Bible-believing church and ask to get baptized in water as soon as possible. Today, the most common way we can make a "statement of faith" is to be baptized in water.

Action Steps:

1. Make sure I am "saved"/know God, by putting my faith in the fact that Jesus came and defeated death by rising from the dead after He was crucified for my sins.
2. Pray the prayer above with conviction.
3. Tell someone as soon as possible that you have put your faith in Jesus.

4. Write down in this book if it is a paper format or write somewhere if you are reading digitally that on today's date and time, that you placed your faith in Jesus Christ as your Lord and Savior.
5. Find a Bible-believing Church as described (the pastor believes the Bible is the perfect Word of God and Jesus Christ is the only way to heaven).
6. Request to get baptized in water as soon as possible. (Ideally, this should be no more than one month from the time you decided to follow Jesus as Lord and Savior.)
7. Attend church as much as possible to learn to grow in your relationship with Jesus.
8. Learn to live a life depending on God daily, spending time in prayer and Bible reading

Salvation is a one-time experience that is granted to you as a free gift of God because of the great price that Jesus paid on the cross. Living out that salvation in this life, though, making it of worth to those around you because of a changed life...that will be up to you. The amount of positive difference you will make to those around you will be determined by how you listen to "your heart" from now on as opposed to how much you "listen to the Holy Spirit" from this day forward.

Thoughts and Questions to Discuss:

1. What does it mean to be redeemed?
2. Jesus sets us free from slavery to sin by His sacrifice on the cross of Calvary. If Jesus paid the price to set us free from sin, how should we respond to this incredible act of love?
3. How should we respond to God's offer of redemption?
4. If God has redeemed us of sin, how should we respond to other people when they sin?
5. According to Romans 10, what must we do to be saved?

6. Are you certain you are saved right now? If not, what is stopping you from getting saved?
7. If you just asked Jesus to forgive you of your sins and be the Lord of your life, what will stop you from fulfilling "Actions Steps" 1-8 above?

PART II

GOD SEES YOU HEALED

CHAPTER 6

New Churches, Bam-Bam *and* Defying Death

GOD SEES YOU HEALED.

God sees you healed

In the year 2000, we saw God do something very special. After landing in Pensacola, Florida, to establish a church in early June of that year, we began to be concerned with the behavior of our youngest son. By November of 2000, the new church group of eleven people had grown to over 50 people, and we were very excited about what God was doing at the fledgling new congregation. Simultaneously, our baby son's behavior was increasingly strange. Andrew Micah Farley, who was at the time 16 months old, had become extremely difficult to control. Andrew had an older brother, and we believed in the proper, loving, careful correction of our children. We never disciplined them in anger, but we did discipline them. Andrew, though, seemed to have never-ending energy. At this point in my life, I had been a youth pastor for almost a decade at large and mega-churches. I had seen a lot of children and teens with attention deficit disorder, hyperactivity syndromes and the like, but my baby son seemed to have far more energy than any other child we had ever encountered.

Increasingly, we noticed that not only did Andrew have an unbelievable amount of energy, but he was exceedingly strong at times. Andrew reminded us of "BamBam" from the old Flintstones cartoon. This child would hardly sleep at night, and you could not keep up with him. As parents, we were both 26 years old and in relatively good shape. When Andrew would get into certain moods, it physically was impossible for me to contain or control him. Remember, Andrew was a baby, sixteen-month-old boy of regular size, but when he would get disobedient or angry, I could not physically contain him. As hard as this is to understand, his 16-month-old arms would often be stronger than my 26-year-old arms (that worked several days a week stocking heavy cases and loading and unloading shelves at Walmart when I was not preaching. [I was in great physical shape]). At times, the nursery workers at church could also not contain Andrew; he had a drive and physical energy that was not normal. When he decided he was going to break out of a nursery door, he would. He did so several times during the middle of church services, with none of the nursery workers being able to control or contain him.

After a few months of this behavior, as parents, we began to wonder if something was seriously wrong. While we always prayed for both of our children, we started to intensely pray about what might be the situation with Andrew. We even eventually considered taking him to the doctor. Often, he would only sleep a very few hours at night (at age 16 months, not at a month or two old). We were getting little sleep and little peace about the child. It is difficult to explain the power he had and harder still for people reading this account to comprehend the level we are speaking of here, so the next story, which is not an exaggeration, kind of lets you understand what we were dealing with as touching Andrew.

In November of 2000, we had prayed about taking Andrew to the doctor about these concerns. One day, as normal, we were having a difficult time controlling him. We were walking up the steps to our porch when we had just been talking and praying about how concerned we were for him. We were discussing whether we should take him to the doctor. At this time, we had just moved to the Pensacola, Florida area a few months earlier in order to start a new church. With limited funds, we had rented a double-wide trailer that was in the back of a lady's yard. The trailer had no garage or shed of any kind, only a large, covered front porch. The porch was the only place to store any type of tools, so we kept our lawnmower on the porch. We owned a 6.5 horsepower gasoline-powered push mower. This mower was relatively heavy and was somewhat difficult for me as a strong, 26-year-old man in good shape to get on and off the porch. (Recently, I looked up the shipping weight of a 6.5 horsepower lawnmower on amazon.com, it showed 80 pounds. So, let's assume the mower on the porch that day was somewhere in that weight range. At this time, Andrew weighed approximately 25 pounds.)

As we were getting ready to walk inside the house, Andrew leaned over and grabbed the lawnmower with one hand. In the next second, he picked it up, raising two wheels off the ground. I remember thinking, "***This is crazy!***" As I was watching him, (I would probably not believe this if I had not seen it with my own eyes - [this true story will make more sense as you continue to read]) he continued to lift the mower and with one hand he lifted it completely (all four wheels off the ground) and threw it a few inches across the porch. Right then and there, we knew that something had to be very different, if not very wrong, and we made an appointment to see the doctor right away.

When we arrived at the doctor that afternoon with Andrew, after getting checked in, he received very speedy care. Once they checked his vitals, they discovered his heart rate was 200 beats per minute, and his blood pressure was also very high. Upon further examination, the physician told us to take him immediately to Sacred Heart Hospital (a large, regional medical facility in Pensacola) to run more tests. Over the next few days, our lives would be turned completely upside down by the results.

In a matter of hours, through several imaging tests, it was discovered that Andrew had some type of large mass in his abdomen. The doctors were not sure what it was, but they did not think it was anything good, to say the least. Surgery, with a team of specialists, was scheduled and we were told that they expected it to be an extensive operation. When the day came to perform the operation (just a couple of days later), most of the new church members were in the waiting room. Surgery started first thing in the morning and continued until the early evening. Every few hours, a different doctor or surgical team member would come to give us an update. This day, a team of several surgeons removed Andrew's right adrenal gland, seven lymph nodes, part of his back muscles, part of a kidney, a portion of the plumbing to that kidney, and a part of his liver. Eventually, the surgery was over, and for the time being, Andrew was alive. Immediately after the surgery, one of the surgeons came to meet us in the waiting room. The female surgeon grabbed my wife and hugged her tightly for several minutes while the doctor cried. The surgeon's profound weeping seemed to communicate to us that even the surgeons believed that surely Andrew would die very soon. He was strapped down in an infant bed with more tubes and monitors going into and attached to his body than a parent should ever have to see. We were told that for several days, he was one of, if not the most critical patient in the entire hospital.

A day or two after the surgery, it eventually became somewhat clear that the baby was moving toward a more stable but still very serious condition, and hopefully, he would live. A meeting was scheduled with the pediatric oncologist (cancer doctor), and those are meetings you never wish on your worst enemy. At the meeting, the doctor had some answers and some news for us. The doctor explained that the surgeons removed the right adrenal gland because Andrew had one of the rarest cancers known to man, an Adrenocortical carcinoma. He explained that the cancer developed into a functioning tumor. Unlike many cancer tumors, which may eventually take the patient's life by growing and pressing into the vital organ and eventually stopping the functioning of a vital organ like the heart, lungs or kidneys - the "functioning tumor" or "living tumor," takes over the organ. Here, the tumor took over the right adrenal gland and caused it to produce adrenaline at an accelerated rate. In Andrew's case, it mimicked the fight or flight response. The fight or flight response is the correct and natural condition of the human body (and some animals) whereby the adrenal glands produce and output large amounts of adrenaline when threatened. This has been used to describe more than one instance, for example, of small framed grandmothers temporarily having the strength to pick up a car when it had fallen on their grandchild. When the body is in the fight or flight response mode, many hormones work together in an almost super-human way to allow the person to flee or fight the threat.

As it was described to us, in Andrew's case and the cases of many other children with this cancer, this can cause the child to have phenomenal energy and strength. This explained the off the charts heart rate, blood pressure, and other vital signs. This was why he had been increasingly difficult to control over the last few months. This was also what killed the vast majority of the people with this disease. We were told there were only 33 other documented cases in the world, and 32 were dead. Interestingly, the vast majority of these were also in young children, less than five years old and they were almost all from the city of Manchester, England. These children all perished in a relatively short period of time over just a few years, all in the 1980s. The British government ripped the town apart looking for an environmental factor, but they never figured out what took the children's lives. Whatever it was, passed just as quickly as it came. We had never even visited England. At the time of this writing in 2020, several websites say there is about one adrenocortical carcinoma per two million people. Even today, this is still an exceptionally rare cancer with an extremely high mortality rate.

As soon as the physician finished explaining the cancer, he immediately went into his next thought. He said, "There is no treatment for this cancer with the exception of removing it. Chemotherapy and radiation make no difference. We took out seven lymph nodes; FOUR WERE EATEN

UP WITH CANCER, so we know the cancer has spread. We will do further tests, but we know the cancer is also in his brain, bones, and lungs. We did the surgery just to extend his life some, but take him home and enjoy him because he will be dead in less than six months." If you know anything about cancer, you know that you do not want one lymph node coming back with cancer, but when you already have an exceptionally rare terminal cancer that has taken the lives of almost everyone that has ever been diagnosed with it, you really do not want to hear that four lymph nodes are also completely taken over by the disease.

The Gospels record versions of an account three times when Jesus was telling the disciples not to worry about what to say when they would be placed before magistrates and government officials when they would get arrested in the future (Matthew 10:19, Mark 13:11 and Luke 12:11). Depending on the translation, Jesus is saying either that the Holy Spirit would give you the words to say at that time, or in other words, that it would kind of be the Holy Spirit actually speaking through you.

> ***In Spirit-filled Christianity, much is said about "yielding" to the Holy Spirit to say what He wants to say through you while speaking in tongues. I have found that even more frequently, He wants to speak things through us in English that may not make a lot of logical sense, but His logic and power are higher than anything a man can come up with!***

I believe the words of Christ concerning the Holy Spirit speaking through us are not confined only to when we get arrested for His cause. There are many times the Spirit will speak through us if we will allow Him and get out of His way. Fortunately, that day, in the cancer doctor's office, was one of those days. As my wife cried her eyes out (it was almost as if someone else was speaking through me), I looked at that doctor and said,

> ***"Sir, the Lord is going to heal my son!"***

The doctor immediately said, "Listen, I see this all the time, you are in denial, but there is no doubt, unfortunately, your son will die in no more than six months." As if I was speaking a different language and he did not understand the first time, I looked at him again, and I believe the Spirit spoke again, ***"The Lord is going to heal my son!"*** At this, the doctor seemed very agitated. He then spoke with all the authority he could muster from behind his M.D. name tag and white physician's coat. He explained that he had been doing this for longer than we had been alive and there was no doubt that the boy would surely die. He now was showing obvious disdain for me and my behavior. He explained that they would be doing some more tests to verify that the cancer had spread to his brain, bones and lungs, but there was no chance this had not happened - on all three counts. He continued that the tumor was not only spewing the cancer throughout the body via the endocrine system, but also explained that the tumor had ripped the adrenal gland apart in the abdomen. The tumor was torn open and leaking cancer into the abdominal cavity. Besides the cancer being transported throughout the body by way of the adrenal gland and being spilled into the abdomen, he also enlightened us that the four lymph nodes eaten up with the cancer indicated that the cancer was everywhere, already. At this, instead of getting into a full-blown fight with the man, I simply said in a little calmer voice, something to the effect of, ***"I understand, but you are going to see the Glory of the Lord. He is going to heal my son."***

Over the next few days, we waited with great anticipation for the results of a test that had to be sent to California for the results. During that week, the oncologist also ordered an MRI of Andrew's brain, a CT scan of his lungs and abdomen, and a full body bone scan to validate his claims that the cancer had spread. The cancer doctor was so very certain of this fact.

A week later, we were called back into the cancer doctor's office. The physician immediately started his speech with, "Do not get excited about what I am going to say." Then he continued, "The tests came back showing no more signs of cancer, but this is impossible. Without a doubt, the cancer is also in his brain, bones and lungs. There is still too much inflammation from the surgery to see the proper results of the scans. I am positive that the test results sent to California were somehow wrong or tainted, so I am going to send it back for another look. Do not get excited because the results are definitely a fluke. The cancer has certainly spread to his brain, bones and lungs."

At this, I looked at the doctor and again said, "Sir, I told you that the Lord was going to heal my son." The physician seemed more irritated with me than he ever had, and said that he would send for more test results as this was simply impossible. Another long week passed, and we were called back into the office. This time, the doctor explained again there was no sign of cancer, but he assured us there was some type of catastrophic mistake with the testing and that someone in the testing laboratory very much needed to be fired. I once again reminded the doctor that, "The Lord is going to heal my son." After a third round of tests, that also showed no more cancer; the cancer doctor eventually quit sending it off. As if this was clearly not enough proof that the Lord had either started or completed a work in Andrew, the physician was certain to explain to us that while these tests possibly were somehow correct, that over the next few weeks, further CT scans and MRIs would confirm that the cancer would quickly return with a vengeance.

In very short order, our son began to be run through large, radiated tubes regularly. At first, every few weeks, he would have either a CT or MRI scan. These became so frequent, that the technicians and nurses responsible for his care during these procedures began to know Andrew and us on a first-name basis. Eventually, one of the sedation nurses would attend our church occasionally. In the weeks after the surgery and the initial post-surgery testing, Andrew was submitted to several scans. Each time, we would have to go see the cancer doctor again. Our visits became adversarial as he had a contempt for me, and I equally had a disdain for him. Each time, the doctor would assure us that the cancer would return. While I am sure he was a fine, dedicated, and disciplined man and physician, I believe that in this situation, it was not actually my spirit speaking through me, but it was often, the Holy Spirit Himself speaking through me. (I am reluctant to even write such a claim and make such claims rarely, but I have no other explanation for the words I shared, the boldness exhibited, and the results that came to pass. All Glory goes to Jesus!) On the other side of these visits, I do not believe that the physician's spirit was speaking either, rather another spirit speaking through him. I am not anti-medicine or anti-science; we appreciate God-given physicians and all the help that a wonderful physician can bring to a hurting individual with the miracles of modern medicine. I can imagine that decades of seeing children die in your practice would harden a man and cause them to believe there is almost never a chance for supernatural intervention. BUT GOD…sometimes does step in and changes prescribed outcomes and alters the future of people, families, churches, towns, cities, regions, and nations! "Jesus looked at them and said, 'With man this is impossible, but with God all things are possible.'" Matthew 19:26 NIV

Eventually, after the surgery, weeks passed, then a month, then months, then we hit the dreaded six-month time frame - that was the "guaranteed" time of death. Six months, came and went. Nine months, a year, 18 months, all came and passed, each with the reassurance from the doctor that the cancer would surely return. Somewhere between the two-three-year time frame, a scan showed something strange in his lungs. Immediately, all medical personnel knew this was the cancer, finally back. The news hit us like a ton of bricks. "Something" was in the pictures of the child's lungs. At this, I told Heather, "We are not going to tell anyone about this. They may not have the faith to believe for it." When the cancer was first discovered, thousands of people in area churches and from across the country were recruited to pray for Andrew. They were told that a baby boy of a young church planter had been given no hope to live after they had been given the diagnosis of a terminal cancer. This time, I did not believe people familiar with the situation would be (for the most part) able to have the faith this cancer was gone.

For about two weeks, we fought Satan in the battlefield of the mind as he assured us that the doctor was finally right and vindicated - this cancer had come back! This time, it was only my wife and I that knew, we did not even tell our closest family or church friends. I knew that if this time, this battle was this incredibly difficult for the parents to fight, how much more would it be for people who were not as invested in the situation. Fortunately, we were almost full-time at the church by then, and we were able to concentrate on our thinking, daily devotions, prayer and fasting as our primary occupation. Finally, some two weeks later, after more tests, it was determined this was not a new tumor or tumors, but it was scarring from pneumonia or some previous lungs infection. By the grace of God, the boy still did not have cancer. This type of scare happened on another occasion, but each time, God was more than faithful.

As time passed by, we grew accustomed to hospital visits, doctors' visits, and the continual scans. Eventually, the months turned into years. About four years into the process with Andrew, the initial cancer doctor, died of cancer himself. I offered to pray for him while he was sick, but he refused to let me pray for him. The years stretched out to make a decade, and after ten years, we were told by a new cancer doctor that, "I am not saying he is in remission from this cancer because you do not go into remission from this cancer. I will say, if he dies of cancer, it will not be from this cancer."

Over 40 days in the hospital initially, over one million dollars of the initial surgery and treatment, a multiple of countless doctor visits to general practitioners, cancer doctors, endocrine specialists, kidney specialists, MRIs, CT Scans and varying tests, and eventually we were told he would live. During that time, the Nemours Children's Clinic (at the time, a large, regional medical team of connected children's hospitals) chose Andrew as one of their cases of the year to highlight in their Nemours Children's Clinic Annual Report. To give an idea of how rare this cancer is, in the same report where Andrew was featured, there were some four to seven cases highlighted for the entire year. Two of the other cases featured were a child who had to live in a bubble because he had no immune system and another child allergic to sunlight. Because, at least in part, to the extreme rarity of the condition, Andrew's medical bills were picked up by the Nemours Children's Clinics and the Children's Miracle Network. (To this day, we often give a small donation when various retailers ask for a donation to the Children's Miracle Network as much like our debt to the Lord, we would not be able to pay that debt). We are very thankful for the Nemours Children's Clinic and the Children's Miracle Network. We recognize, appreciate and are thankful for the many, many teams of surgeons, physicians, nurses and other medical personnel who assisted with great skill and care in Andrew's case. Ultimately, though, we know a miracle occurred that only God Himself could perform.

Amazingly, the healing of this dreaded cancer was not the end of Andrew's healing. After the initial shock of the surgery settled down, we saw all these other physicians in the Nemours Children's Clinic. The endocrine specialist and kidney specialist both explained that if by some chance, Andrew lived through the cancer, he would need specialized care for his kidney and the hormones in his body. The kidney specialist explained that occasionally, the kidneys of such a young child may spontaneously re-grow the missing part and the "plumbing" to the kidney. The kidney with a portion removed and the "plumbing" to that kidney completely healed itself over the next few months and years. (This cannot be properly called miraculous, as it does naturally occur sometimes, but we give credit and glory to God for this blessing none the less!) The hormone specialist explained that with the complete removal of the right adrenal gland, he would probably also need to have hormone therapy to enter puberty when the time came. Interestingly enough, when Andrew reached puberty (alive and well), he went into puberty naturally and normally with no help from modern medicine. In these ways, God proved Himself to be able to heal completely and totally and supply every need for and through His people. We would have been fine to have had some medical and financial complications with Andrew as long as he was alive. Our good God took care of all the medical bills (even though at this time we had no health insurance), and even healed all the auxiliary medical conditions (which are serious enough in their own right). At the time of this writing, Andrew is 20 years old and has little to no known complications from this entire ordeal. **Our God sees you healed!**

Special Note: Our family is forever grateful for the care of the doctors and nurses of the Nemours Children's Clinic and for the financial blessing of the Children's Miracle Network. While we do seek to bring glory to God who did a medical miracle, we do not seek to minimize the wonderful blessing that the physicians, nurses and medical staff made in the care of our son. It was only one doctor we had a problem with. Most or all of the other doctors were supportive. Some were full-blown believers who prayed for our son and did not only depend on their medical skill. Likewise, the Children's Miracle Network paid financial bills that would have been impossible for us to ever repay with care exceeding one million dollars in cost. We had no insurance at this time, yet, the Nemours Children's Clinic and the Children's Miracle Network took care of ALL the medical expense. We still, to this day, frequently support the Children's Miracle Network when they are taking donations at local stores several times a year.

Again, we appreciate the specialized care of physicians, including the lead surgeon, who conveyed to us she was praying the Lord would lead her to do the surgery well. God did a miracle, He also uses people, including physicians, nurses and medical professionals to do parts of His work. It is only the words of one doctor we totally disagreed with, but even then, we do not question his motivation, as he probably just wanted to spare us even more pain thinking our son would die…in the end, though, even doctors are not God.

Thoughts and Questions to Discuss:

1. Do you know anyone that God has ever miraculously healed? Has God ever healed you?
2. Would you consider letting the Lord speak through you even if it may make you uncomfortable or put you at risk for looking foolish?
3. Have you ever "yielded" your will to the Holy Spirit? Have you ever "yielded" your tongue to the Holy Spirit?
4. When Brian said, "The Lord is going to heal my son," do you think he was absolutely certain that would happen, or did it take faith (hope) that it was going to happen? What has stopped you from moving in faith in the past?
5. When you read Matthew 19:26, do you think Jesus was considered normal to people of his day?
6. Does God use medicine and physicians to do His work?
7. What is it in your life you may have been secretly thinking or even openly saying that God is not powerful enough to do?

CHAPTER 7

Misconceptions *about* Healing

Four Myths about Biblical Healing

People believe a lot of different things about divine healing. This is true inside of the realm of Christianity as well as the world at large. Some Christians believe that God does not physically heal any longer- at all. Other Christians believe that it is always God's will to heal people and that if you do not get physically healed, if someone you knew died of cancer, the flu, the coronavirus or just old age, surely you just did not have enough faith. Biblically speaking, we do not see either of these extreme views.

It would be both arrogant and ignorant simultaneously for the author of this book to claim to know why or why not various people are or are not healed. Anyone who thinks they know it all, will be among the most unwise of people. Ultimately, only God knows all, but only He truly knows all. We are told in scripture that…

> *For now we see through a glass, darkly; but then face to face: now I know in part; but then shall I know even as also I am known.*
>
> 1 Corinthians 13:12 King James Version

The New Living Translation, puts it like this…

> *Now we see things imperfectly, like puzzling reflections in a mirror, but then we will see everything with perfect clarity. All that I know now is partial and incomplete, but then I will know everything completely, just as God now knows me completely.*
>
> 1 Corinthians 13:12 New Living Translation

God makes it very clear in His Word that right now, we cannot understand all. The bathroom in the home I grew up in had both a privacy glass in the window on the wall and a glass shower enclosure that was also smoky colored. Each piece of glass allowed light to penetrate the darkness, but it would have been next to impossible to see who was in the bathroom from the outside window and even if you were in the bathroom and someone was in the shower with the shower door closed, you could determine that a person was in the shower, but you would not be able to know who they were exactly. The Bible makes it clear in these scriptures that much of our understanding is now at best hazy, "puzzling" and "incomplete"; however, there is a day coming when we will see clearly and understand what it is that we are going through.

When people unexpectedly die, healing does not come in this life, heartaches of all kinds come, pain seizes our bodies, minds and spirits, dreams are squashed beyond our control and when the world serves up a variety of disappointments and disillusionments, it is easy to say, "See, God does not really love me!" I feel tears welling up even now as I type this page, for those who have experienced deep pain, incalculable loss and suffering beyond what some of us can imagine in this life. We are reminded of the words of Jesus when He said…

> *"I have told you all this so that you may have peace in me. Here on earth you will have many trials and sorrows. But take heart, because I have overcome the world."*
>
> John 16:33 New Living Translation

Jesus understood the grief of this world more than any of us can comprehend on at least two levels...1) As the Son of God, He had a heavenly perspective that currently we earth-only dwellers can dream about. Jesus knew there was much more to the world and universe than what we can see as He had experienced the vastness of the universe, its physically unseen realm and the spiritual warfare that goes on in the heavenliness daily. Jesus knew that the Enemy of our soul was out to steal, kill and destroy us in ways we often forget about or deny completely. 2) Jesus walked through physical, emotional and spiritual pain firsthand that most humans will never experience. From His days being rejected emotionally by His own people and religious system as He taught and loved for their own good, yet they would mostly ignore Him and eventually scream, "Crucify Him!." To the physical torment of the passion week, praying in the garden so vigorously, begging this plan be shelved for another to save humanity He would sweat drops of blood, enduring the beating of the pre-crucifixion torture, the Via Dolorosa (the agonizing route to the place of crucifixion which involved carrying your very heavy wooden cross after you had been beaten extensively with a whip that shredded the back) to the actual crucifixion. To the spiritual torment that is perhaps worse than all of this, when Jesus simultaneously had all the weight of the world's sin on Him and His Heavenly Father momentarily turned His back on Jesus at the moment that Jesus proclaimed, "My God, my God, why have you forsaken me?," Matthew 27:46b New International Version. In other words, Jesus intimately and completely understands pain, suffering, heartache, abandonment, loss and hurt of all kinds. Whether it is the abandonment of a father who walks out on a young family, the lives left in shambles after a divorce, the scene at the cemetery when the small casket is lowered into the ground, or the moment the doctor says the "C" word, Jesus understands and cares.

While going through pain (for example, the grief of losing a loved one) it is a temptation from the Evil one to believe that the people whose loved ones did not die are more spiritual, better than you, or just generally more favored by God, but this is not true. The truth is that sometimes, because of the fallen, wicked, sin-filled world we live in, viruses come, people are born with severe medical problems and sometimes people do not live even though we prayed with sincerity and heartfelt devotion. While the author certainly does not claim to have all the answers about healing...he does think he knows a limited amount and desires to clear up common perceptions that people have about why people get healed supernaturally. We will also look at reasons from the Bible that explain why people do often get healed supernaturally, and share some of the biblical reasons that explain why some people do not get healed.

Four reasons that people sometimes believe other Christians get healed that are not correct, or you could say...

4 Myths about Biblical Healing:

1. **People that receive healing do so because they deserve it or they are good people**
2. **People that receive healing do so because they make promises to God**
3. **People that receive healing do so because they will never sin again**
4. **People that receive healing do so because they are "really spiritual"**

All of the above reasons sound somewhat reasonable (on the surface at least) as to why God would heal people, but the truth is, these are all false.

Healing Myth #1-

People that receive healing deserve it or are good people

If it were true that the people who receive healing deserve it, then a lot of people who died, whose loved ones prayed for them earnestly, would be alive today. We are not to compare ourselves to one another, but we are to compare our spiritual situation only to God. If we were comparing ourselves to whatever the world system considers the worst people on earth to be- murderers, serial rapists, child predators, those who take advantage of the elderly, disabled and vulnerable and whoever else would be in the world's list, then some people look good. If given the choice of who to be left on a deserted island with one of only two people, everyone would choose to be left on a deserted island with Mother Teresa (a Catholic saint who dedicated to helping thousands of poor and neglected people in India) as opposed to Ted Bundy (a prolific and disgusting serial killer who killed dozens of young college girls just for his own pleasure). If those two were alive today and were to both get cancer and one was to die and one was to live, it would be expected according to this myth that Mother Teresa would have recovered and Ted Bundy would have succumbed to cancer. In real life, however, sometimes the Ted Bundys live and the Mother Teresas die. What is interesting, though, as you get to know God, we discover that the "best people" among us are incredibly aware of their very flawed natures. While I only use her as an example and have nothing, but good to say about Mother Teresa…I would dare say, even though I never met her, that she probably realized she had more in common with Bundy than some people would imagine. It is likely that Mother Teresa never murdered anyone, but it is also true that the possibility of murder lived inside of her. We all have the propensity for great good or great evil inside of us. The more we listen to the lusts of the flesh, the more we give into our own depravity, the more wickedness will manifest itself in our lives. It is very unlikely that Bundy, when he was first becoming aware of himself and forming his personality and intellect at the ages of 3-5 years old he said, "One day, I am going to grow up and become one of the most hated, evil, wicked, self-centered people on the planet. I will go down in history as an evil man that will be hated for generations for the many families I will forever shred to pieces with my wicked selfishness." The same could be said for Hitler, Bin Laden, every serial killer and pedophile among us.

It was not that they were initially worse than others, but their choices led them down roads of decision that compounded over time, just like interest compounds. Eventually, unchecked evil reigns supreme, if it is not abated somewhere along the way.

The point here is not what evil exists or why people become serial killers (perhaps the childhood abuse often plays into it, but ultimately only God has these answers), but the point is that when we compare ourselves to the Bundys of the world, we may momentarily feel good about ourselves, but God tells us not to compare ourselves to others. Compared to other regular humans, and especially Ted Bundy, Mother Teresa looks great, but compared to God even Mother Teresa is greatly lacking.

> *Oh, don't worry; we wouldn't dare say we are as wonderful as these other men who tell you how important they are! But they are only comparing themselves with each other, using themselves as the standard of measurement. How ignorant!*
>
> 2 CORINTHIANS 10:12 NEW LIVING TRANSLATION

We see in the New Testament writings of the Apostle Paul from 2 Corinthians it is "ignorant" to compare ourselves to other people. But why is this? Why doesn't it make sense to compare ourselves to extremely wicked people and then feel good about ourselves? It is ignorant because one day to enter heaven we will not be compared to the righteousness or unrighteousness of mankind, but to the righteousness of God Himself. God is entirely righteous and holy...

> *There is no one holy like the Lord; there is no one besides you; there is no Rock like our God.*
>
> 1 SAMUEL 2:2 NEW INTERNATIONAL VERSION

So, the Word of God makes it clear that God is holy and no one is truly holy except for him. We are called to be "holy" in other Bible verses, but we are to understand that our holiness is like the light of the moon at night. We often may say we can see at night, "By the light of the moon," but most of us realize that such statements are just simplified expressions of speech. We learned in primary school that the moon actually does not provide light. The moon simply reflects the light produced by the sun. In a similar manner, the holiness we display as followers of Christ, reflects the holiness of God. Often, I have sat on the dock of my family's bay house in Navarre, Florida to look at an incredible view as the "moonlight" hit the East Bay. The scene was incredibly beautiful, even though the light was not actually produced by the moon.

Our life, is to also produce a majestic image of love, truth, care, and Biblical holiness, not by our own goodness on display, but by a reflection of the Lord's righteousness imparted to us on the cross of calvary and is transmitted to us through the power of the Holy Spirit. The Father's holiness and righteousness is activated when we spend time in His Word, commune with Him through prayer and walk out a life of obedience to His specific direction in our daily routines. When we devote ourselves to be in His Word daily, meditating on it, and being permeated by His will through prayer, we can walk out His purposes in our lives.

When it comes to depending on our own righteousness, goodness and grace, we are reminded often in the Word of who we really are. Psalms 51:5 is just one example…

> *Surely I was sinful at birth, sinful from the time my mother conceived me.*
>
> PSALMS 51:5 NEW INTERNATIONAL VERSION

We were born sinful. We are so sinful that even in the womb, we were sinful. So, when a ridiculous song called "Bad to the Bone" was made popular in 1982 by a since forgotten rock group, George Thorogood and the Destroyers, they were right in their declaration that…

> *"Now, on the day I was born, The nurses all gathered 'round*
> *And they gazed in wide wonder, At the joy they had found*

> *The head nurse spoke up, Said "leave this one alone" She could tell right away, That* ***I was bad to the bone.****"*

In the light of who God is, we are wretched, undeserving, fault filled and just plain sad. We are so bad, that without Jesus, we are "bad to the bone." For this reason, it is unreasonable to think that people who receive healing, while others are not healed (in this life anyway), must have deserved it. When people do receive healing based on the prayers of the saints, the praying Christian played a part in the miracle, they prayed. They asked God to perform the healing, but it was God Himself and His power were displayed in the healing.

If we drive to work in our car today, the car is the vehicle or mode of transportation that physically delivers us from point A to point B, but it is the gasoline in the case of a gas motor or electricity in the case of an electric motor that provided the fuel to propel the car on the road. Without the fuel for the engine, the car would be useless to us for transportation. Similarly, the Christian who prays and receives healing or transmits healing to another human, may be the vehicle that God uses to supply the healing, but make no mistake, the Lord Himself provides the true power in demonstrated healing, whether we speak of the minor healing of a toe, the removal of emotional or spiritual trauma in this life or a major healing from cancer, God provides the fuel for the healing. For these reasons and others, it is a myth to believe that people who receive healing deserve it.

Healing Myth #2

People that receive healing do so because they make promises to God

Have you ever made a promise to God? If you google, "Most common promises made to God?," you will be bombarded, not by the promises that people make to God, but by the promises that God makes to people. This is comforting to know that the Bible is filled with promises made to Christians who have placed their lives in the hands of the Savior. It is my experience as a pastor, though that tells me that as human beings, we often make promises to God. I know of people who, after having an affair, entered the ministry based on a promise to God. I have pastored people who got their life right with God after making promises to God. One person had a heart attack and made a promise to God that if God gave him more time, he would dedicate his life to the Lord. Many years later, he seems to still be successfully and happily serving the Lord. Much could be debated about if these are the best ways to enter God's service. I am especially leery of a public ministry formed greatly based on "making up" for an affair. This at least has the potential to put a spirit of shame, obligation and servitude on the followers of such a minister who did not serve the Lord because of His grace, but possibly served the Lord and made a deal with Him about their soul.

We are not the judge of others with the promises they make to the Lord. I hope if they made a promise to the Lord, they will do their best to keep that promise and certainly through the centuries, many have made life-altering promises to the Lord and have been empowered by the Spirit (remember He provides the gas for the car) to keep those promises. It is a good thing to have integrity in the areas we make promises to the Lord.

However, the truth is, we are not to make promises to the Lord at all. We may be tempted when facing life-altering physical sickness in our own bodies or in the bodies of the ones we love to promise the Lord this or that, if we are healed or our loved one is healed of the sickness of disease. The Word of God directs us not to make these kinds of promises…

> *When you make a vow to God, do not be late in paying it; for He takes no delight in fools. Pay what you vow! 5 It is better that you should not vow than that you should vow and not pay. Do not let your speech cause you to sin and do not say in the presence of the messenger of God that it was a mistake. Why should God be angry because of your voice and destroy*

> *the work of your hands? For in many dreams and in many words there is emptiness. Rather, fear God.*
>
> ECCLESIASTES 5:4-7 NEW AMERICAN STANDARD BIBLE

The content of Ecclesiastes has to do with making vows to pay money to God. The ancient, universal wisdom literature of Ecclesiastes, reminds us in verse four that if we promise to pay God something that we are bound to do so. In verse five, it declares that it would be better to not promise or vow anything at all concerning what we will or will not do for the Lord. Verse six teaches to not let our "speech cause you to sin."

The overall teaching of the passage in Ecclesiastes 5 could be summed up:

1. If you make a vow or promise to God then fulfill it
2. It is best to not make a vow if you will not fulfill it
3. Say little about promises and vows to God
4. If you make a vow or promise to God and do not fulfill it, this can anger God
5. Do not make vows to God lightly, fulfill them if you do

With these sobering verses in mind, we can consider the many promises people frequently make too God. Have you ever promised God you would "be good" or "never sin again" if He would do this or that? When faced with the need for healing, it is always a temptation to make monumental promises you will do this or that, if the Lord will provide healing for your situation. The greater the need for healing, the larger the miracle needed, the greater the temptation to make very large promises to God. They say there are no atheists in foxholes, in other words, when the enemy force is shooting bullets over your head, trying to kill you while you are down in a military trench dug for your protection on a battlefield, even those who supposedly do not believe in God are praying for mercy and protection at that time. Similarly, when the doctor tells you that your child is surely going to die and there is nothing you can do, you will pray and you will be tempted to make mega promises to the Lord that if He will do this healing, then you will do some great thing to pay Him back.

There are several problems with making these types of promises to God during times of major need of a miracle...

Problem One, it is very easy to make a promise and not keep it. The No Action Problem. Even though, we may make it to God, it is easy to forgive ourselves and just say, well, no big deal as soon as the crisis passes.

Problem Two, people sometimes receive healing but do not even acknowledge God by even temporarily thanking Him. The No Thank You Problem.

Problem Three, the third problem with making a promise to God when healing is needed is that often we are trying to "pay for healing" with our good deeds. The No Gift Problem.

Problem One, it is very easy to make a promise and not keep it. The No Action Problem.

The problem here is that people forget to take action on a promise they made as soon as the situation resolves itself and they no longer "need God."

Even though, we may make it to God, it is easy to forgive ourselves and just say, well, no big deal when the crisis passes. In years past in my ministry, I have had the privilege of seeing God heal many people of sometimes very large health issues that could easily have taken their life. Often, these people will come to church frequently before, during and after the health crisis. As soon as the crisis passes though, unfortunately, often, they are back to their old habits. Sporting events, unneeded/extra work, leisure of all kinds, and even sometimes purely evil pursuits all replace the devotion to God that was at an all time high whenever they really needed God to do a miracle. I do not throw stones at these people, as I have experienced this in my own life as well. It is far too easy to forget the goodness of the Lord.

Many in the first camp that make all sorts of promises to God about what they will and will not do to please Him in exchange for this blessing, even though they often forget the promises made, at least at times later in life, these people will often testify of the goodness of the Lord or grant Him praise and honor for His multiplied goodness even when they were not faithful to Him...

> *If we are unfaithful, he remains faithful, for he cannot deny who he is.*
>
> 2 TIMOTHY 2:13 NEW LIVING TRANSLATION

2 Timothy 2:13 is one of the most comforting verses of the Bible. It reminds us that God has a one-way contract. His new covenant with us and His very nature, is not dependent upon the nature of the other person receiving the benefit of the contract/covenant. When Jesus died for us on the cross, He did not die to pay for our sins, if we were good enough. He did not die to forgive us, if we always walked with total integrity. He did not die to pay for our sins, if we would never sin again, but He died for us although He knew we would sometimes not be trustworthy. Jesus died with the complete understanding we often would need His continued grace and mercy. He died while fully understanding our sinful condition, the body of death and untrustworthiness we currently reside in and the wickedness we can commit.

> *But God showed his great love for us by sending Christ to die for us while we were still sinners.*
>
> ROMANS 5:8 NEW LIVING TRANSLATION

What should our response be to such an incredible gift? It should be to give our lives as a pleasing, living sacrifice to God, which is our reasonable service according to Romans 12. However, God gave His life freely because of His great love for us. He did not force us to promise to never let Him down, but He reminds us in 2 Timothy 2:13, that He is faithful to us and He will be faithful to us regardless of if we are faithful to Him. This is a no-lose situation for us. It should not be abused and we would have to wonder about the sincerity of a believer who purposely takes advantage of this incredible promise. Would that type of experience with God be valid at all? The proper response to the promise is to fall in love with God with our whole hearts and tell the world of His mercy, grace and goodness.

Problem Two: people sometimes receive healing but do not even acknowledge God by even temporarily thanking Him. The No Thank You Problem. The problem here is that people forget who healed them or that they were healed at all and have no gratitude.

This is a problem that has existed at least since Jesus walked the earth in the form of man, see Luke 17:11-17. In Jesus' time, there is an account in scripture where Jesus heals ten lepers. Imagine this skin disease has the power to a) ostracize you from society b) permanently mar and disfigure you c) remove you from the ability to enter the temple and be in the community of God's people along with access to the priesthood and in some ways at this time, God Himself and d) ultimately this disease will take your life. What disease could be this devastating in the world we live in today? There may be equally terrifying ailments, but few that would be much worse. Yet, when Jesus healed ten people of this dreadful disease, only one came back to thank Him. In the account from scripture, Jesus asks the man who returns to thank Jesus, "Were there not 10 lepers?" He clarifies that He would have been more than correct to expect thanks from ten lepers.

This seems almost unbelievable that 90% of people would not even say thank you to Jesus for a healing of this magnitude, but my decades of pastoral ministerial experience tell me that this is about correct on average. It is amazing, but often, when people are miraculously healed, they immediately forget it. They reason it away. They determine that it was a mistake, they were misdiagnosed or that they really were not that bad off in the beginning. Others, almost immediately, just forget God. They will intellectually admit, if pinned down, that they probably experienced a miracle, but they simply move on with life and act as if it never happened. I can think of times in our ministry when physicians (who to the best of my knowledge were not Christians) declared that a "miracle" had occurred in the life of a parishioner of the church, and yet, the people involved never had time again to attend church and did not seem to give God praise or credit in other areas of their life as well, outside of church. It is important to say thank you to the Lord. I was fortunate to be taught by good parents at a very young age to say thank you when I received a blessing of any kind, how much more should we show our gratefulness to the Creator and Sustainer of life when He graces us with healing?

The third problem with making a promise to God when healing is needed is that often we are trying to "pay for healing" with our good deeds. The No Gift Problem.

The problem here is that people take what is a gift and try to make it into something they have earned.

It is a very good thing to thank the Lord when He blesses us in any way. It is certainly appropriate and expected to thank the Lord when He heals us. As we see from the Luke 17 account of the lepers, Jesus even rightfully, expects us to thank Him. While a thank you and praise to the Lord is both appropriate and warranted, there is a difference in paying for our blessings and saying thank you concerning our blessings. In the past, I have experienced the favor of being given gifts and the gift giver expressly stating to me that "they wanted nothing in return." I likewise, have given, small and large gifts with no expectation of a payback from the receiver of those gifts. If I were expecting a payback of some sort for giving the "gift," then it would not be a "gift" at all. It would be more of a loan, a pay-off, some type of collateral or something that may be hard to classify, but it would not be a gift. Healing, physical, spiritual, emotional and mental, is not performed to demand that the receiver of the healing "pay for the services of the healer." When we receive medical goods and services from a human health care provider, they normally will require and even need some type of payment. Physicians, hospitals, nurses, urgent care clinics, dentists, chiropractors and the like, they all have bills to pay themselves. Since the health care provider and system have bills due themselves, they will require payment for these services usually. Occasionally, health care providers will travel to third world countries or very poor urban or rural environments in America and render free health care services as a mission of Jesus or as a humanitarian aid project in the name of goodwill to people who cannot pay for these services, but most of the time, these people will need and require payment for services. Surgery, for example, takes resources, knowledge, wisdom, time, physical exertion and preparation to provide a sterile environment. For the finite health care providers, all of these things take a portion of the provider's life, resources, finances, time, brainpower and the physical prowess to actually complete the surgery using their hands and bodies. Since these surgeons and other health care workers are human, these resources are all limited in scope. Even, if the physician is financially independent and they are performing the function as a missions or humanitarian aid project, they are still giving something they can never get back, their limited time. For these reasons, it is vitally important these physicians be paid (at least for their normal work).

On the other hand, with God, things are greatly different because He is not finite (limited in scope) like a human, but He is eternal, all-powerful, infinite (unlimited). When God gives of Himself, He does not sit down at the end of the day and say, "Whoa, I am really worn out!" One of the best possessions I have in life is a Lay-z-boy recliner. I had the privilege to buy myself and my wife one of these wonderful chairs on a clearance sale a while ago. Often, I work hard, and at the end of the day, it is a good thing to come and plop down in that chair, pull the magical side handle and plop back with legs supported by the extended support which magically comes out and then to feel the cushions comfort my back, neck and head as I recline backward. The older I get, the more of a blessing the Lay-z-boys are. With each passing year, no matter how much someone exercises, eats right, works, stays mentally sharp or even communes with the Lord, the frail human body is reminded daily of the wear and tear of time, gravity, age and the resulting lower energy level as each birthday passes.

With God, it is so much different. He never sleeps or slumbers (see Psalms 121:3,4). He never even gets tired. For much of my youth, I thought I would never slow down. I was given the nickname "Spaz" in high school because of the amount of energy I frequently displayed. We were married at the age of 18 and for the next year, I worked three jobs, took at least two college classes and attended church services at least two times a week, often three times a week where I was heavily involved in the children's ministry leading a youth puppet team on Sundays and teaching boys in the Royal Ranger Christian scouting program on Wednesday nights. I hear people say silly things sometimes like they work 130 hours a week and I highly doubt it, but I can honestly say that during those days I worked one full-time job as the night manager of a pizza place in the mall food court, a part-time job of about 20 hours a week at the local Walmart, another part-time job of around 15-20 hours a week cleaning banks in the middle of the night and held down those church responsibilities as well. I was very exhausted all the time, but I imagined that my youthful energy would keep up like that forever. I held up that schedule for about a year. Twenty-seven years later, I realize that one week of that today would probably literally kill me and if not, would most certainly put me in the hospital. If I avoided the hospital, I would fall asleep while standing up for certain by day two. For God, on the other hand, a schedule like that would be child's play.

God never needs us to pay Him back. He never needs His children to "earn our keep." If you could borrow someone else's energy, the Father would never need to borrow yours or mine. Regarding healing, He does not need your good deeds or mine to pay for our healing just as He does not need our good works to pay for His salvation He so graciously provided on the cross. The broken body and blood of our Lord and Savior Jesus

Christ paid for our sin most sufficiently in a manner that can never be repaid. His blood was precious, spotless blood of the sacrificial lamb of Christ Jesus. His sacrifice was 100% perfect, whole, complete and eternal. While the blood of bull and goats under the Old Covenant was only sufficient to temporarily redeem people from their sins for that day, week, month or at most- year…the Blood of Christ is all sufficient to provide forgiveness for our sins once and for all. Many in my Christian faith tradition are erroneously taught and believe that Jesus' work on the cross only covers our past sins, but when Jesus died on the cross approximately 2,000 years ago. Today, when someone sins, or when someone sinned 40 years ago, or if someone sins ten years from now, all of those transgressions were approximately 2,000 in the future from when Christ died on the cross, so His blood covers our sins past, present and future. Not that we should plan to sin or "make provision for the flesh," but it means that if we do sin, we have an advocate with the Father. Jesus knew our human frailty and paid for it long in advance if we will simply submit our lives to Him and accept what He did on the cross of calvary!

In that same covenant deal that God carried out on the cross, at the exact same time, He paid for our physical healing as well. The Bible tells us, prophesying of Jesus' death on the cross more than 700 years in advance of the event that…

> *But he was pierced for our transgressions, he was crushed for our iniquities; the punishment that brought us peace was on him, and by his wounds we are healed.*
>
> ISAIAH 53:5 NEW INTERNATIONAL VERSION

In those words, "by his wounds we are healed," or in the King James Version, "by his stripes we are healed" …the prophet foresaw the beating, the stripes from a whip destroying the back of Jesus. These words are a promise that just as He was, "pierced for our transgressions, he was crushed for our iniquities" = Jesus was beaten for our sins, also, He was also wounded, so we could be healed or by His stripes we are healed. Simple Translation is = Jesus took our punishment for our sins and by the wounds of Jesus, we are healed.

We use a word often in Christian circles, atonement. According to Google's dictionary, *Atonement is: reparation for a wrong or injury; or as used in Christian theology, the reconciliation of God and humankind through Jesus Christ.* More specifically, we are saying that when Jesus died on the cross for our sins He "atoned" or paid for our sins. In Jesus' atonement, He covered both the legal spiritual cost for our sins and for our healing. This is what is meant by the statement frequently said in Christian circles, "Healing is provided for all in the atonement of Jesus on the cross." Just as the atonement provides for our salvation, the atonement also covers our sickness and disease.

Jesus paid for our healing on the cross (Isaiah 53:5) at the same time He provided forgiveness of our sins, we cannot pay for our healing as it has already been taken care of. If we could pay for our healing, we would be doing the work, taking away from the gift of God and the credit could possibly rightfully go to us. Since God is the only one who deserves credit or praise, all the work, all the price and everything was taken care of by Him. If we could somehow earn God's favor for healing by our actions or by making a promise or vow to Him, it might be one reason why God heals, but we can see from scriptures, that the atonement has already covered our healing. The precious blood of Jesus Christ brings salvation and healing, not anything that we have done to merit His favor.

First, for the sake of submitting to scripture and then for these and other reasons not listed, it is always best to not make a promise to the Lord. I knew these things before Andrew got sick and I knew that in the past, I had made promises to God I did not keep. Before you judge me too harshly, have you ever made a promise to the Lord as a child or as a teenager? Now, if you did not attempt to serve the Lord as a child or a teenager, then you really cannot judge me in these areas. For those that have served the Lord, fearfully and seriously, as a child or teenager, then you might understand. I first accepted the Lord at the earliest possible age.

The first time I had an "official" experience when I truly asked Jesus to forgive my sins, accepted what He did on the cross, and believed He rose again was in my grandmother's pre-kindergarten Sunday School at Olive Road Church of God in Pensacola, Florida. My grandmother eventually, faithfully taught that class for over 40 years. In those 40 years, she very, very, very rarely missed a class and when she did, it was only because she was at our summer vacation home in Holley, Florida, where she then attended Holley Assembly of God. I remember Granny faithfully sharing her faith not just in that class, but every day, during my entire life that coincided with hers on the planet (24 years) she would rarely let a day pass that she was not involved in personal prayer and Bible study for three to five hours. This was not an in your face, look at me, I'm so spiritual kind of thing, this was something that only a close family member would witness as she would not do anything much of the time till around 12 noon. Before noon, she would eat, fix me something to eat and piddle a bit, but most of that time was spent in prayer and Bible study. This kind of example, in addition to the model of two dedicated Christian parents and a Christian school education, deeply affects a small child. It was "official" at possibly the age of three or four that I would give my life to Jesus in that class, but I have no memory that did not involve Jesus, God's will, church, prayer, tithing, gratitude, humility and fear of the Lord being a massive part of my family life. When I gave my heart to Jesus in that class, I was serious. Baptized at 5 or 6, I was also serious about dying with Christ and rising again to new life in Christ as I came out of the water.

The Promises- promises, promises, promises

With this type of environment, I was very concerned with the Lord's will and serving Him with my whole heart. It should not be surprising then that on more than one occasion, I promised the Lord that if He would do this or that, I would "never sin again." Now you have to remember that in this case, the definition of sin is important. Some people view sin as "big" things like murder, adultery, rape, stealing millions of dollars, trafficking sex slaves, and molesting children. The problem is that if these are the only things that are sins, then the rest of us can get away with lying, stealing a $50 piece of equipment from work, coveting our neighbor's nice house and certainly there is no problem with a little porn or some misplaced pride in our accomplishments. The issue is that sin is sin. Sin is any time we miss God's mark or standard. Sin is anytime we do not keep Divine law. So, God's law and standard are complete perfection. In other words, God has set up a standard humanly impossible to achieve. In the faith traditions I grew up in, there was no way to reconcile this because we were taught that we must be 110% holy since God was holy. We were taught that ANY deviation from the law would separate us from God and that we would certainly go to hell if we did not fulfill all the precepts of the law. This meant that as a child, I pretty much constantly believed I was going to hell even though Jesus died on a cross so I could go to heaven.

What we did not get in the churches I was a part of was that Jesus really, truly, like 155% paid it all! We would occasionally sing this song, but I think very few people in the holiness tradition I grew up in ever got it. Therefore, many people became a Pharisee. Pharisees were the religious zealots of Jesus' days. They claimed to be righteous (why not, you believed you were absolutely going to hell if you were not righteous), but in reality, Jesus said that while they looked clean and beautiful on the outside, they were actually like whitewashed graves (see Matthew 23:27,28). Jesus explained that trying to appear righteous on the outside would get us nowhere with God. A tomb often looks beautiful on the outside, being clean and beautiful, but on the inside, it is full of dead men's bones and everything that is unclean.

Jesus tells us it is not acceptable to pretend like we have it all together on the outside when on the inside, we are just as dead as ever, but when you are given no real choice except to act like you are perfect in your religious circles, this is often what you will try to do. So, as a child and teen, I tried my best to bargain with God. I wanted to be acceptable to God, but I found myself lacking over and over again. I was constantly told that any sin would certainly send me to hell, and I believed it with my whole heart.

So, I cannot count the times, that by the time I was about fourteen years old, I had made sincere promises to God that I had broken numerous times. These promises went something like this, "Lord, if you will do this thing in my life or that thing in my life, I will never sin again." It's been too many decades now, but I'm pretty sure, at first, these promises were more like, "Lord, if you will forgive me of my sin, I promise, I will never sin again." Oh, how I meant it! Oh, how I desired earnestly to live completely, 100% free of sin. To know perfection in the flesh. And, Oh, how marvelously I failed at this again and again and again. Now, remember, I'm not saying I murdered someone, stole a car, or maliciously planned to destroy someone's reputation, but I am saying, I had impure lustful thoughts, I would be 99% honest, not 100% honest, I was selfish, I was prideful, I was arrogant, I did things without depending on God, I would not use what some would consider curse words, but I would use impure language, maybe calling someone stupid and I would judge people. The problem is, this is sin. It is 100% sin. You can still have a decent society if a lot of the citizens do these sins and others like them, but it is not perfect, it is not holy, it is not righteous and it is not pleasing to a perfect God.

I was a rank and file sinner and I did not want to go to hell, so I made these promises to God that I would never sin again, several times. I spent much of my time as a child repenting of sins. My mother even joked that I was talking to my guardian angel as I was often seen closing my eyes saying something until I was in maybe second grade. I was not talking to an angel or being psychotic, I was asking the Lord to forgive me of my sins over and over and over again. I found that the moment I would find his forgiveness, within normally no less than an hour (and that was a long time), I was again doing something wrong. This fear tormented me day and night. My group's idea of Christianity, had the fear of the Lord is the start of wisdom and knowledge totally down pat, the problem was that the other side of Christianity (grace) was very foreign and to be avoided at all costs.

Anyway, these promises, made me feel even worse. I often believed the lie that God could never forgive me. Eventually, I decided there must be some grace somewhere up there or either I was totally destined to hell because I was so much worse than other people. I must certainly be 100 times worse than other "good" Christians for sure. Thankfully, several decades of serving as a senior pastor, church planter, youth pastor, associate pastor and children's pastor in churches of all sizes, taught me something, I learned these people, even the leaders, in these churches may have been "better" than me, but they certainly had their own boatload of problems and sins. (When I say boat load, we are not talking about a canoe, pool float, or even a whitewater raft that could hold five or six sins appropriately…we are talking cruise liner, container cargo ship, naval destroyer vessels and aircraft carriers…think VERY LARGE boatload of problems and sins).

Eventually I realized that 1) yes, the Lord's standard for us is perfection, but 2) we will never meet this level on our own. If we must meet this level of perfection on our own, we will always fail. Why do radical terrorists sometimes blow themselves up in a pursuit to please an unpleasable God? Because they believe that the only way they can be guaranteed of their god's favor is to martyr themselves. As Christians, we are not supposed to believe this or anything close to it, but some in holiness/Armenian circles, do believe something similar, they believe at least in part that they can never truly know God's love and favor and that they must strive with great difficulty to work hard enough, perform most excellently, strive to worship with ever greater intensity or do enough penance that maybe, just maybe God would forgive them and maybe if they are really, really good, He would actually love them. Just today, as I write this book, I read an account of a once world famous Spirit filled minister that lived in my lifetime, who secretly shared with their family that they did not know if

God loved them and felt they had to work super hard in the ministry to prove to God that they were worthy of His love and favor.

Back to our book, back to our story of healing here, and how God does not heal based on promises made to him...since I had made these earlier childhood promises that I would never sin again, yet, I failed these promises each time and failed, repeatedly. I decided late, now at the age of 26 and as a senior pastor that with my son possibly dying, I could not quickly or carelessly make a promise to God that I would never sin again. I had already discovered in just a little over a quarter of a century on the planet, that no matter how good my intentions were that I was prone to be less than perfect and that if I made this promise once again to not sin, there was a very good chance I would still fail God. I even knew by this point in my life from Bible study that I should not make a promise to God at all and that if I did make a promise, I should keep it. Knowing I was already walking in God's extreme grace, that He had forgiven several unkept promises before (after all, He is faithful when we are not, see 2 Timothy 2:13)...this time, I knew if I would make a promise, it should involve some real, honest, adult, big-boy, soul-searching, that's why it took me three days to come up with a proper promise.

While I promise you should not make promises to God concerning the healing of your loved ones, and while I agree with my own biblical teaching and writing in this very chapter that Jesus paid it all on the cross for salvation and healing, if you do make a promise to God, make one that you can keep. For days, I cried and cried. I argued and wrestled with God Spiritually speaking, Jacob had nothing on me in Genesis 32. I came up with great idea after great idea...

God if you will heal my son, I will never do ____________________.

God if you will heal my son, I will make sure I ________________.

Ok, for real God, if you will heal Andrew, I will never do __________.

Seriously, after thinking about it God, I mean Andrew's life is on the line here, so I will make sure I always ______________________________.

No! Stop! We must not make these kinds of promises to God!

Each time I would come up with some other brilliant thing, some super-spiritual thing, some lack of sin, some sincere desire to please or pay God back...I would always stop myself short of finishing those promises. Each time, the Holy Spirit would gently, calmly and politely remind me of all the sincere promises of the past... I would never miss a day reading so much of my Bible. I would always demonstrate the fruit of the Spirit. I would never lie (even the smallest of white lies). I would never entertain a lustful thought for more than a millisecond. I would never sin again. Now you probably are not this dumb. You probably made maybe one promise to the Lord at worst, but said, well, I will never do that again. Or maybe you never ever made a promise at all to the Lord because you have always been wiser than that, but keep in mind we are talking about the age of five, seven, ten and maybe twelve or thirteen.

After three days of soul searching, I finally came up with this. I thought to myself, this is about the stupidest promise one could ever make. This is so ridiculous, why would He ever accept it.

I finally said with 110% sincerity with tears in my eyes, something very much like this...

Brian Farley's promise to God Concerning His Son Andrew...

"Lord, you know me. You know I am supposed to be very spiritual, but You know more often than not I'm actually pretty unfaithful. You know that the truth is, I often fail You miserably. You know all the promises I have ever made to You, You know I'm sorry for them, but You also know that each and everyone, I failed. You know, You hear more confession from me than probably

anyone else in the world. Lord, I realize now that I am more sinful than I ever thought I was and I ask You to once again, forgive me, wash me, cleanse me and fill me with your power and Spirit…Lord Jesus, I cannot promise You that I will be a good boy. I cannot promise You that I will always hearken to your voice. I cannot say that I will always live the life You have called me to live or do the exact right thing, I find that more often than not I am a spiritual failure of epic proportions, but Lord, if You will heal my son, I will tell everyone that I can when you grant the opportunity that I meet for as long as I live and as long as you give me the ability to do so that ***You are a good God, You are a healing Savior, You are a loving Father and You heal, not because we are good, but because it is who you are to be good, to grant life and to do miracles. You heal because YOU ARE GOOD!"***

Now friends, at the time of this writing, it has been 20 years since that day, and by the grace of God, I have kept that promise. I do not believe that promise is why God healed Andrew, but I believe if you are going to make a promise to God, you should do your absolute best to keep that promise!

Today, I realize this is possibly, one of the only promises He will accept (I said possibly because I'm not God and do not have it all figured out). You see my promise, was not about me. It was not about proving anything to God. It was not about trying to impress the Holy Spirit. It was not about impressing other people. My promise, was simply that I would tell the world who Jesus is. This was something I was already doing. It is something that every Christian is called to do regardless of if our family has experienced miraculous healing or not. I am glad I was not tried in this manner, but I would like to think that I would have still told the world of God's goodness regardless of how the story ended, may the Lord see fit not to change the story I ask humbly of Him. We are all called to recognize the goodness of God and to tell of the goodness of God. When we get to the end of our own "goodness" and we truthfully discover that we come up lacking, we find His grace is sufficient.

> *But he said to me, "My grace is sufficient for you, for my power is made perfect in weakness." Therefore I will boast all*

> *the more gladly about my weaknesses, so that Christ's power may rest on me.*
>
> 2 CORINTHIANS 12:9 NEW INTERNATIONAL VERSION

You see, the promise I made, really required nothing from me at all, at least not anything much! It requires no righteousness on my part whatsoever. For the self-righteous (those who may know they always have it together and keep it together) my prayer may seem a little pathetic. To those, I would say, good for you, I wish I were as great as you, but I'm simply not. However, I am in good company. That company is the company of the Apostle Paul and the company of those who Jesus described as the ones who needed what He has to offer.

Paul said in Romans 7 that the things he wanted to do, he did not do and the things he did not want to do, these are the things he did…

> *[14] We know that the law is spiritual; but I am unspiritual,*
> *sold as a slave to sin. [15] I do not understand what I do. For*
> *what I want to do I do not do, but what I hate I do. [16] And*
> *if I do what I do not want to do, I agree that the law is good.*
> *[17] As it is, it is no longer I myself who do it, but it is sin living*
> *in me. [18] For I know that good itself does not dwell in me, that*
> *is, in my sinful nature. [u] For I have the desire to do what is*
> *good, but I cannot carry it out. [19] For I do not do the good I*
> *want to do, but the evil I do not want to do—this I keep on*
> *doing. [20] Now if I do what I do not want to do, it is no longer*
> *I who do it, but it is sin living in me that does it.*
>
> ROMANS 7:14-20 NEW INTERNATIONAL VERSION

Instead, Paul, under the inspiration of the Holy Spirit explained that even though he was saved, the sinful nature inside of him, still lurked and caused him to do things that in his new nature he had no desire to do (see verses 24-17). Does this sound familiar? Do you ever do things you do not want to do? If so, then you will understand that we need a Savior.

We do not just need a Savior one time to wave a magic wand over us and make us perfect, but we need Him every day to help us serve Him. Our own human frailty teaches us our ongoing need for the Savior. I need you Lord, I need thee. Every day, I need thee. The old song teaches that it is our daily help from the Holy Spirit, which draws us close to the Father, teaches us humility and ultimately conforms us to the image of Christ.

Later in this masterpiece of doctrine, Paul explains...

> *What a wretched man I am! Who will rescue me from this body that is subject to death? Thanks be to God, who delivers me through Jesus Christ our Lord!*
>
> Romans 7:24,25 New International Version

It is our dependence and complete reliance on Jesus that delivers us from otherwise certain permanent death, when this body dies. When we, on the other hand, trust Jesus, we can expect to be delivered through Jesus (verse 25).

Jesus, likewise, did not rebuke people for admitting their need for a Savior, but he actually says that these are the people He came for...

> [30] *But the Pharisees and the teachers of the law who belonged to their sect complained to his disciples, "Why do you eat and drink with tax collectors and sinners?"* [31] *Jesus answered them, "It is not the healthy who need a doctor, but the sick.* [32] *I have not come to call the righteous, but sinners to repentance."*
>
> Luke 5:30-32 New International Version

Jesus was attacked by self-righteous Pharisees (the highly religious people of the day) because He ate and drank with "tax collectors and sinners," but His reply was basically these are the people He came for all along..."I have...come...to call...sinners to repentance." Jesus did not care what anyone thought. He did not come for the religious. He came for sinners. If you are a sinner, you fit the bill.

Many will stop there and say yes, but see, Jesus was talking about sinners before they got saved, because then they will obviously be perfect in Christ and will not have any more sin once they become a Christian. To this argument, first, we reference what Paul (the great Apostle Paul) said in Romans 7. So, if you become perfect, sinless, or almost sinless at the moment of salvation, Paul has been ruled out of consideration for doing a few things, for example, writing the majority of the New Testament, surely, he is too much of a sinner for that. Second, we see Jesus goes out of His way in other places in scripture to make certain that He is saying that Christians are to continually have an attitude of dependence on the goodness of God and not their own goodness. For those who want to claim holiness to such a degree that they never sin again, or that if they do, they have lost out with God, Jesus really aggravates that kind of thinking when He tells parables like this...

> *9 And He also told this parable to some people who trusted in themselves that they were righteous, and viewed others with contempt: 10 "Two men went up into the temple to pray, one a Pharisee and the other a tax collector. 11 "The Pharisee stood and was praying this to himself: 'God, I thank You that I am not like other people: swindlers, unjust, adulterers, or even like this tax collector.12 'I fast twice a week; I pay tithes of all that I get.'13 "But the tax collector, standing some distance away, was even unwilling to lift up his eyes to heaven, but was beating his breast, saying, 'God, be merciful to me, the sinner!' 14"I tell you, this man went to his house justified rather than the other; for everyone who exalts himself will be humbled, but he who humbles himself will be exalted."*
>
> LUKE 18:9-14 NEW AMERICAN STANDARD BIBLE

Have you ever wondered how someone as awesome, sweet, loving and miraculous was so hated by the powerful? Well, this story right here, explains it all. Jesus willingly laid down His life (He could have called down legions of angels), but here is why they wanted Jesus dead. Jesus had the nerve to say that people that were tithe paying, fasters would totally miss out with God if they thought they were better than the "sinners." He turned the whole religious idea on its head and explained that it was the lowly, humble, "sinner" that would be justified with God. Jesus made it clear that, it is the person that knows they are spiritually and morally bankrupt who is truly rich with God.

It is the person that knows they are spiritually and morally bankrupt who is truly rich with God.

If it is an established fact from the Word of God that we all are sinners, continually, in need of a Savior, then it is impossible to pay for our healing, our salvation, or any other favor with God. If we are totally in need of His continual, ongoing grace then we cannot expect that we could ever do anything to merit his healing. We are not healed because of our effort, righteousness, tithe money, fasting or anything else...when healing comes, it is because of the goodness of God.

Healing Myth #3

People that receive healing deserve it because they will never sin again

Some people take the discussion surrounding our unworthiness and our continual dependence on Jesus for our only means of salvation and righteousness and say, "Well, yes, we are all sinners, but Jesus was clearly talking about people before they make a commitment to Him. Once you become a Christian, you will never sin again, if it is the real thing." To this, we can again clearly see that the Apostle Paul would be unqualified to lead the Church with his statements about his lack of on-going holiness. Since we have already covered this, though, let's move on. Not only, did Jesus explain that it is the humble sinner who will be justified before God, but He also says some very disturbing things for those who fall in the "Christians do not sin every day camp." Of all places for Jesus to mess with this seemingly great teaching, He messes with it in what we historically call "The Lord's Prayer." In Luke 11 and Matthew 6 Jesus teaches about prayer. In Luke 11, it is added that Jesus is responding to a disciple's request for Him to teach them how to pray in the same way that John the Baptist taught his disciples to pray. In the narrative of Matthew, it may have been in response to a question, but it may not have been as here, Jesus simply teaches about prayer. These accounts may have been about the exact same time and conversation/teaching that Jesus was having or it may have been two different times where He taught basically the exact same thing. What is certain concerning the Lord's Prayer is that Jesus did NOT teach that Christians will not sin frequently. Instead, Jesus heavily implies that His disciples sin so frequently that every single time they pray that they will need to ask the Father to forgive them.

> *Forgive us our sins, for we also forgive everyone who sins against us.*
>
> LUKE 11:4. NEW INTERNATIONAL VERSION

> *and forgive us our sins, as we have forgiven those who sin against us.*
>
> MATTHEW 6:12 NEW LIVING TRANSLATION

While some translations, may translate the word, here translated as "sin," to something else like "trespass," the idea is exactly the same. We are "sinning" against God so frequently that we must continually come to the throne of grace asking for God's forgiveness. Remember that in both cases, Jesus is teaching how to pray, when we pray. So, the intent is that every time we pray, or at least every day, that we would ask for forgiveness of our sins. Is it not logical to assume that those who believe that a Christian will not sin every day will not also believe that they will need to pray every day? Or is it that the Christians who are so righteous that they do not sin every day, that they have learned to develop this level of piety to the point that they also do it without praying every day? If people are so good that neither do they sin every day and additionally they do not even need to pray every day...do they even need God at all?

If we are not sinners, we do not need the Lord's prayer. Many people that say, you do not have to sin every day will stress that they are not saying you may not sin frequently, but that you do not HAVE TO sin every day. I will accept that Jesus never says you must sin every day. Nowhere in scripture are we told that it is a requirement to sin daily, however, from the Lord's prayer we see that the implication is that sin is so frequent among Jesus' disciples that each and every time they pray that they should also ask for forgiveness of sins as they pray for other things. So, while, it may be possible to not sin every single day, we must accept from the Master's teaching on prayer that sin is always crouching at our door waiting to grab us once again. It is so powerful and its leader (Satan) is such a good tempter, that in the Lord's prayer we are also told to pray that we are not led into temptation, but to be delivered from evil. -Sin is so powerful that we cannot remove ourselves from it on some occasion, but we must be delivered. When something is delivered, a package is picked up by something or someone more powerful than it and it is taken to another place by that person or entity. Likewise, we are so weak, so prone to sin, that in our frailty, we are to ask that the Lord both not lead us into temptation (which He is always willing to lead us to a place of righteousness) and that He will pick us up and deliver us away from Satan's plan. This all again implies that sin, temptation and the avoidance of it, is such a prominent part of the Christian's life experience that we could only say we are not sinners, or that we will never sin again unless we say it with a good dose of pride.

Here we see as well that we will be forgiven our sins in the same manner that we forgive those who sin against us. This is of utmost importance.

In other words, if we are slow to forgive, we will be slow to be forgiven. If we choose not to forgive, then we will not be forgiven. We must not only recognize that we are dealing with the need to be forgiven of sins frequently, but we must also be very free with the forgiveness we offer to others. Healing cannot be deserved by some because they are not sinning or they will never sin again.

Healing Myth #4

People that receive healing deserve it because they are "really spiritual"

While many people will find me unimpressive and rightly so, occasionally, when you preach at a church as the guest speaker and you can tell your greatest preaching stories (true stories), you can come across as impressive to people. People may even think you are spiritually impressive, leading to the false idea that maybe you are more spiritual than you seem. When traveling to a faraway church and sharing the story about Andrew's healing, along with the mystique of being the guy coming into town and telling other powerful true stories, this can magnify this false impression of spiritual greatness. Even though the stories I tell are actually true to life, unembellished accounts of historical events, one must remember that when we come to preach and preach a "great" sermon with "great" stories, these are two or three stories from a whole life and ministry that most of the time was quite unspectacular. If the pastor of every church (who labors week after week, month after month, year after year and sometimes decade after decade in the same pulpit) could just tell their very best life story of what God had done for and through them, if they could preach just their best 1-3 messages instead of the 1,000s of messages they have preached through the course of time at this pulpit, they would also seem rather spectacular. The problem is, that is not reality.

I remember in the 1980s that I grew up in, many of the evangelical, television preaching superstars would only present their very best image always. This was not just about clothing, external looks and appearances and the like, but they would never be "real" when it came to sharing their vulnerabilities, weaknesses and failures. There was one televangelist in the 1980s that was probably ten times more popular and prominent than whoever the top five most successful ministers on media are today combined. In that time, there were normally three channels to watch at a maximum, very limited use of recording devices to record a show, no way to play the show at a later time and only a relatively small percentage of households had cable or satellite channels. This was the way it was in addition to practically speaking there was no internet of any kind except for a few nerds chatting on Commodore 64 bulletin board services over 1200 baud modems, which most Americans did not even know existed.

In this media environment, which is completely foreign to a millennial or generation z-er, if you were a pastor on national television several times a week (with only three or four truly national television stations at the time), you ruled the airways and with it much of America's religious thinking. In this era, a few names reigned supreme and one was set apart from the others. Mostly, all the television pastors of that time went to great lengths to be nontransparent. These leaders did everything to project a powerful, unblemished image. They often went to great lengths to hide their sins, which caused them to sin more and the cover-ups became more and more profound. When several of these men of God fell from their lofty heights through unfortunate sexual and financial scandals, it changed the demands of much of American Christianity.

Prior to the fall of these giants, pastors would never have considered wearing jeans, not wearing ties, or ever discussing their own struggles of any kind. After the scandals, casual dress and a new buzz word would shortly appear across the religious landscape, which has grown and grown for 20-30 years until reaching its now high crescendo, "authenticity." People demanded that their leaders would actually communicate and lead in a manner that admitted they were regular human beings like everyone else. In a search for authenticity, I present this view of why people are not healed because they are "really spiritual." (Whatever that even means).

Yes, my son was really and completely healed of a deadliest of deadliest cancer. Yes, the Lord eventually healed many more people through our ministry of deadly cancers. No, it is not because we are "super-spiritual" or special in any way. In 2012, for one time in my life, I basically fasted for 40 days. Let me explain, yearly I often went on a fast of one day to one full week. Many times, this would last for two to four days. During this time, I would not eat and the entire purpose of the fast, was to hear from God for direction for the church as the pastor and our ministry in general. The idea was to hear clearly from the Lord, get fresh ideas and insight and be able to lead the church in the best direction for the next year to come. Even fasting for one to three days was difficult for me. I am a little embarrassed to tell you, but at times, even when I decided to fast for only three days, I have blown it. On day two, sometimes I would go completely off course. This 40 day fast was, however, quite different.

At the end of summer 2012, I started what I planned to be a three to seven day fast. Prior to this, the longest I ever successfully fasted (completely from no food, but with water/drinks) was about seven to ten days. As a previously chunky boy (husky jeans in the fifth grade), I was very good at eating. It was like a talent and I could have probably won some competitive eating contests, if I had tried out. The fast was a little different, day one was not that difficult. Days two and three seemed a little less difficult than normal. By day four, I sensed that I was probably experiencing something different than I had in the previous years. After a week, two things were clear. One, I was not as hungry or as sick as I had expected to be. In years past, I had often picked up extreme lack of caffeine headaches as at the time I was both massively addicted to caffeine and at the same time was very prone to long, extended, violent, migraine headaches that had even sent me to the hospital on occasions. The second thing clear to me by the first week of this fast was that unlike years past, I was not receiving a lot of Divine inspiration about what the Lord would have me do for the church for the next year.

On days eight through eleven, I was wondering if the Lord was doing something new and different and if He would tell me anything at all about the church. Eleven days turned into 21 days. At this point, I had lost a LOT of weight and even though I had previously been about 20-27 pounds overweight, I did not really have any more healthy weight to lose. On day one to day 21, I was very serious with this. If truth was told, I think once a day for a few days of that time, I would eat one of those little packets of cheese mix which come with a Pizza Hut pizza. I did not eat a pizza, just a packet of cheese mix. We are talking about a little packet that is a little larger than the size of sugar packet or artificial sweetener packet. They come with pizzas, along with other similar packets of red peppers. They are 10 calories total, according to Pizza Hut's website. (Several times during this fast, I would get pizza for others for the family or the church and that packet is what I would eat as a treat. No one else in my family or church was fasting). Yes, I should not have done that, but as you see, I am not claiming to be a spiritual giant. Except for those cheese packets, often after week one finished…for 21 days, there had been no nourishment to the body except for water and possibly an occasion glass of apple juice. On day 21, several people, even outside of my family, had noticed and commented on the rather pronounced, rapid weight loss. I had almost no energy and I had watched on internet videos during this time how several people had recently died on extended fasts. So, on day 21, I waited until after 8 p.m. and I went by a Sonic Drive-Through and got a small vanilla milkshake. Because I was concerned for my health and, let's face it, because I was really, really, really hungry, for the next 19 days, I had only that small shake (daily) after 8 pm. Days 1-21 consisted of no food whatsoever except for 10 calories of Pizza Hut cheese packets here and there. Days 22-40 consisted of one small vanilla milkshake after 8 p.m.

From that fasting experience, I received the clear direction that God was not speaking about the church because I was not going to be at the church for much longer, at least in terms of my tenure thus far. When coming off of that fast, we had been at the church for about 12 1/2 years, after the fast, we would only stay for less than 1 1/2 years more, and about three months of that time was preparing the church for pastoral transition. This was one of the scariest things I had ever done. Leaving complete security and comfort to follow the voice of God. I had done it before, but it had been a long time and I had never been as established as I was at this church. From that fast, I was given the courage to give up the church. It was literally the church of my dreams, I had dreamed of it 15 years earlier, and it had come to pass. During that fast, our 20th wedding anniversary was approaching. The fast happened from late August through the month of September 2012. During the fast, I got the idea that I really needed to do something special with and for Heather for the anniversary. In the past, we had never taken an extravagant vacation and the anniversary gifts were normally very modest. During the fast, I got the idea to ask Heather what she would think of going to New York City for our anniversary. For the next three months, for two specific purposes only, I worked part-time at a fast-food restaurant. Half of the funds from that job, we gave to missions. Half of the funds from that job, we put up for the trip. Our anniversary is in December, but because it is so close to Christmas and as pastors, we are extra busy at Christmas time, we never celebrate our anniversary on our actual anniversary. So as usual, we decided that we would celebrate right after the new year. We went to New York City on vacation from January 1 through January 9, 2013. We stayed on the 43rd floor in a large corner suite of the Doubletree Times Square overlooking all that you could ever want to see. During this trip, we experienced supernatural favor at every hand. Bizarre things that would take another book to explain, but supernatural far beyond belief. The favor was so pronounced that we both noticed it and were astonished by it. On this trip we first heard the Spirit lead us towards New York City. It would take seven years to complete the journey of moving to New York City. Amazingly enough, it was not until writing this book over seven and one half years later that I put together that the fast that I was supernaturally empowered by the Spirit to do (even if it involved small milkshakes at the end)...had set up a calling in a place that was both the scariest place we could imagine and simultaneously the most exciting thing we could ever imagine. It may seem to you right now that the Lord is quiet when actually the Lord is simply preparing you for something all together unexplainable, in a season of your life you cannot even imagine, as you follow his voice.

It may seem to you right now that the Lord is quiet when actually the Lord is simply preparing you for something all together unexplainable, in a season of your life you cannot even imagine, as you follow his voice.

What does all of this have to do with being super-spiritual, not being the reason that people are healed? When you hear that at one time, I was basically, for the most part anyway, able to fast for 40 days and then you hear that this was the same guy who God used to speak and miraculous healing came to his dying infant son and several others with cancer throughout the years...you may say, yes, see, he's super spiritual. He must be pretty disciplined. He must hardly ever sin. Maybe he's better than me?

Truth is, the answer to all of that is a big fat NO!

Now, I have mentioned that it was difficult in the past on more than one occasion to fast. Let me now tell you some of those details. On more than one occasion, I have announced to Heather I would fast for a week or three days or two weeks or whatever. I cannot count the times that when I got really hungry, I did not only break the fast, but I ate too much. So, you go from fasting to the opposite of fasting, gluttony. This means you go from being what some people may call or think is "super-spiritual" to committing what some people consider a "deadly sin." Several occasions I was determined that I would not eat for 2-4 days and yet, on the second or third day, I would lose it.

Here's the one that takes the cake, though…One time, perhaps a year or two before this 40 day somewhat success story, I proudly announced to Heather that I was really going to up my game and fast for a week or two. I cannot remember how long it was going to be, but I know I was talking about at least several days. I started off OK on day one and day two. By the end of day one, I got a caffeine withdrawal headache. By day two, it was really bad. On day three, in a lot of pain, I had a lot of options. As pastor of a local church, I could have gone to the church sanctuary, turned the air conditioner on and some nice, calming worship music and just lay down before the Lord in the cool, soothing auditorium. I could have prayed more and harder. (I did ask the Lord to take the headache away several times and I took some headache medicine.) I could have taken stronger headache medicine. I could have gone to the chiropractor for an adjustment and a massage, which may have helped the headache, as I have experienced that in the past. I could have got in a swimming pool, several of which were available to me, which would have distracted me till the headache passed. I could have simply been stronger and tougher and demanded to wait till the next day because I knew this type of headache would pass. I could have done a lot of "super-spiritual" and better-disciplined things, but do you know what I actually did?

I called Pizza Hut. I ordered a large pepperoni pizza. I had it delivered. (Here is the really sad part, that is also true, I would never recommend it.) I am seriously not proud of it. I am not desiring to be funny, but honestly, I ate the entire pizza in one sitting. Now it was thin crust, but none the less, I ate the entire pizza in one sitting. I went from "super spiritual" to "super unspiritual" in just about 30 minutes. So, this same guy who basically fully fasted for 21 days and partially fasted for 40 days, this same "spiritual giant" who did this is the same guy who broke a fast on the third day by eating an entire pizza. Can God love somebody like that? Can God use somebody like that? You see, it is not our "super-spiritual" state that determines if God can and will use us, it is the goodness of the Lord that brings salvation, healing and all His benefits. Often, we are a part of the equation of healing…will we open our mouths to be used as God's vessel? The same goes for many miraculous things that the Lord does…will we step out on faith and obey His guidance? Will we do the sometimes seemingly strange things He has called us to do? But what we can be sure of is that He can always be trusted and that He is the healer. This explains why we cannot pay for our healing, or salvation, for that matter, with our good deeds. He heals, not because we are "spiritual," but because He is good.

Thoughts and Questions to Discuss:

1. What does 2 Corinthians 10:12 and 1 Samuel 2:2 teach about comparison?
2. What does Psalms 51:5 tell us about how we were born?
3. From Ecclesiastes 5:4-7, what are at least two things we can say about making vows (or promises) to God?
4. Have you ever been unfaithful in your obedience to the Lord? What does 2 Timothy 2:13 say about this? What promise is made in that verse?
5. When we are weak, what does 2 Corinthians 12:9 say happens to God's power in me?
6. According to Luke 5, what kind of people did Jesus associate with?
7. The Apostle Paul wrote under the inspiration of the Holy Spirit in Romans 7:20 that after he got saved, if he continued to do the wrong thing, it was not actually him doing it, but who or what was doing the wrong thing then?
8. Name one thing you learned from this chapter.
9. What was your favorite story in this chapter?
10. Can God use an imperfect Christian?

CHAPTER 8

The Truth *about* Healing

WHY SOME PEOPLE DO GET HEALED

We have seen some of the false reasons God heals people that do not line up with scripture: people deserve healing because of their goodness, people make promises to God and then He owes them, people who got healed will never sin again and people are "really spiritual."

While we probably will never know in this lifetime all the reasons that God does and does not heal people, there are some we can see clearly from scripture…

Four Biblical Reasons Jesus Heals People:

1. ***It is God's Nature to be Good***
2. ***Healing Displays God's glory***
3. ***God is Often Willing to Heal When Asked***
4. ***Healing is Nothing for God***

Biblical Healing Reason #1- It is God's Nature to be Good

Taste and see that the Lord is good; blessed is the one who takes refuge in him.

PSALMS 34:8 NEW INTERNATIONAL VERSION

Although bad things happen to good people (that is another entire book or several large libraries of books), it is also true that God is good. It is not only the subject of countless theology classes and it is not only a major orthodox Christian doctrine, it is the truth, that God is good. Many churches I have been a part of and that you may have experienced love to loudly proclaim the old refrain that, "God is good all the time and all the time, God is good!"

Because of God's goodness, people are often healed. When someone is healed because of the goodness of God, God receives glory, sometimes people are drawn closer to Him and on occasions people are converted to being followers of Christ because of the healing power of the Lord Jesus Christ.

...God anointed Jesus of Nazareth with the Holy Spirit and power, and how he went around doing good and healing all who were under the power of the devil, because God was with him.

ACTS 10:35B NEW INTERNATIONAL VERSION

In Peter's message from Acts 10, God clarifies that Jesus simply "went around doing good and healing all who were under the power of the devil." Why did Jesus do this? In part because He was good.

In Matthew 14, the Bible tells us...

When He went ashore, He saw a large crowd, and felt compassion for them and healed their sick. Matthew 14:14 New American Standard Bible

In the above-cited instance, we see that Jesus heals out of compassion. Dictionaries explain that compassion springs from "pity" for people. Pity is feeling sorry for people because they are miserable. Now, Jesus was and is the God of the universe. He could have chosen to do anything He wanted when He walked this earth, but when Jesus saw pathetic situations, He changed them. Jesus did not and does not walk past suffering and allow it to continue. Jesus heals, God heals, the Holy Spirit heals...because God is good.

Biblical Healing Reason #2- Healing Displays God's Glory

> *Jesus Heals a Man Born Blind*
> *As he went along, he saw a man blind from birth. His disciples asked him, "Rabbi, who sinned, this man or his parents, that he was born blind?" "Neither this man nor his parents sinned," said Jesus, "but this happened so that the works of God might be displayed in him.*
>
> JOHN 9:1-3. NEW INTERNATIONAL VERSION

In the account of the Gospel of John when Jesus heals a man born blind, it is no secret why this man was both blind and why He was healed. Verse two shows both the disciples of Jesus and humans, in general, have a natural tendency to be negative and judgmental. The Bible tells us that the disciples of Jesus ask, as if this is perfectly natural to do so, "Rabbi, who sinned, this man or his parents?" The implication is that in this time, and in this context it was assumed naturally that if someone was born with a serious illness, disability or sickness, probably if calamity of any kind came to your house as well (see the biblical account of Job), then obviously you or your family had sinned. Notice one part of the extreme harshness of the disciple's statement. Did you pick up on their asking not only did his parents sin, but did his sin cause this? What makes this so harsh is that, verse one clearly states he was "blind from birth." While it is good theology that we are all born sinners after the fall of man, it is something else to believe that a baby was so sinful that it was caused to be blind because of its sins inside the womb. Yet, this is the accusation that the disciples make against this child. To assume that the parents were sinners enough to cause their child to be blind is one level of harshness, but to assume that the unborn child showed such a proclivity toward sin is another. I do not have a lot of judgement for the disciples here, because in my younger years, I may have naturally assumed the same type of things as well. It is easy to get so caught up in judgmental attitudes because of our own sins that we can cast this type of guilt and shame upon others, even though, in this case, they were clearly undeserving. Jesus, without hesitation, corrects the statement, the assumption and the problem. Jesus explains that this man was not blind because he had sinned or that his parents had sinned. Jesus declares this man was born blind that the glory of God might be displayed in Him.

When we assume that people are sick because of their sin, we are often assigning a harshness to God and His people that is incorrect, wrong and insulting to God.

As soon as Jesus explained the situation, He went about things immediately to heal the man…

> *While I am in the world, I am the light of the world." After saying this, he spit on the ground, made some mud with the saliva, and put it on the man's eyes. "Go," he told him, "wash in the Pool of Siloam" (this word means "Sent"). So the man went and washed, and came home seeing.*
>
> John 9:5-7 New International Version

Jesus first explains that He is the "light of the world." Jesus brought both physical light to this man by opening his eyes and Jesus brings spiritual light to anyone who trusts in Him for salvation. Jesus started the process of healing by spitting in the man's eyes and instructing what the man was to do to receive his healing. After washing, the man's eyes were healed. (Quick side note: notice that often God instructs people to do something on their own as an act of faith to receive healing or whatever other spiritual gift that God may impart to us.)

If you read the rest of John chapter nine, you will find this man truly brings glory to God and God's goodness displayed in this instance through healing power. Because of the level of miracle displayed here, the man quickly becomes the discussion of both his neighbors and the religious pharisees. It would have been one thing if this man once had sight, and then had it restored. In today's modern medical situation worldwide, one might think that he possibly had some type of injury that damaged the intricate inner workings of the eye that was restored. While this would be incredible as ever, in this case, the man had no working eyes whatsoever! What did Jesus do with his spit and dirt? Did He grow the man's optic nerves? Did He connect things that were not connected at birth? Whatever He did, it was a miracle hard to comprehend, but it was one that got the attention of both those who hated and loved Jesus. When Jesus does a miracle for the Glory of God, it will get people's attention.

This man was born blind that God's glory would be displayed in Him. That is a powerful statement...that means there are sicknesses and diseases that exist and are allowed to continue because one day, God is going to heal them, and through this, bring Glory to Himself that others may be saved.

You might say, "Isn't it awful mean of God to allow someone to be blind for however long this was before God healed Him?" This account requires an eternal perspective. This life, even if it is very long in the way we count time as humans, it is actually very brief in the light of eternity. If we lived to be 125 years old, it would just be a moment in the scheme of infinity.

For our light affliction, which is but for a moment, is working for us a far more exceeding and eternal weight of glory, while we do not look at the things which are seen, but at the things which are not seen. For the things which are seen are temporary, but the things which are not seen are eternal. 2 Corinthians 4:17,18 New King James Version

Even the terrible situation of being blind for many years, pales in comparison to spending eternity in an incorruptible body in the presence of Jesus!

A quick search of scripture shows that God does this type of thing, allowing seemingly terrible things to happen for the sake of His glory, possibly much more often than is at first apparent, even to the Christian observer. Just two chapters later, Jesus declares that Lazarus' death and, more importantly, Lazarus' resurrection was actually pre-ordained for the Glory of God…

> *But when Jesus heard about it, he said, "Lazarus's sickness will not end in death. No, it happened for the glory of God so that the Son of God will receive glory from this."*
>
> JOHN 11:4 NEW LIVING TRANSLATION

So, even death of a loved one can be for the Glory of God, that again, as with the "problem of evil" (bad things happens to good people), could be another book or library of books, so we will move on. What we do know from scripture is that, often, God heals, to show His glory!

Biblical Healing Reason #3- God is Often Willing to Heal when Asked

> *The Leper is Cleansed When He had come down from the mountain, great multitudes followed Him. And behold, a leper came and worshiped Him, saying, "Lord, if You are willing, You can make me clean." Then Jesus put out His*

> *hand and touched him, saying, "I am willing; be cleansed." Immediately his leprosy was cleansedAnd Jesus said to him, "See that you tell no one; but go your way, show yourself to the priest, and offer the gift that Moses commanded, as a testimony to them.*
>
> MATTHEW 8:1-4 NEW KING JAMES VERSION

The account of Jesus Healing this particular leper is also recorded with extremely similar wording in Mark 1:40–44 and Luke 5:12–14. In all instances, the statement that, "If you are willing" is mentioned. It is very clear that one of the points of this healing was to demonstrate that not only was and is Jesus often willing to heal people who ask for His healing, but He was willing to heal a leper who asked.

In this historical account, we see that not only does Jesus heal someone who recognized that the healing was simply a matter of if Jesus was willing or not, but we see that Jesus- comes into the personal space of a leper, speaks to a leper, touches the leper and heals the leper.

These actions are phenomenal. I grew up in America from the 1970s to currently, I find myself in late April 2020 living in New York City at the time of this writing, in the midst of the coronavirus outbreak. Before this situation, there was never anything in my lifetime in America that could even be compared to leprosy. However, there are some similarities here.

Both leprosy of Jesus' time on the earth as a human and the coronavirus plague in 2020 in New York City are: possibly a death sentence, one of the most feared illnesses on the planet, when they do kill you they kill you with special torture, people with these diseases would and will face discrimination, they both stopped and stop you from attending public worship services and they were both highly contagious.

For Jesus to even get near this man was astonishing. Besides the possible danger he presented to Jesus, just by his presence, he was also religiously unclean. To come in contact with someone who was unclean would make you unclean, therefore removing your ability to go to the temple as someone who was "unclean." The diseases that fell under the category of "leprosy" at the time were so dreaded that you had to scream "unclean" if people got near you. When you had leprosy, at best you were to become part of a leper colony where only others with leprosy lived, and at worst, if there was no leper colony, when you die of the disease (as with covid-19) you would be forced to miserably die alone. The disease of leprosy was so dreaded because certain strains of it slowly rotted away the limbs and body of the infected person. Many having symptoms of losing toes, fingers, feet, hands and other parts of the body before they died. It is frightening to even think of the disease because of its cruel disfiguration and isolation it caused. Today, most of these diseases have been eradicated by modern science or the prognosis for them in developed countries is hundreds or thousands of times better than in AD 28 or 29 in Israel. Jesus tells the man after the healing event to, "tell no one" possibly because of the effect of the news spreading about a leper maybe or maybe not being healed. It was so devastating that Jesus told him to go have the priest declare him clean before he did anything else. The toll of leprosy on the man and the societal implications for him, are truly hard for modern-day people to understand.

When you consider the seriousness, contagiousness and other devastating ramifications of leprosy in Jesus' time, it adds new light to the idea that God would be willing to heal this man because he asked to be healed. The description of this healing shows that Jesus was not only willing to heal when asked, but He was even willing to heal those who were untouchable. The man says to Jesus that if you are willing, "you can make me clean." Jesus still today, often physically heals when people ask in faith, but He is also willing to cleanse people who need to be cleansed. Whether it is leprosy, sin, addiction, another disease, or whatever the case may be, Jesus is often willing to heal and cleanse those who ask in faith.

Many churches today believe that Jesus no longer physically heals whatsoever. If I attended one of those churches that did not practice, believe in or "allow" healing, I would leave immediately if I needed a miracle. And by the way, you cannot stop Divine physical healing by not "allowing" it. The pharisees and other religious leaders of Jesus day tried to stop Him from healing 2,000 years ago, without success I might add, and many religious leaders try not to allow religious healings today. There may be a multitude of reasons this seems reasonable (false teachers, lack of teaching about healing or incomplete teaching about healing which can lead to false hope, pure scandalous "in it for the money faith healers") to not allow healing in your church, but at the end of the day it is unbiblical and it is cruel to many people in churches who may otherwise be healed.

When you surround yourself with people who do not believe in healing, you set yourself up to not be healed. This account clarifies that 1) Jesus wants people to ask him to heal them and make them clean and that 2) when they do ask, He is often happy to heal. You stand in direct opposition to the will and majesty of God when you tell people that God no longer heals. When our son was diagnosed with the rarest of cancers, we protected ourselves from people who had negative, death affirming things to say. From arguing with the doctor who pronounced the death sentence, to kicking pastors out of his hospital room who wanted to pray for the family's "comfort" since he was probably dying anyway, we had to protect the seed of faith that the Lord had given to us. It was impossible to listen to any negativity from people about the situation because faith must be cultivated carefully. It only grows in carefully protected environments.

God is often willing to heal, when asked, but if He is not asked, why would we think He would heal? If God will heal people with leprosy in a time that it was a death sentence and made you a public outcast, then why wouldn't God heal people today of a variety of ailments from the smallest to the largest, if He is simply asked?

There are many reasons that still today, people do not ask to be healed by Jesus. As a pastor, I have heard many of them. Some we have already discussed.

Reasons not to ask to be healed:

"I'm not good enough to be healed"

"I don't deserve to be healed"

"I'm not spiritual enough to be healed"

"I brought this on myself by my own foolishness"

"I'm too great of a sinner to be healed"

"I don't even deserve to be in God's presence, much less to be healed"

"This is too big a thing for God"

(Really? Bigger than leprosy in AD 28?)

The list of reasons could go on and on. I have been told as a pastor by someone who smoked that we shouldn't pray for them to be healed of lung cancer because they had been a smoker. However, I can say I have seen God heal at least one smoker of a serious lung disease. (Now that kind of blew my mind years ago when I first saw that- God is a mind blowing-ly good God!) You just cannot overestimate God's goodness. Occasionally, as He sees fit, He heals smokers of lung cancer. I wonder, would he heal more if they asked? Maybe you would not heal smokers of lung cancer when they asked if you were God. If so, well, I'm glad you are not God. God is God, He can do what He wants to do. Now if you have any question about it from reading this book and not knowing me…if you smoke- QUIT. It just might kill you of lung cancer. It is a bad idea. It is a bad and smelly habit at best. BUT- if you are a smoker, and you get lung cancer, I will pray with you that God in His mercy just might heal you. Do you know why I would do that? Because God is a good God, one trillion times better than you or me. Sometimes He heals people of things even that they brought on themselves and if you ask, you never know, He just might heal you. If you don't ask for healing, your chances of being healed are very low. If you surround yourself with people and especially pastors who assure you that you will certainly not be healed because you brought this on yourself, and if they don't believe in healing anyway, then the chances of you being healed are exceedingly low. In that case, I would just put my life in the doctor's hands, not that I am against physicians or all that they can do, I am thankful for that. However, God is greater than any earthly physician, He is the Great Physician while all other physicians are only "practicing medicine" they haven't even perfected it yet after all these years.

From the description of the interaction and healing of the leper, one can easily get the idea that God actually likes to be asked things by His creation. I believe that is the way it is. We were made to fellowship with our Creator. We miss out greatly as human beings that never fulfill our fullest potential when we live lives not dedicated to the plans and purposes of our Creator. I also get the feeling from scripture that while He does not "need" us, at least not in the same way that we "need" Him, the Father, Son and Holy Spirit love to hear from their children. As a person in midlife now, I can tell you that we love to talk to our young adult children when we call them now, but it is especially sweet to get a call from your children. To know that the ones that the Lord used our bodies to create, would take the time out of their busy day to remember and call their old mom or dad, just to say hello, this is a great thing when it happens. God feels the same way, when His children take the time to speak to Him, seek His guidance, acknowledge their dependence on Him and request His favor, he often rewards with His blessings and sometimes physical, emotional, spiritual and mental healing as well. God can do anything, but often what He does on earth is partially determined in a small way by His children who sincerely pray that line of the Lord's prayer, that "His will be done on earth as it is in heaven." When we seek His will and ask for His healing, He loves our fellowship and may very well be willing to heal, if only we will ask.

Ask God to heal you. Ask if He is willing to heal you, there is a chance (and maybe a pretty decent chance with a milli-teaspoon of faith involved) that He will say, "Well, you know what, I am willing, and I am going to heal you!"

Biblical Healing Reason #4- Healing is Nothing for God

This portion of this book is being written from New York City in April of 2020 (the global "epicenter" of the coronavirus) with the local news reporting 500-799 deaths in the city each and every day. We are reminded constantly that the health care system here is under incredible strain. At this time, the Naval Hospital ship "Comfort" is in the port of Manhattan. The Javits Center (large arena) has been converted to the largest emergency field hospital in the nation with thousands of beds. Central Park has a temporary hospital of tents set up with many patients on ventilators and a staff of all volunteer nurses, physicians and medical staff from the Samaritan's Purse organization. Other temporary hospitals have been built all across the city and state while medical workers have been flown and bused in from all around the country to temporarily assist with the effort to keep overcrowded intensive care units in each hospital operating. The hospitals are full of ventilators keeping the critically ill coronavirus patients alive. The cost of this is staggering. The expending of energy and resources to deal with this is mind-boggling. The money to fund all of this comes from 2.2 trillion dollars of money the government just "magically" printed to keep the country going while most of it has been under a month or so of a "lock down." All of this in an effort to try and slow the spread and "flatten the curve" of deaths of the virus.

While the money expended is one thing, the resources that hospitals are using is another entirely different situation. Every day on the local news, besides the hundreds of deaths in the city being reported, the backlog of coffins in temporary refrigerator trucks being used as morgues because the morgues are full, there are doctors and nurses crying on the television nightly. These doctors and nurses are expressing their grief and the toll it is having on them personally. They are pleading with people to stay home so the spread will hopefully slow down. For the last several days ambulances can be heard almost constantly outside our apartment window. The mental, physical, emotional and spiritual energy being put forth by these health care professionals is hard to imagine. They are courageous heroes. Tonight on the news, a physician in the city said that on his shift last night, during the night, he pronounced six people dead and made it sound as if that had become somewhat normal.

A story a few nights ago covered some hospital janitors. They were being praised for consenting to come in for low wages and clean the hospitals they know are full of the virus. Things are so bad in New York City, I received word about some things I ordered online that were to be sent through the mail. These packages could not be sent because the post offices and the US postal system had to be shut down in several places in the city. A piece of electronics I needed to do a live stream is in the Philadelphia Pennsylvania Post Office, and it has been there for several days. They have so many sick mail handlers, they simply could not deliver it right now, so it is just stuck in limbo.

In the environment of New York City during the coronavirus pandemic of 2020, the thing being stressed on the news is they knew it would kill a lot of people, but beyond just trying to save as many lives as possible, they were going to mainly be concerned with not overtaxing the health care system. Basically, what they are saying is that if everyone goes into the hospital for coronavirus at the same time, they cannot handle this many cases and the system, for lack of a better term, collapse because it is just too much strain on the buildings, people, personal protective equipment (masks and gloves) supply and finances needed to handle an epidemic of this proportion. Another way you might say this, is that this mass healings (or attempt at healing anyway) is too much for the health care system, but healing is not too taxing for God. The situation with healing and Jesus is entirely different...healing is nothing for God. Physical healing is nothing for God.

> *[40] On the other side of the lake the crowds welcomed Jesus, because they had been waiting for him. [41] Then a man named Jairus, a leader of the local synagogue, came and fell at Jesus' feet, pleading with him to come home with him.*

[42] His only daughter, who was about twelve years old, was dying. As Jesus went with him, he was surrounded by the crowds. [43] A woman in the crowd had suffered for twelve years with constant bleeding, and she could find no cure. [44] Coming up behind Jesus, she touched the fringe of his robe. Immediately, the bleeding stopped. [45] "Who touched me?" Jesus asked. Everyone denied it, and Peter said, "Master, this whole crowd is pressing up against you." [46] But Jesus said, "Someone deliberately touched me, for I felt healing power go out from me." [47] When the woman realized that she could not stay hidden, she began to tremble and fell to her knees in front of him. The whole crowd heard her explain why she had touched him and that she had been immediately healed. [48] "Daughter," he said to her, "your faith has made you well. Go in peace."

LUKE 8:40-48 NEW LIVING TRANSLATION

In the above account from Luke 8, we see Jesus on his way in verses 40-42 to heal Jairus' daughter. In verse 43, Jesus is interrupted on His way to perform the other miracle that would become Him bringing Jairus' daughter back to life. This is one of the few cases, where the description of a miracle by Jesus is interrupted by another miracle. Most descriptions in the Gospel records are of Jesus going somewhere and healing someone and then moving on. Sometimes, people interrupt Him, but in this case, the woman boldly and some could even say rudely, inserts herself into Jesus' life. Jesus is going to perform a miracle for a leader of the local synagogue, Jairus. This man had important political and religious standing in the community. This miracle would possibly be seen by some as "more important" due to the predominant community standing of the man involved.

In verse 43, we see an unnamed woman in the crowd inserts herself into Jesus' life and day. The Word tells us she reaches out, touches Jesus' robe and is immediately healed from bleeding that she had been battling for twelve years prior. Jesus knows that someone has taken power from Him, after asking who touched Him and then being scolded by Peter for the seemingly stupid question since thousands of people are probably knocking up against Him, He says, "No, somebody touched me on purpose and I know it because healing power went out from me." Then the woman begins to fear (trembling) and fell to her knees explaining that she was immediately healed. She was probably overtaken by fear of what Jesus might do to her. She knew that instantly something the physicians had not been able to remedy for more than a decade, had been miraculously healed in less than a second. What other power did this man possess that He could unleash on her in punishment for taking His power without asking?

Amazingly, Jesus does not punish her. He does not take her healing back since she seemingly just took it without asking. He does not even scream at her or rebuke her in any way. Instead, he says, "Daughter...your faith has made you whole. Go in peace."

Incredible! Jesus allows the woman to basically "get away with stealing Jesus' power." How cool is that? This story seems to imply that you can sometimes order your miracle. I do not mean, "order" as in God MUST do this or that we tell God what He is going to do. I think of order in the sense of sitting down at a dinner style restaurant where the waiter or waitress comes up to you and asks for your order. Just as simple as you can enter a Waffle House and order a waffle and hash browns, this lady seems to have just decided that Jesus would give her healing. She had been to all the doctors with no assistance and now she would go to Jesus. Surely, she had heard of the string of miracles that Jesus was responsible for as recorded in the Gospels. How many others had she heard of since St. John says that if everything Jesus did was recorded in print, there may not be enough books in the world to hold them? (see John 21:25) The woman had heard these things and she ordered her miracle.

As if this supernatural occurrence was not enough for Jesus to do in one day, what makes this event even more incredible are the circumstances that surround it. Again, this was a messy miracle account in scripture. This was not the healing marvel of the day (Jairus' daughter that Jesus was on His way to visit), this was the side note to the main event. To the woman involved, it was no side note, she had after all been suffering for twelve years, but compared to what Jesus was about to do, this was a side note. Let's be honest, we do not want anyone to suffer in any way, but a woman with a bleeding problem (as terrible as it was), it was not killing her... at least in twelve years, it had not killed her. There was another twelve-year-old event that was happening at the same time. It kind of makes you wonder how close in time these events coincided, twelve years earlier.

At some point, twelve years earlier in time, both the woman started bleeding and a baby was born. To be exact, Jairus' wife, delivered their little baby girl. In the same year (maybe the same month, who knows, maybe the same day), one woman had her life interrupted by an event that would bring her pain, suffering, anguish and inconvenience for the next twelve years, but across town somewhere, another woman would deliver a child. The pain of childbirth would soon be forgotten for the joy that would become the little girl. On this day, twelve years later, the women's experiences would be opposite. One woman in pain, would be set free from the pain. Another woman, who was experiencing some anxiety from a sick child, would feel monumental pain when that child died, but by the end of the day, Jesus would turn both women's mourning into gladness.

> [49] *While he was still speaking to her, a messenger arrived from the home of Jairus, the leader of the synagogue. He told him, "Your daughter is dead. There's no use troubling the Teacher now."* [50] *But when Jesus heard what had happened, he said to Jairus, "Don't be afraid. Just have faith, and she will be healed."* [51] *When they arrived at the house, Jesus would let no one go in with him except Peter, John, James, and the little girl's father and mother.* [52] *The house was filled with people weeping and wailing, but he said, "Stop the weeping! She isn't dead; she's only asleep."* [53] *But the crowd laughed at him*

> *because they all knew she had died.* [54] *Then Jesus took her by the hand and said in a loud voice, "My child, get up!"* [55] *And at that moment her life returned, and she immediately stood up! Then Jesus told them to give her something to eat.* [56] *Her parents were overwhelmed, but Jesus insisted that they not tell anyone what had happened.*
>
> Luke 8:49-56 New Living Translation

Jesus left the woman who had been bleeding and simply told her to go on about her business in peace (kind of like, "Hey I'm good with you, no problem") and then immediately goes on down the road and raises the child from the dead in verses 54 and 55. What is noticeably amazing about this is that Jesus never stops to recharge. He does not say after the woman took his healing power for the bleeding issue, "Hey, wait a minute, that power is not for you. I need that to go to Jairus' house. His daughter is far sicker than you. In fact, she is going to die and I am going to need enough power to bring her back to life! Now give that power back, right now!"

If Jesus had been working in the flesh only, this is the kind of response we might have expected. Like we have already noted, physical healing by mere mortals in the earth requires lots and lots of power and resources. Physicians are normally some of the brightest and best minds among us. Their modern training shows they are definitely at least among the most disciplined to get through medical school and residency, but no matter how gifted, bright, talented and dedicated they are…they are still limited in power, scope and ability. Every doctor, may not get a lot of sleep, but sometimes, they will have to sleep. Every hospital, think of it, the hospitals in New York City, arguably some of the best and most advanced in the country, still could not handle the coronavirus epidemic of 2020. More staff, resources, ventilators, hospital ships and extra hospitals set up in civic centers and tents were required to just get through a tough time of trying to help many people stay alive at once. On the other hand, Jesus had so much power available to Him that He could, on the same day- 1) heal a woman of bleeding that apparently had not been on His agenda for the day and then 2) bring a dead girl back to life.

I am thankful that today I have not been asked to stop a woman from bleeding with this problem for twelve years and all the doctors in that time could not cure her. It would certainly be more daunting of a task, though to be asked to bring a twelve-year-old back to life. For me, and you, this is inconceivable in our own power. For Jesus, however, this was not the case. For Jesus, He had plenty of spiritual, healing virtue or power to heal both the woman with the issue of blood and to bring the young girl back from the dead. For Jesus, it was basically "nothing."

What seems incredible, impossible, monumental or implausible for us as finite human beings is basically "nothing" with God. God's batteries never run out. Unlike me, He never gets so tired at around 2 p.m. that He has to wonder will He be able to stay awake until it is time to go to bed at night? As a matter of fact, He never sleeps or slumbers and what is impossible for you and me is totally possible with God...

> *Behold, He who keeps Israel Shall neither slumber nor sleep.*
>
> Psalms 121:4 New King James Version

> *...The things which are impossible with men are possible with God.*
>
> Luke 18:27b King James Version

So, you might say, well, that's nice, but it doesn't apply to me; however, you must understand that when Jesus walked on the earth as a man, He was totally God, but he chose to not use His divinity. (see Philippians 2:5-8). Not that Jesus was not fully God when He walked the earth, He was 100% God and 100% man, but He chose to voluntarily not work independently of the Holy Spirit while He walked the earth. If this were not true, then John 14:12 could not be true which says...

> *Truly, truly, I say to you, whoever believes in me will also do the works that I do; and greater works than these will he do, because I am going to the Father.*
>
> JOHN 14:12 ENGLISH STANDARD VERSION

Did you get that from John 14? Jesus said that we will do these works He did and that we will even do greater works! What an awesome promise! One that is most often ignored by Christ followers.

Most people say instead, "Well, I mean I am not Jesus! Sure, Jesus had the power to walk the earth because He was the son of God and do things like raise the dead and heal all sorts of people, but I am just a regular person who believes in Jesus." Many people think like this. Even many Bible believing Christians think like this, but the truth is that you have this very same, unlimited, God-power ***living inside of you*** if you believe that Jesus is Lord, God raised Him from the dead, He is alive today and you have placed your faith and trust in Him to save you from the power of sin, death and the grave...

> *And if the Spirit of Him Who raised up Jesus from the dead dwells in you, [then] He Who raised up Christ Jesus from the dead will also restore to life your mortal (short-lived, perishable) bodies through His Spirit Who dwells in you.*
>
> ROMANS 8:11 THE AMPLIFIED BIBLE

If you are a Christian, the same power that raised Jesus from the dead dwells in you right now! The Bible declares this power will one day restore your temporary bodies back to Life through the Holy Spirit who is living in you right now! The Holy Spirit's power is unlimited. He raised Jesus from the dead and He can raise people from the dead, even today. In the future, this same power will raise all to life who died in Christ Jesus. (see 1 Thessalonians 4:13-18)

Now, if we are working only in natural power, even the best natural power, (remember the earthly physician's illustration of weakness), we are very, very limited at best. Occasionally, the natural and the supernatural intersect and God grants new knowledge to doctors or scientists, which propels the human race forward, but when working in our current natural knowledge and power we are very limited in scope and practice of healing. We may be 1,000 times better prepared for sickness and disease than we were 100-300 years ago in the medical field, but we are still very limited. On the other hand, when humans work in God's power, we are no longer limited because what is impossible with us, is totally possible with God.

Years ago, when my son had his cancer diagnosis and the doctor declared death over him, if I had been working in my own power, holiness, goodness, knowledge, wisdom or even if I had what was then the best medical knowledge in the world about this cancer, then I would have been limited to the option of death only. However, when we allow the Spirit to speak, when we walk in His power, His authority, His boldness, His knowledge, His goodness, His holiness, then we are walking in the supernatural and an entirely different dimension of spiritual power is available. I stress again, that we are not in complete control of this by any means. We do not determine who lives and dies, but when we yield our bodies and mouths to allow the Holy Spirit to speak through us, you never know what He will do or what the result may be. What we know, is that if it is God speaking through us, then Jesus will be glorified and we will not.

There have been a few times in my life that I was aware during, and had more understanding after the event, that God was physically and powerfully working through me to heal someone. Many times at the front of a church altar area during a church service, as I touched the abdomen of someone and prayed for them that cancer would go and leave their body, while it was not like a projector screen or anything you could see perfectly in the natural, sometimes, the best way I could describe it was I could almost see inside of the person in the spirit and as we prayed, and rebuked cancer, you could almost see with spiritual eyes, the cancer shriveling, dying and being removed. Each time, I was nervous about the whole thing. After my son's healing, I realized that it was up to God and not me. Later, as I prayed publicly for more people who were then healed, I became a little less nervous about it, but to this day, it is something that I do not take lightly. I do not take it lightly when I stand as a conduit for the Lord to heal through and I never will. I am, however, realizing that God wants people to trust Him for healing, we can stick our necks out for God. We can walk out on faith, and if we did it with a sincere heart, attempting to glorify Jesus, not ourselves...all I can say is that He has never let me down yet. And, He never will- by faith. If it was my power, then I would have no reason to trust in it for such great things. If it was my power, I am just excited when enough energy is created to pump blood through my heart, operate my brain and organs and help me walk, talk and do what is needed to be accomplished through the day, but in God's power, by faith, anything can be accomplished. Healing may be monumental for me and you, but never forget, ***healing is nothing for God.***

Thoughts and Questions to Discuss:

1. What does Psalms 34:8 tell us about the Lord's nature?
2. Matthew 14:14 teaches us that sometimes God heals people because of His what for them?
3. In John 9:1-3, why did Jesus heal the blind man?
4. In 2 Corinthians 4:17,18, what does the Bible teach us about our current problems?
5. What was the biblical reason given for Lazarus' sickness and temporary death?
6. In Matthew 8:1-4, the Leper knew that if Jesus was __________, He could heal him.
7. How can we find out if the Lord is willing to heal someone or not?
8. What stops us from asking the Lord to heal us?
9. After Jesus healed the woman with the issue of blood, did He have enough power to do any other miracles on that day?
10. In John 14:12, what kind of works did Jesus say those who believe in Him would do?

CHAPTER 9

Five Reasons People DO NOT Get Healed

(EVEN SOME VERY "GOOD" PEOPLE DO NOT GET HEALED)

5 Reasons People Do Not Get Healed

1. **It was their time**
2. **They hate people and/or walk in unforgiveness**
3. **They put the doctor's word over God's Word**
4. **They love being sick**
5. **We don't know, but God does knows and He is loving, kind and trustworthy**

We probably all know someone who loves the Lord, serves and trusts Jesus with their whole heart, yet they lost a loved one to some death, sickness, disease or other unexpected tragedy. These people often totally agree that God is good, He is willing to heal, He heals to display His glory and they may even believe that healing is nothing for God, yet, they did not experience healing.

Now it would be unwise, arrogant, prideful and judgmental to presume that we know all the reasons that God does and does not heal people. This statement or one like it has been repeated several times throughout this book in the author's attempt to clarify that he makes no claim he has all the answers about healing or how God always works. A few years ago, as I preached about my son's miraculous healing, a man jumped up and stormed out of the auditorium I was preaching in. He was so incredibly mad and displayed this anger toward me. I discovered that he was upset because they had prayed for their son's healing and he ultimately was not healed in this life, which led to his earthly death. I realize today that the parents were not really upset with me, but with God Himself. I had not pronounced judgment against them as if I claimed to understand the reasons their son was not healed. I make no judgment about how much faith the family had or if they held up a certain standard or biblical doctrine...ultimately, God chooses who to heal and not heal. This book is intended to help with some areas we can clearly see from scripture about why SOME not all people are healed and not healed according to scripture. My prayer is to be of assistance to some people in need of healing. If someone falls into one of the next four categories discussed concerning why people are not healed, I hope that instead of that person turning their hostility toward me, God or any other, that they will instead examine their own heart and ask do any of these things need to change. Remember, if what is being presented is backed by the Word of God, the Bible, then the author is just the messenger. The God of the universe has made several things about healing plain in His Word. While it will always be controversial with some, the Bible does clearly let us know some things about healing. These areas of knowledge do not only cover some reasons why we are healed biblically, but they also cover some of the reasons that people may not be healed.

5 Reasons People Do Not Get Healed

1. It was their time

> *And as it is appointed for men to die once, but after this the judgment*
>
> Hebrews 9:27 New King James Version

This is simple and straightforward. There comes an appointment that all of us have in God's appointment book...we are appointed to die. The Word continues that after this, we will be judged. Two things are clarified in this verse. One, we will die. Two, we will be judged. If we know Jesus, and are trusting Him with our lives, for the forgiveness of sins and for justification with the Father, we will die only once and when we are judged, Jesus' blood will cover our sins and we will be counted as righteous. If we are not following Christ, we will be judged unrighteous, and we will eventually die twice. Once on earth, and once in eternity in a terrible place we call hell that Jesus has no desire for us to go to. For the purposes of this writing on healing we will focus, though on those simple words, it is appointed for men to die once.

These words make it crystal clear this is an appointment. God is not like us, He does not miss appointments, and this appointment ultimately set by Him for all of us will be kept. Sometimes, we pray and pray for the appointment time to be changed and He seems to change the appointment. Other times, He does not change the time. While I believe in Kingdom living, power in our words and the authority of the believer, make no mistake, God is God.

Sometimes, when people die, it does not seem like the right time to us left here on earth. If we were in charge, we would have postponed this time frame. However, if we will trust God, his appointment for us and our loved ones can be trusted. Remember that even if the timeframe seems very pre-mature to us, this life is just a vapor.

> *Yet you do not know [the least thing] about what may happen tomorrow. What is the nature of your life? You are [really] but a wisp of vapor (a puff of smoke, a mist) that is visible for a little while and then disappears [into thin air].*
>
> JAMES 4:14 THE AMPLIFIED BIBLE

If we live five years or 125 years, compared to eternity, never-ending years, this life is just a momentary puff of water vapor and it is gone. Now, no one desires the death of a young child and no one wishes this tragedy on anyone else, not even their worst enemy, but in the light of eternity, it is at least somewhat more understandable. To us, the death of a child is an unimaginable, heartbreaking tragedy and if you have experienced this devastation, I am so sorry, I grieve with you in spirit. However, if one lives to be 11 or 98, the life we now live is so very temporary.

The younger a person is when they die, the more heartbreak suffered because, at least in part, we think of all of the "what ifs?." The life milestones that will never come. There will be no graduation, no wedding, no first job, no promotion, no grandchildren from that child, but when this child is in the presence of God, they do not suffer, they do not cry, they do not mourn, they do not hurt, they can breathe well, they walk and run with ease, and most of all, they are in the presence of their Heavenly Father who cares for them with a greater care than that of the even the world's best parents.

Other times, at seemingly younger ages, but not that of a child, the reality is still harsh. Sometimes the person was in the middle of a promising career. It seemed like they were destined to help many others, yet they were taken in unexpected ways. Is it possible that their purpose, even though it seemed on the surface that their life had so many twists and turns left still to be completed that Jesus said, "They need to be in my presence now."?

Death is such a cruel enemy we do not welcome the temporary separation it causes even when it is an "expected" and "normal life time" death. I remember as a young pastor at Dowling Park Church of God in

Live Oak, Florida the statement made when a woman in her 90s peacefully passed away. I believe the saint of God was possibly 94 years old. Her daughter came to me and posed this question, "Why did she have to die?" At the time I was about 23 years old, so 94 seemed a million years away, I was young, full of life and energy constantly and could not comprehend what seemed like an unwise question. Fortunately, I had enough of the Holy Spirit operating in me that day to say nothing and instead just showed love with my presence, care and concern. The truth is though, on that day, I wanted to say, "Are you serious? She had to die because she was almost 100 years old." Now at almost 46 years old at the time of this writing of this book, I see 94 as not nearly as old as it used to be. I can also see with the benefit of experience and time now that while at 23, I could appreciate that she loved her mother, I could not comprehend her emotion. At 23, I primarily focused on the obvious life aging process and wondered how she had not prepared herself for this. Since then, I have buried all of my grandparents and a step-grandmother after burying the first grandmother. Some were as young as 69, others were in their 90s. Yes, before they died, I had considered that they would probably die before me, but I still was not totally prepared for the separation. A couple of them even had an extended dying process (we knew for weeks or months that if God did not do a life extending miracle, they would surely die), but even then, you are just not prepared for the separation. The more we love and like that person, the more we grieve. I was especially close to one of my grandmothers, I looked at her as a spiritual giant (which she was). I looked at pictures of her hanging in our hallways after she died wishing I could get spiritual advice from her on more than one occasion. Like many of you, when some of my loved ones died, I still on more than one occasion actually picked up the phone to call and speak to them after they died when for just a temporary, fleeting moment, I would forget they were gone and for now, I could not speak to them. As I write, I think of how much I do not want my family or friends to die and I pray they do not. The reason is that I know a little of the sting of death. This pain of separation is magnified hundreds or thousands of times the younger the loved one is and the more unexpected the death is, but we can trust Jesus' plan. We can know that while we never know the appointment time exactly, there is an appointment time coming for all of us.

We can take comfort as well that when that time comes, the separation of a loved one who died in Christ will not be as long as it seems in the natural. All we have to do to recognize this is to consider how time works, even in this very brief life we now live. Time works differently at different ages in life and it moves differently depending on what is happening in our daily lives. We all have heard and the older we are, the more we know it is true...the older we get, the faster time goes. Now science may claim that time is constant, and in a way, I suppose it is, but in the application of how we experience time, it is certainly not constant. For a young school child, to think of a month or a week or month of school passing before summer or Christmas break comes, this can be quite torturous. When I was in kindergarten, the day took FOREVER to pass until I could get back on the bus and make it home to watch an afternoon cartoon on the television. Amazingly, the shows on the television that were 30 minutes long, seemed to only last for 2-3 minutes.

As we get older that same week that once seemed like years to the third-grader waiting for the final day of school to come, so they could experience the freedom of summer...now at 46 years old, a week often seems to pass by in an hour, an hour can pass in three minutes. In basic training in the United States Air Force, the time passed by ever so slowly while I was experiencing the torture I voluntarily signed up for that is boot camp, yet when it was over it was just a moment in time. This paragraph is written during the New York City Lockdown (and to some extent worldwide lockdown) of the 2020 coronavirus pandemic. On social media, many people discuss not knowing what day it is, or this has been forever... yet, anyone with wisdom knows that as soon as this passes, whenever this passes, it will have simply been a brief season that either we squandered away or did something productive with our precious gift of time.

I know some people that for years lived in the "good old days." Anytime you got around them, this old friend would talk about how things used to be so much better decades ago than it was now. It can sometimes make you feel warm and fuzzy to reminisce with old friends about times gone by, but truth is that now is the new good old days and what we do with them can never be recaptured later. We should remember this as we consider that we all have an appointment coming. That appointment will come faster than we expect. This appointment may mean we or other people do not get healed in this life, but if we are trusting Jesus with our eternity, everything will be alright. What are now years, decades and lifetimes to us is just a moment in eternity. When people are not healed, it is often simply because it was their time.

> *"O death, where is your sting? O grave, where is your victory?" The sting of death is sin, and the strength of sin is the law. But thanks be to God, who gives us the victory through our Lord Jesus Christ! Therefore, my beloved brothers, be steadfast, unmovable, always abounding in the work of the Lord, knowing that your labor in the Lord is not in vain.*
>
> 1 CORINTHIANS 15:55-38 MODERN ENGLISH VERSION

2. They hate people and/or walk in un-forgiveness

While Christians of various backgrounds believe a myriad of differing minor doctrines, there are some that should be universal among us. Loving people, should certainly be among those doctrines, but some people who claim to be Christians think it is acceptable to hate certain groups of people.

The Google dictionary defines hate as a verb as "feel intense or passionate dislike" or "have a strong aversion to." As a noun, the definitions include "intense or passionate dislike" or "denoting hostile actions motivated by intense dislike or prejudice." One true story that illustrates this perfectly involves the last definition there where "prejudice" is involved.

My background is in churches which are often described as "holiness" churches. You would think this would mean that one could expect the leadership of those churches to attempt to act like God since we claim that our "holiness" comes from God's "Holiness." Amazingly, sometimes people think they can be in leadership at any Christian Church, much less a "holiness" church and still hate people.

When I was 26 years old, I was pastoring Harvest Christian Center in Cantonment, Florida. When a 26-year-old is pastoring, he will often find lots of older people looking to "help" him pastor. Sometimes, they are actually trying to "help" and other times, under the guise of "helping," they are trying to mold the church in their direction and vision. Occasionally, these people's help may be spiritual and godly and it may line up with the pastor's vision for the church, which can create a win, win situation, but more often than not, it will cause division and be counter-productive for the church. At other times, the people's leadership is NOT needed and it is a tool of the enemy to attempt to destroy the church.

One day, as I was pastoring, a man walked in the back door of the church. This man came to the front before service, shook my hand and introduced himself. He explained that he used to go to the church years before, but had left. (Even though we had recently taken over this facility, officially closed the previous church, changed the name and moved forward with new church government and four times as many people in the church as before the old church was closed...some people in the community wanted things to be the way it had been some 20 and 40 years earlier.)

Imagine this now, as he introduced himself...he explained that he had been in lay leadership as a board member of the church before and God had called him to be my board member to lead the church. This man had not attended the church for years and no one there now even knew who he was. I politely shook his hand and ignored his comment. I knew this comment was at best foolishness.

Over the next few weeks, he attended all the time and did everything to push his way into leadership. I let him cut the grass, but discouraged him anytime he suggested he should be in leadership. I knew something was wrong, but I could not tell you exactly what it was. It was hard to put your finger on exactly. During this time, many healing miracles discussed in this book were manifesting in the church, and I think it is factual to say that some were being discussed in the community. On more than one occasion, people over the next few years said that they had attended because they heard that people had been healed of cancer in this church.

It was not too long before we discovered the issue with this new person who desired to be a board member, he and his entire family were full-blown racists. Now in the year 2020 in America, the term racist is sometimes very liberally thrown around. For some people, anytime a disagreement occurs between people of two differing skin tones occurs, often one of them calls the other one racist. Often, prejudice would probably be a better term. It certainly may be true that racism was involved, but I think there are fundamental differences in "prejudice" and "racism." In Air Force Basic Training, I had an African American Technical Instructor (often called your Drill Sergeant). This man taught early on in basic training that every person of every color had certain prejudices, and that at the time at least, the United States Air Force would tolerate some prejudice, but would tolerate no racism. The drill sergeant's definitions were something like this. He said it was acceptable to be prejudice against someone based on you not understanding something about them or the culture they were a part of because of the difference in your skin color. He chocked this up to ignorance of difference. He explained that prejudice concerned pre-judging, and sometimes that pre-judgment would be correct, and sometimes it would be incorrect. He explained that he was not necessarily speaking of dictionary definitions for the two terms, but working definitions. While prejudice was pre-judging of another race, racism was hatred of another race or believing one was superior to another race.

It should not be misunderstood that prejudice should be encouraged or allowed within the bounds of Christianity or the Church, but prejudice and racism at least can be very different things. In the Fruit of the Spirit, there is room for neither. Having said these things, understand that the man in this story was not prejudice by these definitions, but truly racist in any and every sense of the term.

After a few months of being around the church, I suppose he thought he had earned my favor from cutting the grass and doing some other physical labor type jobs on a volunteer basis now and then. I was not leading him on, he would just show up and ask what he could do. One day, once a little time had passed, he took it upon himself to have a talk with me about what was wrong with the church and how I could fix it. I thought he would surely give me a rant about the music since we were doing all modern, worship music and the former church that met at this location had been strong into classical Pentecostal hymn singing. If not that, I thought he may criticize that he and others were not in control of the church. If not that, maybe it was that I was using the New International Version of the Bible as opposed to the King James, but it was none of these…this man decided to plainly tell me on this day in the year 2002 there were too many black people in our church. As if the amount or percentage of people mattered negatively at all, remember that in a church of about 100 people at this time, altogether there may have been 3 or 4 people of the black and brown persuasion. The man then actually stunned me with what he said next. I had seen racism in white churches in the South before. A church that I was the youth pastor at in Montgomery, Alabama was literally destroyed by racism in the leadership in the mid-1990s; however, the people in these former churches, no matter how evil their intentions may have been, they actually had enough sense to disguise or attempt to hide their sin. They hinted around at things for the most part. This man on the other hand, explained words I have decided are too hateful to even put into print in this book. While he did not use the notorious "n" word, he actually used language and stated false facts far more evil and wicked than that word. The extent of his perceived superiority, hatred and the false narrative he told me about all "colored people" that day was actually shocking. I calmly explained to him that what he was saying was evil, wicked and false. I also explained to him that the Bible clearly stated that his perceived Christianity was entirely false and that on top of that, God Himself called him a liar...

> *If someone says, "I love God," and hates his brother, he is a liar; for the one who does not love his brother whom he has seen, cannot love God whom he has not seen. And this commandment we have from Him, that the one who loves God should love his brother also.*
>
> 1 John 4:20,21 New American Standard Bible

In 1 John 4:20, God clearly states that if you say you love God who you cannot see, but you do not love your brother who you can see then you are a liar. There are some verses in the Bible that people argue over the meaning. Some verses that you might interpret a number of different ways. This verse is extremely straightforward, though. This verse is not exclusively about racism or prejudice, it is about if you hate anyone, for any reason, who you see, then you cannot love God who you cannot see.

People hate others for a million reasons, but none of them are acceptable to God. Hating someone because of the color of their skin is completely illogical. Hating someone you have never met simply because of variations in skin tone, hair texture, facial features or whatever else may be encompassed in racism is completely illogical. Notice, though that the verse does NOT say, but if someone gives a good reason to hate them, then that is acceptable.

Racism is foolishness, sinful and there is no place for it in the Kingdom of God, but hating people for what the world calls "good reasons" is also not allowed in the Kingdom. What if someone stole something from you, can a Christian hate them? How about if they beat you, are we allowed to hate that person? What if they raped you, or raped your spouse? How about if they sexually molested you as a child or if they molested your child? Or there is the ultimate, what if they murdered your child?

Those are all extreme reasons, that many people would say are perfectly fine to hate someone over, but in the Kingdom, even these extreme examples are not good enough. When Nelson Mandela became the president of

South Africa after the apartheid legalized racial system was overthrown, he led by example forgiving people who had enslaved him and led the country (black and white) to forgive one another. In some ways, perhaps the apartheid system was worse than slavery, as it was common knowledge that white people would kill blacks and there would frequently be no justice whatsoever, similar to the despicable black lynching of the American South only a couple generations ago. In South Africa, whites killed blacks with no regard for human life, treating their pets with more respect.

When Mandela was released after being in prison for 27 years and having been tortured in prison for much of that time for his opposition to apartheid, he called for forgiveness. Mandela knew that if there was any hope for the New South Africa to survive, the only way forward was forgiveness. After his call and example of forgiveness, when the country was reformed and he became president, forgiveness was modeled and taught so vigorously there are countless stories of redemption that came out of the new country. In what would become years-long race wars, many whites killed blacks and blacks killed whites. Murder and war are an unfortunate part of unchecked human nature. What is remarkable is the stories that grow from these murders in the light of forgiveness. Many people who once fought on different sides of hate, came together and eventually not only lived in harmony but worked side by side. Most remarkable, there are multiple stories of people whose close loved ones had been murdered by each other, yet they found it in their heart to forgive and then worked together in a business for years after. One such true story involves a woman who employed a young man after apartheid ended. They became not only employer and employee, but the young man became like her son. What is incredible about that story, is that a couple years before, during apartheid, the young man murdered the woman's son. In a beautiful and truly supernatural choice of forgiveness, with time, the murderer became like a son to her.

What does all of this have to do with healing, you might ask? Forgiveness is just the opposite of hate when it comes to healing. Healing does not grow in an environment of hate. In hate, sickness, disease, and death of every kind can flourish, but in forgiveness, healing grows, life flourishes and restoration can be accomplished. Whether it is the healing of a physical human body, a sick family relationship, a divided church, or a broken country like South Africa, forgiveness breeds healing, while hatred destroys it.

During the time this racist man was attending the church, his son came down with cancer. I was asked to go pray for the son with cancer. I went to the house. Before I prayed for him, I asked how he felt about the racism that his father so boldly held dear. He explained that he was in exact agreement with his father. I explained what has been discussed in this section of the book. I encouraged him to repent of his racism and hatred. He would not. He asked me to pray for him anyway. I explained that I would pray, but I had no reason to believe that he would be healed. I prayed. The man lived for a few days after the prayer. I was not present on the day that the man died. I pray that he repented and received forgiveness. Do we KNOW with certainty this man died because he was a racist? Certainly, we do not. Do we know with certainty that hating your brother will hinder your prayers for healing or any other request? Certainly, we do.

3. They put the doctor's word over God's Word

Generally speaking, physicians have a properly earned place in most societies of respect. We all know that physicians spend over a decade of their lives involved in higher education, learning the anatomy of the human body. In America, as with most countries, to become a physician, one has proven that they are among the most intellectually talented among us. The grades required in high school to be accepted into a rigorous undergraduate pre-med university speak to the aptitude of the student. This requirement that the students stay at their peak performance continues on through medical school and the required residency as a learning internship. One can assume that all physicians are very intelligent, very academically disciplined, or probably most physicians have both a high intelligence quotient combined with the ability to remain focused on their academic pursuits with a level of discipline not common among other mere mortals.

Since there is a compelling case to be made that physicians are normally pretty smart and disciplined cookies, and if you have been raised with good morals (respect your elders, respect authority), then it is very understandable that what doctors say would be taken seriously. Physicians are not only bright, disciplined and worthy of respect, but more importantly, they are the health experts. They are the ones that, by theory, should know much more about the mechanics and structures of our bodies. When they speak about our bodies or especially when they speak about a specialized part of our body they have spent many more years studying as a specialist…in general, we would be very wise to listen to them.

So, generally speaking, properly trained medical doctors should be respected and their advice should be taken to heart. This is true, probably something like 95% of the time. However, if the doctor's word does not line up with God's Word, this is when we should be cautious not to take everything they say to heart.

Many doctors will go out of their way to not give "false hope." These realistic doctors will quote statistics about the disease and/or condition we may be dealing with as a patient. This is understandable, that the physicians will want to let us know treatment options, what people can normally expect when diagnosed with an ailment and how to plan for the immediate and longer-term future. There is certainly nothing wrong or out of the ordinary with this line of information coming from a competent physician. On the other hand, some physicians are naturally very pessimistic and will go out of their way to give us the worst of the worst-case scenarios because of the not wanting to give "false hope" line of thinking. When this happens, I would look for a second opinion from a doctor with a more positive outlook on life in general.

If possible, it is best if you can find a physician who 1) is a practicing, Bible-believing Christian and 2) believes in both modern medicine as a gift from God AND believes in faith and divine healing as well. These physicians are likely to aid in your healing much more than a doctor with no faith or especially one who is anti-God or anti-faith.

When a physician speaks death over your situation, remember that no matter how smart they are, what rank they graduated in their medical school or if they are nationally ranked in their field, at the end of the day they are "practicing medicine." Medicine is an ongoing, ever learning science which does its best to help the healing of many ailments and for this, we are grateful. At the same time, God is the Great Physician. He is not practicing when He steps in and heals. God is the Creator and Sustainer of life. He can restore, heal, grant extensions of life and ultimately, He is the One who can take both body and soul for eternity.

> *Do not be afraid of those who kill the body but cannot kill the soul. Rather, be afraid of the One who can destroy both soul and body in hell.*
>
> Matthew 10:28 NIV

> *By his power God raised the Lord from the dead, and he will raise us also.*
>
> 1 Corinthians 6:14 NIV

> *I can do all this through him who gives me strength.*
>
> Philippians 4:13 NIV

When an earthly doctor says that you will surely die, yes, we realize, that this certainly may be the case, but if God contradicts that word with His will and says, "*No, you will surely live!*" ...then you will live. If we take the doctor's word as the authoritative word and it settles deep within our spirit, then we can be almost guaranteed that what they say will happen. The power of faith, the power of what we believe cannot be underestimated. If we take the Word of the Lord at face value and let it settle in our hearts and spirits, then there is no limit to what He may do. Yes, we will all die one day. Yes, this may be the time, but if God says otherwise, then this will NOT be the time, regardless of what the doctor says. Respect physicians, generally speaking, listen to a physician's medical advice, use the gift that God has given us in physicians, but do not put the doctor's word over God's Word. Medical doctors are practicing, God is the Creator and Sustainer of life.

4. They love being sick

There is no reason to spend a lot of time, space and words on this point, but the truth is we all know some people that love to be sick because of the attention they receive from it. Some people would not know what to do, if they did not have a different sickness every week. While many people are legitimately chronically ill totally beyond their control, there are at least a few people who like sickness, or the appearance of it. For those people, God will not take their sickness from them.

5. We don't know, but God does know and He is loving, kind and trustworthy

We can clearly see from scripture the reasons some people may be ill. Simultaneously, there are certainly people who become ill, have a lot of faith-filled prayer on their behalf, but die regardless. While a part of the answer for "Why did this happen?," goes back to number 1, it was their time, we also often, simply do not have all the answers on this side of eternity. It is never the place of a Christian to judge someone who has died. It would be both arrogant and foolish to think that they did not have enough faith.

What we do know, if someone has died while they were trusting Jesus and praying and believing for a miracle, they will be fine eternally. Everyone who dies in faith in Jesus, will go to heaven. In heaven there are no broken bodies. In heaven, we will be in the presence of Jesus eternally. In heaven, all wrongs will be made right.

> *'He will wipe every tear from their eyes. There will be no more death' or mourning or crying or pain, for the old order of things has passed away."*
>
> REVELATION 21:4 NIV

The Bible does not ignore the harsh reality of life in this world. Earthly life can be harsh, brutal and extremely sad at times. As humans, we will probably all, at some time, experience loss, loneliness, death of a loved one and the suffering associated with thousands of illnesses, but through it all, we can trust we have a Savior who has walked with us and understands the pain and heartache of life on earth. Not only did He say that one day, He will wipe those tears away, but He also made it clear that this life is sometimes very difficult...

> *I have told you all this so that you may have peace in me. Here on earth you will have many trials and sorrows. But take heart, because I have overcome the world."*
>
> JOHN 16:33 NLT

Jesus not only says that in life we will "have many trials and sorrows," but he also reminds us we can take heart because He has "overcome the world." We do not know why, sometimes people are not healed in this life, but we know, if we trust Jesus it will be worth it all one day. We are also promised in John 16:33, that when things go south, we can "take heart" that Jesus has overcome the troubles of this world.

We do not always know why God does not heal, but if He chooses not to heal in this life, we will be healed in the next. We can also take solace in the fact that when the situations in life do not seem fair, God is always more than fair.

We can take heart that God is never fair...He is always more than fair. For example,

> *For the wages of sin is death, but the gift of God is eternal life in Christ Jesus our Lord.*
>
> ROMANS 6:23 NIV

This verse tells us that the wages (what we have earned) for sin is death. Earlier Romans 3:23, has told us that we all have sinned, so we have all earned death. The end should be right there, that we all must die.

However, that is not the end of the story, instead, the verse tells us, that God gives us eternal life in Christ. This is an example of how God is never fair, He is always more than fair. This is great to remember that when circumstances look like God is "unfair" this is only a temporary viewpoint. If we will think eternally, we can see that even though we do not want to experience death, in time, God will make it up to His children. In time, eternal life and resurrection will happen for all who have trusted in Jesus.

We may not always know why God does not always heal, but we can always trust Him:

- Know that He is more than fair
- Eternity will redeem many sad situations and answer many difficult questions
- Jesus promised these sad times would come, but He has overcome the world's sadness if we will trust in Him
- One day, He will wipe away every tear from our eyes

Thoughts and Questions to Discuss:

1. According to Hebrews 9:27, what appointment do we have?
2. What happens at some point after we die, according to Hebrews 9:27?
3. 1 John 4:20,21 tells us that if we say we love God, but hate our brother, we are a what?
4. If we love God, who else will we love automatically?
5. Are medical doctors "Gifts from God?"
6. In general, should we respect and honor medical doctors?
7. Who has the final word in our lives?
8. Revelation 21:4 promises us that what will one day happen?
9. Is God fair?

CHAPTER 10

Helps *for* Healing

FIGHT SATAN, GARBAGE IN/GARBAGE OUT, SPEAK LIFE

Helps for Healing...

In these formative years of healing ministry, we discovered a lot of things connected to healing. They are not special revelations, besides the Bible, they all find their footing in the pages of scripture, but it did not seem like I heard these concepts a lot before experiencing them personally even, though I spent my entire life in Pentecostal churches and Baptist schools. During the years we fought the battle for Andrew's life during the cancer struggle, God taught us several things along the way. We learned first hand: you must fight Satan's words, garbage in equals garbage out and we must speak life.

Help for Healing #1 - Fight Satan

A candy apple red, 1998 Plymouth Breeze. I remember it like it was yesterday. I had bought the car about a year earlier when I was still working at a large church as the youth pastor in Phoenix, Arizona. My previous green

1994 Honda Civic EX with the power sunroof, leather seats and loaded out package was a nice car, but I had made a mistake that forever changed it. While backing down the ramps to unload the car from a U-Haul car dolly attached to the back of a moving truck, I slightly miscalculated and drove the car off the ramps. The 18" or so fall, did not seriously damage the car visibly, but there was a problem you could not see. Apparently, it had jarred the air conditioner in such a way that it would never work properly again. After taking it to two auto air conditioner garages and replacing several parts, the car still would not consistently produce cold air. This was problem enough where we were living in north Florida, but as we moved to Phoenix, Arizona, air conditioners are almost NEVER optional, so I traded in my beloved green machine for the 1998 Plymouth Breeze.

The little car was kind of sporty in a cheap, American car sort of way. One thing it definitely was though, was red. As a matter of fact, it was bright, candy apple red. I loved that color and the color is probably 75% of the reason I had bought this car. Our little Plymouth Breeze was the cheaper, inferior version of its identical triplet sisters in the Chrysler Cirrus and Dodge Stratus of the time built on the exact same frame, but those otherwise identical cars had better interiors, exteriors, engines and drivetrains. It turned out to be the last mid-size Plymouth car ever made as Chrysler discontinued Plymouth a couple of years later. I remember when I purchased it, after having driven around in an often hot (broken air conditioner) Honda Civic for the last few months, that I had the dealership tint the windows very darkly all around. I did not want any chance of heat in this car in Phoenix and I thought it looked "cool" as well. Remember, I was 25 years old when I purchased it. I have distinct memories of purchasing a year-long car wash pass, as I took it to the car wash weekly and kept it immaculately clean. I had after all, just landed the job at a megachurch and I was very insecure about so many things. I thought keeping the car looking good, might be important at my new church position since at my last large church job, I was told that my car was not good enough for church standards, but that's a story for another book.

Twenty years later, I remember a lot of details about that little car. I still know the radio was pretty sad, the hubcaps betrayed any thought of the car actually being cool, later the air conditioner would break in it as well, but this time, I had purchased an aftermarket warranty and had a complete $2,000 air conditioner rebuild for only the cost of my $100 deductible. On top of all those details about the car, Heather reminded me (while I was typing this book) that our oldest son Aaron also one time vomited up pizza in the back seat as well, but even that was not the most memorable story from that old red car.

I can tell you the exact place it happened. There is a highway overpass in Pensacola, Florida, that is a part of Brent Lane very near the entrance of Pensacola Christian College. This overpass became a treacherous place for me to drive one late evening on my way home. If you drove off of either side, you probably would have died. I'm not sure how tall it is, but it is tall enough for a road and a train to pass underneath. Now this overpass was not the site of a wreck in the Red Plymouth Breeze, but it was the site of a battle.

This event on that overpass was still several years away from the time that everyone has an advanced video camera in their cell phone. No one was even texting yet. If you had been in the back seat and if you would have had a video camera to record the events of this night, I imagine that 1) you would have been scared to death as a passenger and 2) you might have been able to get this video to go viral for the crazy man in the driver's seat that the video would have captured.

On this evening, I had just left Sacred Heart Hospital where our baby boy was in the hospital fighting for his life. The diagnosis of the deadly cancer that would "certainly take his life in no more than six months" had just been pronounced very recently. We had at this time, no positive or encouraging word in the natural whatsoever that confirmed or lined up in any way with the Word that the Lord would speak through me to the cancer doctor that the "Lord is going to heal my son!"

There are often times that the Word the Lord gives is out in front of what is going on in the natural. Sometimes in the 2020s when you make a video to broadcast via livestream on the net, your words will "be off." The video image will lag behind the audio, or the audio will lag behind the video and the lips "will be off." Sometimes a Word from the Lord is like that as well and there is a time of "God lag." Unlike a video normally off for only a part of a second or a few seconds, the God-lag time can be hours, days, weeks or sometimes years. King David experienced a time of about 15 years or more of God lag between his anointing to be King and his actual coronation. Joseph experienced a God lag time of 14 years between when he dreamed of being a powerful ruler and when he would be promoted from the prison to the palace. During this time of God-lag, you must hold on to those Words with all your heart.

In these first few days, we simply knew that his condition was extremely critical. I imagine, even though they have never told me so, that most of my family probably thought I was a little crazy at what I had said to the doctors. The science, the medicine, the natural state of things all said, Andrew is going to imminently die. God said, "Andrew is going to live."

On this night coming home from the hospital, I was by myself. I cannot remember if Heather had left before me to take care of our other son Aaron, or if she was at the hospital. We, or a grandparent were there basically 24 hours a day. What I know is that it had been a particularly hard day at the hospital and things looked very grim. It was very dark outside that evening and it must have been pretty late, because fortunately there were not a lot of cars on Brent Lane which is a very busy road traveled by thousands of cars daily.

I was feeling pretty emotionally wasted. I had been bargaining with the Lord, trying to come up with a promise as I discussed earlier in the book. It had been long day after long day at the hospital, mixed with trying to hold together a struggling new church work which had just had our first official launch church service less than a month earlier. On this night, someone spoke into my ear.

As I was driving up the overpass, I heard in my spirit, not in my natural ear, the sound of a sweet, still voice. It sounded, in some ways, very much like the Holy Spirit. I had drifted into a vision like state. I'm not saying it was a trance or I was asleep or anything like that. It was more of a daydream that someone else was playing and I was having a difficult time controlling it. The thoughts were so pervasive and seemed as if they had been implanted supernaturally. The vision was so clear, I was having a very difficult time concentrating on the road. I clearly could see and hear myself presiding over a funeral. In front of me was tiny casket and I could see myself holding it together as I spoke. At this time in my life, I had already presided over about 200 funerals, so it was something I was accustomed to as a part of my profession. This, however, was not just another funeral of a church member or someone from the community whose family just called a large church to ask someone to do a funeral for their loved one unconnected to any church. I always do my best to take very special care to put together a funeral with focused preparation, attention to detail, prayer and listening to the family, this is so very important, you only get one chance at a funeral. It is one thing to do someone's funeral you are not related to and to do a close family member's funeral. This was my baby boy Andrew's funeral, and it was in the very near future. The voice said, "You will give God glory when you speak at your son's funeral and show everyone how you have held it together so well with God's help." For just a moment, the voice sounded correct. It seemed right. After all, isn't that what rational Christians plan for? I mean, don't we know that while we know God can heal, in reality, He hardly ever does miraculously heal, right? Displaying the fruit of the Spirit is more important than miracles, right?

Since the mind and the spirit work at such a faster pace than the mouth and ear, this communication and internal conversation that probably would have taken 30 seconds to a minute in real-time to occur, if audibly spoken, this all happened in probably less than 3 or 5 seconds. It took less time than it takes for a car traveling at about 50 miles an hour to go from the bottom to the top of this relatively short distance of the highway overpass. By the time the bright red American wanna be sporty car's hubcaps reached the top of the overpass, a full-blown war had broken out in that Plymouth Breeze.

I know the car swerved as I yanked the steering wheel as I literally screamed out loud with my lips, tongue and everything my lungs had in them, "Get the **** out of this car devil!" (I referenced the place of eternal fire where Satan will spend eternity, I do not use this word as a curse word on a normal basis by any means, I was speaking literally to this hellish entity). A millisecond earlier, at the speed of thought, I played through me calmly speaking at the funeral. For that half-second, I wondered was this God preparing me for this tragedy? A half a second later, I realized this was not the voice of God at all. This was the work of Satan Himself. God's Word clearly warns us this is a scheme of Satan commonly used...

> *And no wonder! For Satan himself transforms himself into an angel of light.*
>
> 2 CORINTHIANS 11:14 NKJV

That night, there was a decision to be made. Now, I put out a disclaimer again, I do not know the exact specifics of how divine healing works. While I have listed some things we can clearly find from scripture about why some do and do not get healed, as I stated then, I back up again now, those are just a few examples, but ultimately God is sovereign and we cannot know His ways fully in this life. For now, we see through a glass darkly (see 1 Corinthians 13:12). Having re-emphasized that, I wonder, was the decision made that night pivotal for Andrew's recovery? Once you accept something, it often becomes the way it is. It is very difficult to believe against all hope that your son will live when every single medical authority tells you they will definitely die. It is very difficult to believe that your son will live when all of history about this cancer also tells you that your son will die very shortly. It is very difficult to believe that your son will live when Satan himself or at least his demons, invade your mind to remind you that your son will die. It is even more difficult to believe if you listen to what the world tells you, you must quit believing because all this stuff is just a fairy tale anyway. BUT...

WHEN YOU HAVE A WORD FROM GOD, YOU **STAND ON IT**.
WHEN YOU HAVE A WORD FROM GOD, YOU **PROTECT IT**.
WHEN YOU HAVE A WORD FROM GOD, YOU **CULTIVATE IT**.
WHEN YOU HAVE A WORD FROM GOD, YOU **LISTEN TO IT**.
WHEN YOU HAVE A WORD FROM GOD, YOU **REPLAY IT.**
WHEN YOU HAVE A WORD FROM GOD, YOU **REPEAT IT.**
WHEN YOU HAVE A WORD FROM GOD, YOU **DECLARE IT.**
WHEN YOU HAVE A WORD FROM GOD, YOU **REMEMBER IT.**
WHEN YOU HAVE A WORD FROM GOD, YOU **TREAT IT AS MORE VALUABLE THAN ANYTHING THAT COMES AGAINST IT.**
WHEN YOU HAVE A WORD FROM GOD, **YOU HAVE POWER, AUTHORITY AND LIFE.**

I wonder, if I had said, well, yes, let's be realistic. I'm not special and my family isn't special, let's just accept this must be God's will…would Andrew have lived?

You see, when you grab hold of a Word of God and it is contrary to everything that is normal and sane, then you look really crazy. That Word is like a greased pig. While, I am a city boy, and I have never held a greased pig, it is my understanding they are very difficult to hold on to!

That Word is bombarded daily by every lie of the enemy, which tries to displace the Word in your heart. The Word of God is often quieter, softer, more subtle and less obvious. This is because power, truth and life does not have to defend itself, just as God doesn't have to defend Himself. God is God, all by Himself. He is not insecure. He is not fighting a battle. He is not afraid He is going to lose.

Satan, on the other hand, is a defeated foe. His time is extremely limited. His power is incredibly weak compared to the Lord. His goal is to take down as many as possible with him before the age we currently live in expires.

If I had accepted that Andrew would die, there would have been little if any more praying for this miracle. Had we accepted this was his fate (did you notice that fatal and fate sound a lot a like?) and we could do nothing about it, then the battle would have been over. We could have gone back about daily life. We could have quit spending the mental energy to pray, fast, believe and protect the Word that the Lord had spoken to us. Life would have been much easier, but instead, we fought with as much mental, emotional and spiritual energy as we could muster up. (AGAIN, others who have lost a loved one, certainly DID NOT care any less or simply accept the fate easily of their precious one. Many people had an appointment with death and there was nothing that could have been done. We are not more spiritual in any way than anyone else, ultimately, God's goodness and mercy healed Andrew). My point is that, in this instance for example, if you accept something as the Lord's will when it may not have actually been the Lord's will, a million things change and if from that moment forward, the prayers and faith toward that end quit, then the Lord, from that moment forward has no obligation to heal or do whatever act He was previously being asked to accomplish.

How did I know for certain this sweet, calm voice was the voice of Satan? How can you tell when the Holy Spirit is speaking as opposed to a foul spirit? The foul spirit will cause fear, while the Holy Spirit will cultivate faith.

When you have a Word from the Lord, hold on to it. Satan Himself may come as an angel of light, but do not let him steal your Word. The next time Satan gets in the car with you, tell him where he can go.

Help for Healing #2 - Garbage in/Garbage out

From a very young age, I have always been a little nerdy (or maybe a lot nerdy). When I was in youth ministry full-time, I realized there were a lot of youth pastor tools I did not have in my ministry toolbox. I remember visiting a youth conference where the youth pastor had really big muscles, wore super cool clothes, he had a chiseled chin, Fabio type fabulous hair and talked like a super cool California surfer boy dude even though he was in Montgomery, Alabama. I had spent several years, on and off, trying to build my upper body in the gym, but while I had massive leg muscles (that no one cares about) I simply could not get the arms and chest no matter what I did. While hopefully, I did not look like a dog, when I was with my guy friends as a kid and teen, the others would always be noticed by the girls while I was the leftover. I remember thinking at that youth conference with Mr. Cool Youth Pastor, that if I was going to build a youth ministry of any size, I might not be sure how, but I wasn't going to do it from the cool factor. Later, I would be used by God to build several youth groups that would reach hundreds of kids and even had some sporadic events with thousands of teenagers attending. I did it with the nerd factor instead.

I was born in 1974, right as this new-fangled thing called the personal computer was being birthed. By the early 1980s, much of middle-class America could either afford a Commodore 64, an Apple II, a Coleco Adam or some type of IBM clone. During the late 1970s and the early 1980s, a variety of competing machines were released by all sorts of companies. Many were so weak, that virtually nothing could be accomplished on them and the game selection on many was beyond pathetic. Certain computers had "keyboards" that were flat and each key was like a sticker. To "type" on them was a special kind of torture. Depending on your age, you might not realize that in the late 1970s and the early 1980s, computers were not common. They were not taken for granted; they were incredibly "cool" to nerds. They were predicted to be the "wave of the future" and what the smart people would get involved in if they were going to be successful. A cousin that lived a couple of doors down first had a Texas Instruments "computer" in about 1980, but it was very weak and mainly played a few incredibly primitive video games. Then another cousin that I was close to named Angel was the first person I knew who owned a computer that I was close enough to, to go to her house and play with the computer for hours on end. We both grew up in my grandparents' home. She lived there full-time and I got on and off the school bus there daily, lived with my parents the rest of the time and also lived there during the days over the summer. We were very close. She was super cool in my eyes. If you wondered if she was super cool, all I can say is that in 1978, she bought an Atari 2600...and let me play it for hours. Defender, Space Invaders, Pac-man...for hours. In 1981, Angel got a Commodore Vic 20. It was pretty impressive. Then in late 1982, while I was in third grade, an event changed the course of my life forever. Angel bought a Commodore 64. While many think of the Apple II as the computer of the early 1980s, it was twice the price of the Commodore. So, while Apple ruled the school computer lab education space, for many young, nerdy Americans, the Commodore 64 swept the nation and took a special place in our hearts. Angel was about 12 years older than me, and she treated me like her little pet. When she got this new computer, she immediately had me over at her house to both show it off to me and to let me play with it for hours. The Commodore 64 would soon sweep the nation as a powerhouse game machine, truly use-able personal computer for many applications and for me, a programming machine that included the BASIC operating language.

Angel and her roommate ran a flower shop owned by my family. They lived in a mobile home that was literally about ten feet away from the florist and it was simultaneously in the back yard of the florist with a fence protecting an 8-year-old kid from any would be no gooders. Occasionally, I would be at Angel's house with the computer for hours while she would work in the flower shop. During this time I was introduced to "type in" games. In the late 1970s and early 80s, a popular new pastime emerged in America. "Type in" games were found in computer nerd magazines. Magazines would contain sometimes, pages and pages and pages of code you could type in to BASIC on your Commodore 64. Other magazines had similar code for IBM, Apple and several variations of the BASIC programming language. Today, when you want to copy a page or two of text on a computer, you simply high-light it, and press Command C or Control C depending on which system you are in and then paste it in the new place you want it to appear. However, in 1982, when you wanted to move hundreds of lines of computer code, you typed character after character, space after space, number after number and symbol after symbol. When you completed this sometimes monumental task, you would be rewarded with a play-able video game. In the standards of 2020, these games would be mocked and ridiculed by today's third graders to say the least, but in 1982, to be able to create your own knock off version of "Frogger" or some other really wonky game that involved moving blocks supposed to be military tanks or whatever the case may be, was basically magical.

The Commodore 64 was so magical that I would get more and more involved in computers and computer programming. In 1984, my dad who was always into electronics, bought me a Coleco Adam computer. These computers had experienced a disaster at launch time in 1983 the previous year. They had so many problems that stores had something like 80% returned immediately as defective. In 1984, to get rid of these now discontinued machines, the local Zayre store was selling a package for less than $200 with the computer, tape data drives, keyboard, printer and software. The machine we purchased had no problems and I continued learning BASIC programming. By 1985, my dad purchased a Commodore 128 (this was the 64's rarer big brother with twice the memory and other computer modes built-in). This was a serious computer in 1985 standards and I wore it out playing text-based adventure games (another story for another book) and I continued my affinity for computers in general. Later in high school, I would win two Florida statewide "Computer Literacy" competitions, taking first place from 8,000 students and this would land me a job at a local computer company. After high school, I enrolled in the United States Air Force in Computer operations and repair. After doing well at Air Force computer technical school, I was chosen for a special duty assignment due to academic achievement, where I spent the next two years working with the programming and maintenance of robots. I used my computer fluency in the early to mid-1990s to bring PowerPoint presentations on big-screen televisions (which hardly anyone had heard of in 1995 and 1996) to present the Gospel in churches. My computer nerdism, was now benefiting the ministry as well.

The only problem with coding in 1982-1986 (which was "programming" back then, no one used "coding" until a couple of decades later) was that it had to be EXACTLY CORRECT. The last time I programmed anything was well over a decade ago, but by the 2000s, programs called "compilers" existed. These programs helped with much of the work. Today, all kinds of programs exist to build upon in computer game programming, for example. In 1983 though, something as simple as drawing a couple of lines on a screen could be a complex set of instructions that would be very time consuming to perform. While I am sure coding can still be very tedious work, in the early 1980s, programming was often an incredibly painful experience.

One of my most hated experiences was seeing the words "Syntax Error." For people who worked in computers during that time, syntax error was probably the most common issue you had with running a program correctly. After spending what could literally have been eight or twelve hours to type in a game code or a code for something actually useful, if even one character was wrong, the entire game would not work. Often, this manifested itself by the game not starting at all. Other times, this would not be noticeable until you were actually attempting to use the program or game. Somewhere in your use of the program, a command you entered via text keyboard or by pushing the joystick in a certain direction, would often cause the computer to lock up or issue another "Syntax Error." Syntax "is the set of rules that defines the combinations of symbols that are considered to be a correctly structured document or fragment in that language."[1] If even one rule of the language is broken, it will not work. While I am not sure how it works in the 2020s, in 1982, if one space was not in place, if one comma was misplaced, if a long string of numbers like "378556091234" was mistakenly typed as "378566091234," then you produced a Syntax Error. Remember, these pages and pages of code, were not logical words or phrases, but sets of numbers, commas, symbols and other technical and tedious lines of confusing text that only made sense to the computer and the people who understood the programming language.

[1] "What is Syntax?". *www.computerhope.com*. Retrieved 2019-08-05.

After hours of work are completed to play your masterpiece of a game, if there was even the slightest of errors, you would instead only be rewarded by the error. These "Type-in" games and programs, if they were pages and pages long, could sometimes be real, small masterpieces (for the time and the technology considered). What would take an average kid, teen or young person in their twenties a day or two to type in, might have taken the original true programmer a month or two to write, perfect and then submit to the computer magazine.

When running these games after all that work, you would sort back through the code and find the error on whatever line number of code it was and spend the time to correct it. After you finally got that finished, invariably, if it was a long set of code, another error could show up later. If you had five pages of complex code, you could be sure that you would have multiple errors. Computer nerds would help each other look for the errors and fix it so they could enjoy this game masterpiece together. Then there were the exponentially more maddening situations where the code in the magazine was printed incorrectly. On more than one occasion, people placed code in national magazines with an error in it that more code had to be originally written to correct. Even more fun, was if someone had forgotten to save the code before running it. If you ran a type-in code that contained a syntax error then this could often result in locking up the computer in a way that could not be remedied without losing the code, if you had not saved your code during the process, then all of your work was lost.

While some of these games were simple, some were very long and complex, all had one thing in common...whatever you put into the computer, was what you got out of the computer. The "Garbage In, Garbage Out" (GIGO) statement has been used in computer circles for years. It is widely debated who first coined the phrase and who first put it into print, but the concept is very sound. A computer is just a machine without feelings, whatever you put into it will be processed and it will produce results based on those instructions. If you provide bad quality instructions, then the computer will produce negative results. If you produce good quality instructions that match the capabilities of the machine, then you will reap high quality results.

Garbage in, garbage out can also describe the physical body. As we all know, generally speaking, if we provide our body with a low-quality diet, then we will reap low-quality level health. If we eat only junk food, then there is little hope we will live a healthy life. If we eat high-calorie foods in too much quantity, without much exercise to compensate for this then we will produce the outcome of being overweight.

The mind and the spirit of man are no different. There may be an exception to a rule here and there, but garbage in, garbage out, is true of computers, bodies, minds, spirit and any other type of system that both inputs and outputs products of any kind.

In the realm of healing and faith, garbage in, garbage out is a vitally important concept. I took a good bit of time to set up garbage in, garbage out, even though I feel sure most readers will have quickly known what I am talking about. The reason, is because I really want you to think about the concept because it is so important. In Divine and faith healing, especially in "large" or "miracle needed" type situations GIGO is so important.

Jesus reminded us that in this world we will have trouble (see John 16:33). The world is an automatic set-up for serious difficulties. The pain, negativity, sin, sickness and chaos of the world is always and automatically working against faith, healing and hope. You do not accidentally flow upstream. You have to work against the flow.

In healing and all matters of faith, this is why it is so important to only take in the right things. When I was a child, the churches I grew up in were always talking about what we put in our spirits and minds. To be honest, I am not sure if they got the reason you should not put the wrong things into our spirit correct, but the concept was still sound. The churches I attended literally taught that if you listened to any secular music, you would go to hell. They taught that if you watched a soap opera, you would go to hell. They taught that if you went to a movie theater, you would go to hell. The list went on and on and on and on.

Today, I do not believe you can biblically teach that if you go to a movie theater or listen to a slightly objectionable song, you will go to hell. It is the blood of Jesus Christ applied to our lives that saves us and prepares us for heaven or hell, not media. However, paying close attention to the media we put into our minds is very important. All media, basically either glorifies God or glorifies the world system. There may be middle ground occasionally, but most media is good or bad. Media not specifically designed to glorify God, often is filled with the messages of the world. The world teaches death, depression, hopelessness and sin. Most media, even though it may not be totally dedicated to Satan or totally dedicated to the Lord, has the Spirit of one or the other.

From 1994 to 2009, the television show ER (Emergency Room) aired on American television sets. From around 1994 to the year 2000, Brian and Heather Farley watched most episodes of ER. ER differed from a lot of television from the 1980s. In the 1980s, before "reality tv" took over the airwaves, television time slots were filled with pre-scripted shows. Many of these shows were dramas or comedies. Most television shows of the 1980s were a special escape from reality even more so than pre-scripted shows are today. Before the explosion of the internet, the world was a much more sheltered place. In America, most of what was on television was relatively tame. On network television, nudity, curse words, extreme violence and the like were scarce. You could almost bank on the fact that in the 30 minute or 60-minute time-slot of the show you were watching, that by the end of that show, regardless of drama or comedy, most of the problems of those character's world would be neatly wrapped up. Often this would conclude with sappy music, people making up, fathers having a stern "talking to" with their wayward teenagers who then hugged and made up. Broken relationships (sensual or otherwise) were almost always mended before the final credits rolled with your favorite television theme song playing in the background, which made you feel all warm and fuzzy on the inside. ER, did NOT follow this pattern.

Most television shows before ER were predictable, even medical television shows were pretty predictable. What was so neat about hospital and medical shows in the 1980s was that, since it was on American television where decency ruled, the sick people in the hospital almost always recovered by the end of the show. And doctors are intelligent heroes, so they would almost always have the incredible procedure or new medical idea that would save the patient's life just in time. Before the last commercial, you knew that little Sally who had been bitten by the poisonous snake while at girl scout camp would be happily hugging her mom as the music played and the words rolled over their hugging faces because just in time, the snake anti-venom was flown in on a special flight from Canada by the daring doctor who had to travel there on his private plane to make it happen! The End...everything is wonderful. The problem with ER was that it was more realistic. In ER, an emergency room set in Chicago, the third-largest city of our country...people died, and people died almost all the time. This stinks, this is kind of like, what is the word I am looking for? This is kind of like, life, real life...where people really die all the time.

Apparently, this formula worked. ER aired 331 episodes, 15 seasons, won numerous awards and surpassed three billion dollars in television revenue, according to Wikipedia. The problem with this is what they call the law of diminishing returns. By season six or seven, if you had watched a lot of ER, you had seen a WHOLE bunch of people die. So, to satisfy your audiences' taste for death, you have to up the ante. The law of diminishing returns states that what satisfied you yesterday, based on excitement, thrill, pleasure, etc., will not satisfy you today or tomorrow...you will have to up the ante. So, what did the writers of ER do? They started killing off the doctors. We know that physicians die untimely deaths in real life just like everyone else does, but did we really need to see fictional Dr. Mark Greene die?

When the writers killed off Dr. Greene, that was it for me. I imagine that for many that were regular viewers of the show, that may have been a big disappointment for them as well. For me, it was not just that a television show had killed off a main character, it was much more. We were at almost that very same time, going through one of the seasons of medical unknowns just a few months into the diagnosis with little Andrew.

We were still constantly being told that Andrew would definitely die imminently. It was around the six-month mark at this time. Just as plain as could be, the Holy Spirit spoke to me, that I was not to watch ER again. This was not a command for my church members, I am not sure if it was a command at all, but it was a direction.

Now at this time, we did not watch a lot of television, to begin with. ER, I would say, was about the only thing we did consistently watch at all. Was God going to send us to hell for watching ER? Were we going to lose out on our relationship with Jesus if we watched ER? I do not think this was the problem. When the Spirit spoke to me, and it wasn't English He spoke, it was in "feeling," "urging" or "unction" that He spoke, what He said was, "Quit taking in any unnecessary death." I had specific instructions to limit our spiritual, mental and emotional intake of death.

Now obviously, this was not about my pastoral duties of praying for and comforting the dying, leading and attending funerals or performing graveside services. I still needed to perform the essential parts of my calling connected to death, and over the next few years, I performed many funerals and I was present when several people died. Until you are told not to take in any unneeded death, though, you probably have not noticed how much of our media and the culture, in general, is fascinated by death. We would assume there would be a fascination with death, fear and horror movies and other shows around Halloween, and there certainly is, but the amount of death on television and now the internet all the time is more than you would imagine. Over the next few years, we immediately quit watching ER and most other television. Probably 30-50 times over those years when we waited for the all-clear on Andrew's condition (this was a ten-year period), I turned off televisions because a fictitious or factual death was reported either on a fictional drama or the actual news. Not that we were in denial that physical, earthly death was a fact of life in this world, it was that we were denying it in Andrew's life. The more you think about something, the more you are drawn towards that thing.

For us, we were to limit our exposure to death. This extended a thought I had experienced many years prior in 1989 when I watched Stephen King's "Pet Sematary" film. The film caused nightmares and fear. From that moment forward, I vowed to never watch a horror film again. For me, taking in fear is simply not something I find beneficial, enjoyable or entertaining. I will not judge anyone who chooses to watch these things, but I cannot imagine that anyone needs more fear in their lives. Maybe it is because I am an adventurous person that I invite enough real fears in life naturally because a person of faith is always walking on the edge of the unknown. If you choose to bring more fear and death in your life, that is your business. For me, I was told to quit taking in any unneeded death and I already knew that for me, taking in unneeded fear was not good for me. The things we watch, listen to and experience do affect us. If we are not careful, things can rattle us, get in our spirit and hinder our progress with God.

Whenever you want to move forward with God, in life, power, leadership, growth, discipleship, consider that what we take in directly affects what we can put out. Garbage in, garbage out. If you are constantly taking in streams of fear and death, then it will be somewhat more difficult to believe for life and faith. If we are taking in foul language, it may be more difficult to produce love language. If we are listening to discouraging words, it requires more of the fruit of the Spirit to produce encouraging words. When we take in anti-God rhetoric, it is a source of friction to push against when called to produce a faith-building message and life.

If you, or if you are believing for a loved one, for healing, it may help to limit your intake of death, fear and negativity. Instead, focus on healing scriptures of the Bible. Promises of the Bible have the exact opposite effect of death narratives. For many years, I often read over and concentrated on healing scriptures from the Bible. While the list can be rather exhaustive, here is a brief list you could compile for yourself. Others facing life-threatening illnesses have recorded healing scriptures and played them back over and over on a loop while they were in the hospital. Do not underestimate the power of the Word of God. It is life.

Here is a small, partial list of healing scriptures in the King James Version to avoid any possibilities of copyright issues, but you can look them up in your favorite translation and read them, quote them and declare them over your situation. Much larger lists can be compiled from scripture (you may want to start with studying the healing miracles of the Gospel accounts of Matthew, Mark, Luke and John), but this list is a starting place to declare healing scriptures. The more you say them, out loud into the air is best, the more you will build your faith and change your thinking. Remember, you need not have "super faith," even the smallest amount can move a mountain. All you have to believe is "God, just might, actually heal me or my loved one," and the door of faith-filled possibility is opened...

> [1]*Is any sick among you? let him call for the elders of the church; and let them pray over him, anointing him with oil in the name of the Lord: And the prayer of faith shall save the sick, and the Lord shall raise him up; and if he have committed sins, they shall be forgiven him.*
>
> JAMES 5:14,15 KJV

> *A merry heart doeth good like a medicine: But a broken spirit drieth the bones.*
>
> PROVERBS 17:22 KJV

> *The Lord openeth the eyes of the blind: The Lord raiseth them that are bowed down: The Lord loveth the righteous:*
>
> PSALMS 146:8 KJV

> *And ye shall serve the Lord your God, and he shall bless thy bread, and thy water; and I will take sickness away from the midst of thee.*
>
> EXODUS 23:25 KJV

Fear thou not; for I am with thee: Be not dismayed; for I am thy God: I will strengthen thee; yea, I will help thee; Yea, I will uphold thee with the right hand of my righteousness.

ISAIAH 41:10 KJV

Beloved, I wish above all things that thou mayest prosper and be in health, even as thy soul prospereth.

3 JOHN 2 KJV

And whithersoever he entered, into villages, or cities, or country, they laid the sick in the streets, and besought him that they might touch if it were but the border of his garment: and as many as touched him were made whole.

MARK 6:56 KJV

When he was come down from the mountain, great multitudes followed him. And, behold, there came a leper and worshipped him, saying, Lord, if thou wilt, thou canst make me clean. And Jesus put forth his hand, and touched him, saying, I will; be thou clean. And immediately his leprosy was cleansed.

MATTHEW 8:1-3 KJV

And, behold, a woman, which was diseased with an issue of blood twelve years, came behind him, and touched the hem of his garment: For she said within herself, If I may but touch his garment, I shall be whole. But Jesus turned him about, and when he saw her, he said, Daughter, be of good comfort; thy faith hath made thee whole. And the woman was made whole from that hour.

MATTHEW 9:20–22 KJV

Surely he hath borne our griefs, And carried our sorrows: Yet we did esteem him stricken, Smitten of God, and afflicted. But he was wounded for our transgressions, He was bruised for our iniquities: The chastisement of our peace was upon him; And with his stripes we are healed.

Isaiah 53:4,5 KJV

And when he was come into the house, the blind men came to him: and Jesus saith unto them, Believe ye that I am able to do this? They said unto him, Yea, Lord. Then touched he their eyes, saying, According to your faith be it unto you. And their eyes were opened;

Matthew 9:28–30 KJV

But that ye may know that the Son of man hath power on earth to forgive sins, (then saith he to the sick of the palsy,) Arise, take up thy bed, and go unto thine house. And he arose, and departed to his house.

Matthew 9:6–7 KJV

And the whole multitude sought to touch him: for there went virtue out of him, and healed them all.

Luke 6:19 KJV

Then Peter said, Silver and gold have I none; but such as I have give I thee: In the name of Jesus Christ of Nazareth rise up and walk.

Acts 3:6 KJV

Help for Healing #3 - Speak Life

The tongue can bring death or life; those who love to talk will reap the consequences.

Proverbs 18:21 New Living Translation

> *Death and life are in the power of the tongue, And those loving it eat its fruit.*
>
> PROVERBS 18:21 YOUNG'S LITERAL TRANSLATION

> *The tongue has the power of life and death, and those who love it will eat its fruit.*
>
> PROVERBS 18:21 NEW INTERNATIONAL VERSION

> *Death and life are in the power of the tongue, and they who indulge in it shall eat the fruit of it [for death or life].*
>
> PROVERBS 18:21 THE AMPLIFIED BIBLE

It's so important, I put it in the book four times, in four translations...

> *Death and life are in the power of the tongue: And they that love it shall eat the fruit thereof.*
>
> PROVERBS 18:21 KING JAMES VERSION

...Make that five translations. Death and life are in the power of the tongue. Did you get that?

What is in the power of the tongue?

Two things: 1) DEATH and 2) LIFE

As a church child of America in the 1980s and 1990s, I have heard this statement so misused and abused and, more importantly, cheapened. Let me make clear, that I do believe it is God's will to prosper people and that if you follow biblical principles of generosity, wisdom, tithing, giving, and stewardship, you will experience God meeting all your needs. Often, He also adds many wants as well. However, no matter where you live on the globe, these principles will work. God will meet the needs of every person who puts His plan of management into practice. He will provide the basics to His children. That does NOT mean that everyone will be or should be rich. It does NOT mean that everyone should or will have a 2,500 square foot house at minimum with a $100,000 automobile parked in the driveway. There is nothing inherently wrong with wealth, but Jesus gives many warnings about it. It has led many people away from the Lord, and it will make it extremely difficult for many to enter the Kingdom of Heaven. Wealth without extreme generosity is very, very dangerous. Generosity in the presence of wealth keeps the steward of that wealth remembering it was never truly their wealth in the first place and that they have been blessed to be a blessing. Extreme generosity in the presence of extreme wealth keeps the steward of that wealth remembering that it was never truly their wealth in the first place and that they have been very blessed to be a very big blessing. The power of life and death being in the tongue, working with the biblical principles of generosity and wealth management combine to mean that extravagance and needless opulence, may be produced and may be a bi-product of the principles of stewardship of the Word of God. Some people use the principle of the power of the tongue to produce wealth. (Preachers flaunting extravagant lifestyles for no reason.) The point to mentioning all of this is not really about wealth, but to point out that, yes, as many have discovered, what we speak into the air, can and does affect our wealth, credit, net worth, transportation, food, clothing, and inheritance to leave for children, but that is NOT primarily what this verse is about.

We cheapen the meaning and priority of Proverbs 18:21 when we transform it and especially when we limit it to be concerned primarily with financial wealth or poverty. Again, Proverbs 18:21, concerns two things primarily 1) DEATH and 2) LIFE.

The fruit of what we say, will change our life. It will change our health and it will also change our wealth, but are you wealthy or poor if you have a billion dollars, but you do not have your physical health? All the money, property, cars, clothing and the world's greatest food has little value, if you are dying.

When told that your baby son is dying, it does not matter how big the pastor's church is, what car they drive, what neighborhood they live in, how many people they employ, if they were wearing a tailor-fitted suit on Easter Sunday, all that matters is that your son is dying or living. A part of the healing equation is what is said over the patient. Whether that patient is you or someone you care deeply about, what is said over them, to them and by them is of utmost importance.

The Word of God must be used in context. For example, much of the Old Testament of scripture contains Hebrew law, which was primarily designed to protect Israel to ensure the advent of God's Son in the form of Jesus, born to the virgin Mary at just the right time. This law was completed in the permanent sacrifice that Jesus made on the cross of Calvary for the sins of the world. This is the reason that today, Christians are not required to keep religious parts of the law, for example, admonishments against wearing different types of thread in clothing. However, Proverbs (or you could say Principles) was located in the Old Testament, but it has little to do with the Old Covenant. Proverbs and Ecclesiastes are a part of universal wisdom literature. The Proverbs are timeless and are as applicable today to anyone as they were to an Israelite 2,700-3,500 years ago. So, when we read that the power of life and death is in the tongue, this is not a special promise only for those who know God. This applies to everyone, and it applies all the time.

An illustration of the power of this principle of the power of the tongue was covered by the New York Times in 1989 in an article entitled ""Health: Psychology; Doctors find that surgical patients may still 'hear' despite anesthesia" by Daniel Goleman."[2] The New York Times article cites medical studies from medical journals and major universities who have researched the issues. The article explains that researches have confirmed

---

[2] "Health: Psychology; Doctors find that surgical patients may still 'hear' despite anesthesia" **By Daniel Goleman, Oct. 26, 1989, accessed online Google search, May 13, 2020. https://www.nytimes.com/1989/10/26/us/health-psychology-doctors-find-that-surgical-patients-may-still-hear-despite.html**

that patients can often subconsciously recall much of what was said to them while in surgery. This is not to say that they were awake, aware or in any pain during the surgery, but in a state similar to what people experience in hypnosis possibly. People should in no way read this and be afraid to have surgery that is needed. The hypnosis description is my communication, not the article's, but it is a fair assessment of what is described. Unconscious patients were told random facts like the blood pressure of an octopus and many were able to recall this bizarre fact after surgery. Others had it suggested to them that in an interview after the surgery that they would pull at their ear. The patients who were told this, tugged at their ears five to six times more than those who this rather unique behavior was not suggested to while being operated on. Also, patients who were told, "*You'll want to get up and get out of bed to help your body recover earlier*", recovered faster than those who were not told this information. The article ends with the suggestion that what is said in an operating room is so important, that at a minimum, the physicians should say, '*We're pleased with the operation," or, "You'll be feeling very well quite soon"* over their patients.

Both naturally and supernaturally, it is apparent that the human body responds powerfully to what it said to it and over it. The words somehow, in a way currently only known by God, sink deep into our inmost being and affect everything about us. This is possibly why the Bible has so much to say about the power of the tongue and our speech. Inside your mouth, you hold a force that can shape your world and the worlds of others. One of the greatest lies of the devil is the old children's statement so neglectfully taught as truth to millions, "Sticks and stones may break my bones, but words will never hurt me." Although we can let the foolish, hateful, wicked and terrible words of others roll off our back, if we take those words in and do not combat them with God's Word spoken over us and to us…those words cannot just hurt us, they can kill us, destroy our dreams and stop the entire destiny of nations!

For this reason (*the tongue has the power of LIFE and DEATH*), we should carefully monitor what is being spoken over us, to us and about us. This is all the more true when believing for miraculous, Divine healing.

The more lethal the situation is, the more important that we observe and guide the words spoken.

Words of death or life come from at least four groups of people when we are in a situation needing healing...family, friends, physicians and pastors. During our years of believing for Andrew's healing to be manifested, we dealt with all four groups.

In Hebrew, the word for "power" in that verse, "Death and life are in the POWER of the tongue," can be properly translated, "the force and ability sufficient to accomplish a task; state of domination over a less powerful object." This implies that there is so much force, power and ability in your words that it can dominate a less powerful object. In other words, when forceful words are spoken by other forces, some of those false words, false narratives put in place by Satan and hell, must be forcefully overtaken by a more powerful Word. You will have to choose if you will allow that more powerful word to come out of you at that time.

I am not a muscle-bound pastor. Probably, no one has ever said, "You know that Brian Farley's physical presence really scares me." Quite the opposite, many times, people have said to me you look like a "nice guy." I think twice or more in my life, people who did not know I was a pastor, guessed that I was a pastor. Anytime someone has ever guessed anything about what my place was in life, it has always been something rather non-threatening, docile, calm and maybe even boring. However, when you put the Spirit of God in any size package, when you allow your frame to be overtaken by the God who has the power to speak LIFE or DEATH, when you understand that the same power that raised Jesus from the dead is living inside of you...then you scratch the surface of understanding that NOTHING can stop the Word of God, bundled up inside of you. You might be a seven-foot-tall, 350-pound muscle-bound basketball player at the height of their peak performance at 25 years old or you might be a physically frail 97-year-old, 100-pound lady, when you fill yourself with the Word of God and His Spirit, you become a force to be reckoned with spiritually and this translates to the natural world as well. Your words have the power to dominate less powerful words.

Four Groups You Will Probably Have to Deal with their Words in Healing Situations:

- Family
- Friends (including church members)
- Physicians
- Pastors

Dealing with family speaking DEATH OR LIFE

Fortunately for Heather and me, when Andrew was under the greatest attack, it was amazing to see how my family reacted. Our family, like many others, had several people known to be super dedicated to the Lord, positivity, joy and blessing. I will not say who, because they are wonderful people, but some in my family could at times be known for not being very positive (this includes myself at times, especially in the past). When Andrew became ill, though, it was amazing to see as if a switch was flipped in several close family members. All of us who could sometimes be known for being negative, became positive. Without saying a word about not saying negative words over the baby, everyone in my family (at least when I heard them speak) said only words of faith and positivity. I said several times, announcing early in the process we would only speak words of faith and that nothing else would be tolerated, but I give all glory and praise to God because EVERYONE I can remember in my family all spoke words of LIFE. It is amazing how a family can be somewhat messed up, but God can still use them. No one in my family (including myself) was or is perfect, but for speaking positivity and life over Andrew, they all were supernaturally empowered to do so. My immediate and extended family have many problems like all families, but one thread that runs through the family is Jesus. The whole group, had and have some type of connection with Jesus, believing and trusting in Him. When you are talking about a group of 20 or more people, there are different levels of dedication to the Lord, varying degrees of immediate intimacy versus backsliding from the

Lord and there were virtual Bible scholars as opposed to those who spent little time at all the Word, but all of these people, generally speaking, trusted the Lord. What a blessing that turned out to be.

If you are going through a situation where your family is opposed to the Lord, then your situation from this standpoint may be difficult in the natural, but it is not impossible. God will grant you a special grace needed to overcome discouraging words of doubt, darkness and death. There may be some family members you need to distance yourself from if possible, you are not called to hate them or blame them, but there are even some family members you may not be able to pay as much attention to in this situation.

While, I was blessed to have a supportive family and extended family, I believe had I encountered people, even in my family who had spoken extreme negativity or death over Andrew, that even those people would have encountered an opposing word from me. Their word of darkness could not be allowed to overcome the words of LIFE.

If family speaks words of death over your situation and you are not ready to accept this as the only outcome, then immediately counteract that by saying out loud words of life. Speak healing scripture over your situation and claim the promises of the Lord.

Friends (including church members) speaking DEATH OR LIFE

Another group you will deal with about whether they will speak Words of life or not are your friends and this includes church members. Hopefully, your friends and church members will be more than supportive and speak words of life over the situation. If your friends and even church member friends do not speak words of life, then first, ask them to speak only life over the situation or not say anything at all. If their behavior continues, then eventually you will have to make the choice of whether to stay in a close relationship with them, at least during this time. Often, friends and family will be very well-intentioned because they are just trying to be "realistic" or help you "prepare" for what may happen. It is my belief that if you are over ten years old and you are reading this that you have already found out that the world is a harsh place, people die, we are dealing with the effects of sin in a fallen world and there is enough negativity and death in the world without adding to it with our words.

I also take a moment to separate church member friends from regular friends. If you are reading this book, there is a great chance that you attend church regularly. If you attend a church that does not believe in healing, I would suggest changing churches. If you are not sure where your church stands on healing, then ask the pastor. Some churches teach that supernatural healing absolutely does not occur today. They usually mix this with the belief that no supernatural events or gifts happen today. I would run from this church as fast as I could. This church will do everything to dampen your faith in the name of being rational. Many churches in the world will at least claim that they believe from time to time healings occur. This is the minimum doctrine I would tolerate, but if you are looking for healing, you really must be in a church that believes that divine/faith healing is for today and that while it may not be the norm in the natural, healing is something that we should expect to see from time to time. This is the type of church you should be a part of, a church that believes in, prays for and encourages faith in the strong possibility of healing today.

Amazingly, sometimes in full-Gospel, Spirit-filled, Life-giving, Pentecostal and Charismatic churches even then people will be discouraged from believing in healing. This could be for a number of reasons. Please know that you need to surround yourself with people believing for a miracle, no matter where you can find them as long as they are Christians who trust in the name, power and life of Jesus Christ and none other. I want to reiterate that if your church is not believing with you for healing because you will not accept medical treatment, I would NOT recommend ignoring them at all. If there is a treatment for cancer or whatever the disease or ailment you are dealing with, please do not think of the medical community as your enemy.

> *"Every good thing given and every perfect gift is from above, coming down from the Father of lights, with whom there is no variation or shifting shadow."*
>
> JAMES 1:17 NEW AMERICAN STANDARD BIBLE

James 1:17, clarifies that every good and perfect gift comes from Father God. So, medicine, is a good thing and we believe that it is from God as a gift to His children. Many stories I know about people not using medicine or medical treatments for the sake of believing in God instead end badly. Please do not take this book as an anti-medicine writing, it is not.

If you can find a church that believes in the power of healing, this is probably one of the best places to surround yourself with like-minded individuals during a time where you and your family need a miracle. If the friends or church members speak words of death over the situation, then combat this with Words of Life immediately and continue to do so when you are alone or with your immediate family.

Physicians speaking DEATH OR LIFE

First, a word about physicians, personally speaking:

Obviously, physicians are, generally speaking, as stated in chapter 9, among the brightest minds in society and if they are not among the brightest minds in society, they are without a doubt among the most disciplined people on the planet to have passed the rigorous schooling and training that takes roughly a decade of preparation to complete. Probably, most physicians are among the brightest minds AND the most disciplined people academically at the minimum. Because of this truth, along with many people's good belief in respect for authority and authority figures, physicians sometimes are tempted to pick up a God complex and some give into this belief they are as smart and powerful as God. This belief, if taken to heart, can make these otherwise very intelligent and extra disciplined individuals among the greatest fools on the planet. In the defense of physicians, this is certainly not the case for the majority of physicians. In fact, a few years ago, Heather worked as an ophthalmologic technician for Dr. John Cox in Huntsville, Alabama. Dr. Cox, is the opposite of all of those negative possibilities mentioned. Dr. Cox is a great example of someone who works at the top of their profession, is a brilliant physician, a super hard worker, caring, honest, truthful, very medically competent, compassionate, and yet is exceedingly humble and committed to Christ Jesus even though Dr. Cox sits at the top of the social ladder. Dr. Cox's practice partner, Dr. Heather Estopinal, is another example of a great physician who also does not think they are God, but trusts in God. These physicians are involved in missions work, are committed to their local churches and the Cox's treated us as friends in their homes on many occasions even though Heather was an employee. Many, if not most, physicians are worthy of great admiration and often, these physicians are strong believers in Christ.

As discussed in the proceeding section on friends and church members, this book is NOT opposed to physicians or traditional medicine. The author takes prescription medicines daily that assist in his day to day life. Once again, medicine and medical treatment is a good thing. We thank God for physicians, nurses and medical workers who help us recover using education and skills they spent years of their life learning.

Now that the groundwork is laid, physicians and medicine are usually a gift from God, physicians can also, at times, be very confrontational with the patient because they are very certain that the person is dying because of past medical experience. If you knew that you would definitely die on a certain week, you would probably want to know that. The same is true for the loved one of someone who is almost certainly going to die in a relatively short while. The physicians who look at medical records, statistics, past studies and trials...especially if they are a specialist in a field they have been practicing in for decades, will want to let you know the truth about your situation and the facts about your situation. When a physician says that 95% of the people in your situation die in two weeks time, or something similar to that statement, they may very well, just be presenting facts. It would be irrational to hate the doctor for telling you information such as this. As long as what they are telling you is true, then they are probably just trying to let you know the truth, so you can get your final affairs in order. It is good to have your final affairs in order, spiritually, financially, mentally and in every way. This can be done, though, regardless of believing you are imminently dying or not.

There is, however, a great difference in a physician saying that 95% or even 99% of people in a certain situation will die of this condition in two weeks time or less and that you will definitely die in two weeks time or less. A physician may be intelligent, better informed medically than you, they may have statistics, they may just try to stop "false hope," but if a physician tells you or your loved one will definitely die in a certain period of time, then they have overstepped their bounds. Physicians are not called to be prophets of doom. Physicians are not called to predict the future with certainty. When they step outside of "most likely," "commonly," "statistics show" and into "he will definitely die," "you will definitely die," "you will definitely not recover" ...they have overstepped their grounds. If they simply added words like, "he will definitely die without a miracle," "you will definitely die unless God supernaturally intervenes" or "you will definitely not recover without massive help from the Big Man upstairs," then this is an entirely different scenario.

It is understandable that doctors may not feel like this is appropriate, but if you are dealing with a life and death situation, then you do not have time to be concerned with how doctors feel about things. The cancer doctor in our situation literally verbally sparred with me every time we met in his office for several years. I do not know if he hated me, but he certainly acted like it. I cannot speak to his motivation, but I can speak to his actions and words. This doctor, would argue with me again and again. He claimed that my son would not live, he spoke that the tests would not come back in a positive manner, he claimed that the cancer would return and he spoke all of these things with absolute certainty. Now, I am not saying he wanted my son to die, or that he was a cruel individual, I assume that he simply wanted to not provide "false hope." I certainly hope he wanted our son to live, but these were not his words.

A few months or years after we started this cancer journey with Andrew, I saw commercials on television for "Cancer Treatment Centers of America." I do not claim to know anything about these centers. I have no idea if the quality of their care exceeds most cancer hospitals, specialists or centers and I do not know if they practice what they preach. There is a great amount of information for and against Cancer Treatment Centers of America easily accessible on the internet. This book is not intended as a recommendation for Cancer Treatment Centers. Some people say that Cancer Treatments Centers of America are purely for profit and offer a lot of "false hope." I simply have no first hand or even second-hand information about them, but I do know that they have the best commercials I have ever seen for a cancer treatment center in the world. If they live up to the spirit of what their commercials preached from 2005-2012 or so, then I love their approach to treating cancer.

One of their commercials famously said right smack dab in the middle of the commercial for some form of ultra-serious and often fatal cancer, the physician is quoted concerning one of these patients, "I didn't see an expiration date stamped on you." Then the patient shares a story of how they lived years beyond the normal life expectancy for that type of cancer. The internet criticism of the Cancer Treatment Centers of America is these stories are rare and that they seem to conclude that they are common. I cannot judge that. I know that people could say this book is written primarily for profit. Someone could say this book claims that anyone could be cured of anything at any time if they believe hard enough, and this claim would be blatantly false. I do not claim it is easy to be cured of cancer or anything else. I do not say that everyone will be healed in this life. I do not desire to mislead anyone ever about healing or anything else, but I know that GOD CAN HEAL, even when there appears to be no hope whatsoever.

The statement that Cancer Treatment Centers of America (CTCA) makes about, "I didn't see an expiration date," is NOT FALSE. It is not false or incorrect to simply state the obvious. It is not a bad idea to try alternative treatments if traditional treatments are failing and it is certainly not illogical to cling to the supernatural power of Jesus' healing, especially when the natural world has little or no answers. The CTCA may or may not just be in it for the money, but they are completely telling the truth when they say that physicians and other medical experts do not know when someone is going to die. Only God knows when someone is going to die.

It would seem that many physicians who deal with critically ill patients believe that one of their greatest responsibilities is to not provide "false hope" to a family or individual of a possibly terminally ill patient. There is a great problem with this thinking though, hope is NEVER false when God is involved!

> *Jesus looked at them intently and said, "Humanly speaking, it is impossible. But with God everything is possible."*
>
> MATTHEW 19:26 NEW LIVING TRANSLATION

Google defines hope as- a feeling of expectation and desire for a certain thing to happen. If you take this first definition as the definition for hope, it is impossible to have "false hope." Hope is defined as an "expectation" or a "desire" for a certain thing to happen. If we are only dealing with "expectations" or "desires" then it is impossible to have false expectations or desires. An expectation or a desire is not something that is tangible, to begin with. It is just that, it is something we at best expect and more likely, just desire. It is not false hope when someone purchases stock on the New York Stock Exchange because they believed that the company of which they are purchasing a small share of will perform better in the future, which would increase their investment. It is not necessarily foolish for someone to invest "hope" and money in the stock market. If they are not unwise, then the investor will know not to put their money in the stock market if they cannot afford to lose some or all of it. If they wanted a lower risk proposition, they would have invested in a saving account, bonds or something that is less volatile and safer.

Similarly, when someone invests in spiritual, emotional and mental "hope" they are not investing in a sure thing. If faith didn't require faith, it wouldn't be faith. If hope wasn't hope, it wouldn't be hope. Hopefully, most or all people who invest themselves spiritually, emotionally and mentally hoping to heal understand that it is hope. Ultimately, God controls the outcome and no one can manipulate God to do their bidding. However, there is no such thing as "false hope" even in the natural. Then when you involve God in the equation and the healing power of Jesus, there is certainly no such thing as "false hope." Humans can live with a lot of things, including disappointments, pain, regret, the effects of sin, losses of all kinds, illness, bad cancers and the list goes on and on, but humans cannot live for very long without hope! When you take hope away, you take away something of immeasurable value. Hope is as important as the latest, greatest medical treatment for any illness, and I believe sometimes, it is more important.

If a physician says that you have no hope, maybe you should prepare a will just in case, but never prepare a will without also planning a major vacation for at least a year away at the same time. If a physician speaks death over you and you do not believe this time schedule they are laying out is God's will, then mitigate that doctor's word by speaking life back over yourself and proclaiming what the Word of God says about healing over you. (Read those healing scriptures out loud, every day, several times a day).

When do you give up? When do you quit believing for healing in this life? Well, you have to hear from the Lord on that. Most would say at the death of a loved one. While I have not yet seen a dead person raised back to life in my life personally, I know it has happened and does happen and I have laid my hands on a dead body and asked to bring them back to life. No, they didn't come back to life, yes, I am sure the doctors at West Florida Hospital thought I was a fool asking for a minute alone with the body, but I am certain you will never be used by God to raise someone from the dead if you never lay hands on a dead person and ask God to raise them from the dead. I'm still believing to see it before I die, if not see it many times. Why would you put this in the book? Because it is what happened and everything else in this book is what happened as well. Possibly, I will one day write a book from personal experience about raising people from the dead in Jesus' name as well. And guess what, I wasn't mad at God when the church member who had just had a massive heart attack on the golf course did not come back to life, I just assumed it was his time. And guess what, the family was not mad at me either for praying for the dead guy. You have to be willing to put yourself out there for Jesus if you will ever see real miracles. You have to walk in faith if you will ever see God do some crazy, awesome stuff in your life and ministry.

If doctors speak death over your situation, speak life back over it unless you desire death at that time.

Pastors speaking DEATH OR LIFE- Kicking Pastors Out of the Hospital Room

Have you ever kicked a pastor out of your hospital room? In as polite a way as possible, I have.

Believe it or not, you may need to be careful about pastors praying over you in the hospital. If they are praying over a broken pinky finger of your thirteen-year-old who jammed it while skateboarding, there is probably not a lot at risk here. If you are praying for your life to continue over a dire diagnosis and you need all the faith you can get, you will want to align your faith with someone who is walking in Spirit power. This false, "false hope" narrative is a really powerful thing. It has caught on to the medical profession so well, that it is easy to pick it up as a pastor. Even though I am authoring this book, it is easy for me to want to fall into it as well. As a pastor, you see people very, very ill often. As a pastor, even if a church member does not call the church for small medical emergencies... even in the largest of churches and even with the most low maintenance of church members, when someone is gravely ill, normally they will call the church for prayer at the point of death and when the person is young or generally not expected to die, they are all the more likely to (rightfully) call the church. This truth means that pastoral staff are often faced with desperate medical situations. Some of these people will die and some of these people will live. So, what is the point in calling the pastor? Well, there are many good reasons, but two of them include 1) comforting the family and being a companion to them and 2) actually believing with the family for a miracle.

Every time I go to the hospital or train someone to go to the hospital, I ask the Lord to help me that I will be of real spiritual and possibly physical help to the person I am visiting. I was ministerially trained in an environment where the pastor of a large church often talked about how many years of his life he had spent in hospitals with families. Hospital visitation was a large part of his church growth strategy and it had been successful. This gentleman had built several churches to more than 500 people in weekly attendance and much of the growth could probably be directly accredited to the amount of time that the pastor spent in the local hospitals with parishioners. The pastor had figured the hours and days out, and he often stated that he had spent thirteen years of his life visiting the hospitals.

While it is very appropriate for pastors to visit hospitals and while it has many good benefits for the hospital patient, the church and even the pastor, hopefully, the reason the pastors visit is more than emotional ties, church strengthening and spiritual well being of the injured party. Hopefully, at least occasionally, the person in the hospital is physically healed. Possibly, the pastor at the hospital prayed or assisted the prayers of the person who was sick to pray toward physical healing of the sick person with an aim at bringing glory to God. With the benefits that hospital visitation can bring to churches, pastors should not get their eyes off of the reason we visit people that are sick. Hopefully, a part of this is to see the people healed. I think it is an easy trap for pastors to fall into that we are some type of social worker mainly and then secondarily, we are there to pray for physical healing. Although the sick person's spiritual well being is far more important than their physical well being, let's not forget that we serve a God of miracles who can manifest His glory in the miraculous if we are open to this!

When Andrew was extremely ill, he had just been out of intensive care for a day or two, we had many hospital visits from pastors of all kinds. The baby was so ill and his diagnosis was so grim that the word had gotten out in local churches and many churches were praying for him. We were thankful then and now that many of these churches prayed for him. We believe that many of these churches' fervent prayers from people we did not even know played a part in his healing. God is not limited by time and space in prayer. He can heal someone 3,000 miles away and 21 years from now, prayer is not limited like our finite bodies are limited. For this, we are forever grateful.

During this time that Andrew's story was circulating in many local churches, several pastors I knew well, some that we were familiar with and some that we did not know at all dropped by while they were at the hospital visiting their own church members. This is a practice I occasionally do as well. I will never forget one of those visits which probably upset a couple of visiting pastors.

If this pastor, who is a very real person, reads this sometime in the future, I pray they will understand my mindset and forgive me, but they need to understand that at the time, their feelings were not my primary concern. The pastor I speak of, is a good man who works hard at his ministry position, has increased his church attendance greatly and is dedicated to his flock. I appreciate the pastor coming by since they probably had no intention of ever benefiting from it personally and were trying to assist the larger Kingdom of God.

One of those days, just a day or so, out of intensive care, Andrew was still in a very, very touch and go type state of living or dying. We were in a time we had just been recently told in the last seven days, probably five times or more that Andrew was definitely going to imminently die. This was repeated over and over forcefully by the cancer doctor and was obviously something that had been shared with the medical staff. We were in a spiritual and mental fight for Andrew's life. After all, Satan has not come to hurt your feelings, injure you or let you know that he is your more powerful big, bully brother…Satan has come to steal, kill and destroy (see John 10:10). Satan's aim is to kill, He is a mass murderer and He is on the loose in the world today. Can you imagine if a psychotic serial killer who was not at all repentant and had full intentions of killing as many people as possible walked in your life, house, church and hospital room to kill your infant son? Would you do everything you could to protect your son? Or would you agree with others who seem to take the side of this homicidal maniac?

While Satan may not have had a knife, gun or poison to put in one of Andrew's medical intravenous drips…he did and does have a poison that is even more powerful when it comes to the battlefield of the mind and spirit, unbelief. This poison is a killer of millions in the past and will continue to ravage the world until Jesus returns. If Satan can steal your faith in Jesus, and in this case, the healing life of Jesus, then the devil can rob you of your miracle.

In this state of mind and this heightened state of spiritual awareness, I was much like the mama bear who instantly protects her cubs. In this situation, two pastors walked into the hospital room.

It was near the end of the day, possibly between four and six p.m. Like every other day for the last week or so, and like every other day for a total of 46 days to come, either Heather or I was at that hospital 24 hours a day, seven days a week with a few exceptions in the later weeks when we would let grandparents take a shift here and there. Remember, we were not just there to see how sick the kid might be, but according to the cancer doctor and the surgeons, he could die at any time.

Into this environment, two pastors (the senior and the associate pastor) of a local church walk in. They do not know me really and I do not know them, we each know of each other and our local churches. The pastors are a part of a group supposed to believe in divine healing, in fact, the denomination they are a part of teaches that divine healing is one of the four most important doctrines of the entire Bible, setting it apart with three other doctrines as the four most essential from a greater list of Sixteen Fundamental Truths. I would expect that people who represent a group like this, would clearly pray for healing, real, physical, miraculous healing. That is not what we experienced.

They made some polite small talk for a moment and then asked if they could pray for Andrew. The prayer was something like this, "Lord, we thank you that you comfort us in times of need. We appreciate that you are here with us in the darkest of hours. We know that you can do anything, but we pray that you comfort this family right now. Be with them no matter what happens. You are the God of the brokenhearted." Now, almost 20 years have passed since that prayer, so I am certain these are not the exact words spoken, I am trying to represent the basics of the prayer without exaggeration. What I can tell you with certainty, was this prayer was NOT about healing. This prayer was not about a miracle-working God. What I can assure you is that they had not asked me what we believed for or how we were praying. I know with certainty from the words of the pastor that the prayer had little or nothing to do with asking God for healing...this is not up for debate, the pastor's words literally had nothing to do with healing except for possibly a token something like "we know you can do anything" sandwiched between lines and lines of would you comfort this family.

The way I heard comfort that day was the problem. Comfort is something you give someone when everything is wrong. Now, this pastor did not necessarily mean that our son would die, but it sounded that way to me. He may have simply meant that our situation was terrible (and there was no denying that it was) and whether God healed our son or not, it was still a situation that needed comfort. On that day though, all I could hear was a man saying our son was most likely going to die, there was no prayer of agreement that he would live. There was no asking for a miracle, on that day, I did not have time for that. It sounded as if the pastor had joined the ranks of the medical professionals who had pretty much given up on our son as far as living a regular life span. He was in the hospital to recover enough to take him home where we could "enjoy him for a couple of months or so" before he died.

In those minutes of prayer where this pastor of a church who was supposed to believe in real, physical, miraculous, divine healing (just like my church), a church where you are expecting the world to call you a fanatic, the pastor jumped on the comfort the most likely dead bandwagon. On that day, I did not have time for this. I could not handle the spiritual strain of one more person adding to the pathetic lament of the cancer doctor, on that day, I had had enough. I walked up to the pastors with their hands on the bed and on Andrew, I took my hands and grabbed their wrists, pulled them off of Andrew and said something like, "I'm sorry, but you are through praying for him," and asked them to leave. They were both visibly upset, but I said, "No, I'm sorry, I need you to go. My son is going to live."

I get it, this is the kind of thing that people will think you are spiritually nuts for. I understand that this type of thing hurts people's feelings and does not put you in the camp of being a great compassionate pastor. Could I have been nicer about it? Possibly. Would I have handled it differently now? That's hard to say, nearly 20 years have passed since the incident to the time of this writing. I was 26, young and brash. I was on a mission to see my son saved. I believe I was often led by the Holy Spirit during the process and several times, I had to forcefully speak more dominant words of life over words of doubt and death.

Now, I am in good company with these types of "insane" actions. There was a great movie called "*Breakthrough*" that premiered in 2019. It chronicles the true story of a mother, Joyce Smith's fervent prayer life and words of life over her son that had fallen through a frozen lake. She was bold and probably what the world would consider a little crazy acting after the accident. When she was told there was no chance of her son's recovery after being under the freezing water for 15 minutes before any attempts to resuscitate him were made. The boy, did eventually miraculously make a full recovery. In the film, she is portrayed as rudely throwing out people from the hospital that had already started acting like the boy was dead even though he was not completely dead. Later in the story, she apologizes for her actions. I think that her actions were nothing to apologize for. Either you are going to believe (and put the things, people and systems in place to protect that belief) or you are not.

In Matthew 9, Mark 5, and Luke 8, the Gospel writers give us the account of Jesus rebuking "mourners" before He raises a girl from the dead. Jairus, a synagogue leader's daughter has died. Before Jesus gets to the house, mourners have arrived. These are probably not mourners as we think of today. These were most likely people who were playing sad musical flutes and wailing to get paid by Jairus to show the importance of his daughter at the time of her death. These people definitely caused a mood of death, despair and grief. The Luke narrative explains that Jesus rebuked the crowd of worshippers, telling them, "Stop the weeping! She isn't dead; she's only asleep." Luke 8:52 New Living Translation

Mark 5:40 explain that Jesus did more than rebuke the mourners, in these two accounts the Greek used to explain His actions describe that Jesus- expelled them, drove them out, threw them out, or sent them out. In Matthew 9:24, the Greek describes that Jesus told them to "go away, withdraw or leave."

> [23] *When Jesus arrived at the official's home, he saw the noisy crowd and heard the funeral music.* [24] *"Get out!" he told them. "The girl isn't dead; she's only asleep." But the crowd laughed at him.* [25] *After the crowd was put outside, however, Jesus went in and took the girl by the hand, and she stood up!* [26] *The report of this miracle swept through the entire countryside.*
>
> MATTHEW 9:23-26 NEW LIVING TRANSLATION

Now Jesus is Jesus, didn't He have the power to raise this girl from the dead without rebuking the mourners? Couldn't He have been nicer and respected the feelings of the flute players and women wailing at the top of their lungs over the tragedy of this little girl dying? Couldn't Jesus have performed this miracle without the seeming harshness towards these people?

Perhaps, but when Jesus was encountered by people who brought opposition to His greater mission, He rarely left you wondering how He felt about things when you listened to His fierce words and sometimes exceedingly strong actions. When the Pharisees propped up their "self-righteous actions" as the means to heaven, Jesus called them dead men's tombs full of rotting corpses! When people were selling animals for sacrifices at the temple, He came in and furiously knocked over the money changer's tables! When mourners were declaring that this girl was dead and gone, Jesus rebuked them and drove them out of the girl's presence!

While Jesus certainly had a high emotional intelligence, He also was not at all shy to turn off all political correctness and face people clearly aligned with the wrong side of spiritual things in order to get His Kingdom tasks accomplished.

Jesus knew that when the atmosphere is wrong for spiritual healing, at best it makes things very difficult. When the atmosphere and the belief of the people about miracles is completely wrong it can even hinder the miracle from taking place…

> [4] *Jesus said to them, "A prophet is not without honor except in his own town, among his relatives and in his own home."* [5] *He could not do any miracles there, except lay his hands on a few sick people and heal them.* [6] *He was amazed at their lack of faith.*
>
> Mark 6:4-6 New International Version

If Jesus "could not do any miracles there" (Mark 6:5), how much more useless are regular folks like you and me to perform miracles if the atmosphere is one of complete unbelief? You must change the atmosphere if you are expecting to see a miracle. Jesus not only lived it, but he taught it to his disciples. In Acts 9:36-41, Peter does the exact same thing.

Before a woman can be brought back to life, Peter asked all the sad people to leave...

> *36 Now there was at Joppa a certain disciple named Tabitha, which by interpretation is called Dorcas: this woman was full of good works and almsdeeds which she did. 37 And it came to pass in those days, that she was sick, and died: whom when they had washed, they laid her in an upper chamber. 38 And forasmuch as Lydda was nigh to Joppa, and the disciples had heard that Peter was there, they sent unto him two men, desiring him that he would not delay to come to them. 39 Then Peter arose and went with them. When he was come, they brought him into the upper chamber: and all the widows stood by him weeping, and shewing the coats and garments which Dorcas made, while she was with them. 40 But Peter put them all forth, and kneeled down, and prayed; and turning him to the body said, Tabitha, arise. And she opened her eyes: and when she saw Peter, she sat up. 41 And he gave her his hand, and lifted her up, and when he had called the saints and widows, presented her alive.*
>
> ACTS 9:36-41 KING JAMES VERSION

> *The room was filled with widows weeping and showing him the coats and other clothes Dorcas had made for them. 40 But Peter asked them all to leave the room; then he knelt and prayed.*
>
> ACTS 9:39-40 NEW LIVING TRANSLATION

The case here does not seem to be professional mourners, but legitimately sad widows who were friends with this woman. They very much loved this woman, but Peter still asked them to leave. Peter knew that if they had already written her off as dead then their sadness would infect the environment and might dampen his belief as well.

In the moment that a new miracle is needed,
It does not matter:
how many miracles you have seen Jesus perform,
how many miracles you have been used
by Jesus to perform yourself,
if you saw Jesus come back from the dead,
if you saw Jesus ascend to heaven....

In the moment that a new miracle is needed, the present, the "now moment," and the weight of the now, is powerful...the now causes us to forget all that we know about the miraculous workings of God and if the now moment is filled with grief, despair, doubt, fear and death...it will be very, very difficult to speak LIFE enough to overcome the DEATH in the air.

In these moments, you must remove as much DEATH as possible to make as much room for LIFE as possible. If Jesus had to rebuke the mourners and clear the room and if Peter had to clear the room to change the atmosphere, what would make me and you believe that we can see God do a miracle without at times being forceful and clearing the room?

Jesus paid the price for our healing when He died on the cross. But he was pierced for our transgressions, he was crushed for our iniquities; the punishment that brought us peace was on him, and by his wounds we are healed. Isaiah 53:5 New International Version

Jesus paid the price we could never pay for healing. It was His spotless, perfect Blood of sacrifice on the cross that would make it possible for us to receive healing. Sometimes if we desire to walk in the blessings of that healing and experience miracles today, we may have to pay a much, much, much, much less, almost inconsequential price of setting the environment so we can be in a mental and spiritual place of faith conducive to walk in this healing. Jesus took on the form of man, was beaten, ridiculed, tortured and murdered, we may need to ask some people, physicians, church members, family members, friends or pastors to leave. We may have to open our mouths and be willing to look foolish in the world's eyes, but really it is certainly no price to pay that deserves any comparison to the incalculable price that Christ paid for our salvation and healing on calvary. If you desire to walk in the miraculous, know though that you may have to stick your neck out, open your mouth, use your tongue to boldly speak, tell some people to get out and maybe even inadvertently offend some folks along the way.

Remember, when people speak death, you must choose to speak life and speak it with power. Do not let death settle in your spirit, soul and mind. Believe on, speak and repeat the Lord's Words of life.

Thoughts and Questions to Discuss:

1. How can Satan make himself appear according to 2 Corinthians 11:14?
2. If Satan can transform himself, how do we know when he is speaking and when the Holy Spirit is speaking?
3. What is the computer programming term that can also be applied to our spiritual lives?
4. Have you ever noticed that when we eat bad (excessive junk food) as opposed to when we eat healthy that our body feels totally different? What kind of spiritual diet should we be consuming to be in peak performance spiritually?
5. One of the best ways to increase our spiritual vitality is to intake large chunks of the word of God. If you are sick, try praying the healing scriptures included earlier in this chapter once or several times a day. Praying them out loud is best.
6. What two powers are held in the tongue?
7. Do you believe that the tongue literally has the power to heal?
8. What four groups of people will you need to have a plan for how you will deal with them if they speak death over a serious medical situation?
9. Can you trust all pastors to speak life over you?

CHAPTER 11

How to Pray *for* People in Dire Medical Situations *and* What is needed *for* a Miracle

As stated in the last chapter, when you are in the hospital, believing for a miracle when all the odds and all the doctors are against you, what you do not need is a person who comes in at least seeming that they are not in agreement with your faith. This section hopes to provide some direction on how to practically pray with and for people who need a miracle and the amount of faith that is needed to receive a healing miracle.

How to pray for people in dire medical situations...

When praying for and with people in desperate medical situations (the medical establishment has written them off, there seems to be little hope, they have been told they are terminal), *first, find out what the person and/or the family is believing for.* The Bible talks about agreeing in prayer...

> *I promise you that God in heaven will allow whatever you allow on earth, but he will not allow anything you don't allow. I promise that when any two of you on earth agree about something you are praying for, my Father in heaven will do it for you. Whenever two or three of you come together in my name, I am there with you.*
>
> Matthew 18:18-20 Contemporary English Version

Jesus promises that when people "agree" about something, there is tremendous power released. When we agree on earth, God the Father in heaven, will do it. From this, we can walk away with the concept that before miracles happen in prayer, there must be agreement. If two people are praying about a situation and one person is praying to one end, and the other is praying in the opposite direction, then they will likely not have a miracle outcome. This demonstrates why it is important to first find out what someone or a family is praying for, especially in a dire medical situation, before someone prays for a miracle or before someone stops praying for a miracle.

For example, some people who are older and have been battling a disease for years and years, have decided they are completely fine with going to heaven, and going to heaven soon. If these folks have decided in their heart that this is what is best for them, then would it be right to pray for physical healing? We do all know that we have an appointment with death at some point. For many people, they have settled the issue in their heart, have peace about the situation, feel good about what has been accomplished in and through their lives and are almost looking forward to seeing Jesus. This is especially true of believers who have buried several loved ones and all the more true of very long-term marriages of senior citizens. In these cases, it may be counter-productive to pray for miracles.

Once you find out what a person and family is believing for their situation, there may be a great freedom to pray with reckless abandon for the person. If you discover that the family has decided to pray, fight (spiritually, medically and in every way) for a miracle, no matter what the odds, it is easy to link your miracle faith with theirs. In these cases, I would not quit praying in agreement for miracle healing until the patient is in the ground. To come in and pray prayers of "comfort" for the family with the person in the intensive care unit would be just as inappropriate as speaking and believing for a life-extending miracle when someone is believing and even desiring to go home to be with Jesus.

A third group of people experiencing dire medical conditions are looking for spiritual guidance. Some families and individuals are not sure what they should pray and are seeking the guidance of someone spiritual to help them sort it out. For these people, I would explain that we believe in a miracle-working Savior. I would also explain that we all know we will die eventually, so God has not let us down if the situation goes south in the natural.

So first, when praying for people in dire medical situations, find out what they are praying and believing for, and second, if they are not sure what they are believing for offer, them the formula for what type of faith is needed to receive a healing miracle.

What is needed for a miracle...

When we pray for miracles, God is not asking us that we be 100% sure this miracle is absolutely going to happen. In fact, (see Matthew 17:20), Jesus says that if you have faith the size of a mustard seed that you can tell a mountain to be moved and it will move.

> *Then the disciples came to Jesus and asked privately, Why could we not drive it out? He said to them, Because of the littleness of your faith [that is, your lack of firmly relying trust]. For truly I say to you, if you have faith [that is living]*

> *like a grain of mustard seed, you can say to this mountain, Move from here to yonder place, and it will move; and nothing will be impossible to you.*
>
> Matthew 17:19,20 The Amplified Bible

What can we learn from this? Jesus does NOT say we need big faith to move mountains. In fact, Jesus says that mustard seed size faith is all that is needed to remove mountains. A mustard seed is a little speck. It can be as small as 0.039 of an inch. It can be less than 4/100 of an inch across. And the verses' context here was that Jesus said that the disciples could not cast a demon out because they did not have mustard seed size faith. He was NOT saying their faith was small, He said that if they had mustard seed size faith then they would have been able to not only cast out demons, but they could have moved mountains as well. I have told many people that this means, all we must believe for a miracle of healing or anything else to occur is to believe that it is a real possibility. God is not saying we must have this unshakeable, superhuman faith, He is saying, if we had even the smallest amount of faith there is unlimited power in that. So, if we can just open the door of our hearts and minds that God just may do a miracle of death-defying healing, at that moment, it becomes more than possible that it just may happen! If you can just believe that you might be healed, then that is just the smallest amount of faith, and Jesus says it can move a mountain. If you are closed to the possibility of a miracle, then a miracle, is almost surely not going to manifest. If you just have the idea that God maybe could, or maybe will, perform a miracle, then you are moving toward mustard seed faith and anything can happen. What is needed for a miracle? Just being truly open to the idea that God certainly may and very possibly will do this, opens the door for miracles. Instead of trying to convince someone that a miracle is probable, we can lead them to the idea, that however unlikely in the natural that a miracle may occur, with God, it is possible. When this happens, we are halfway to a miracle.

Thoughts and Questions for the Chapter

1. Have we asked what the people we are praying for in dire medical need are believing for in this situation?
2. What does the Bible say about agreement in prayer? see Matthew 18:18-20
3. What does Jesus say about the amount of faith needed to do incredible things? see Matthew 17:19,20

CHAPTER 12

True Stories *of* Miraculous Healings that will Build Faith

ROBERT, JACK, SALLY, TED, SAMANTHA

Robert

Every year for Thanksgiving, the church I pastored held a pre-Thanksgiving Tuesday night service. Usually, we had Wednesday night services, but found that with Thanksgiving being the day after, almost no one would attend since they were busy with pre-holiday preparations or they were already out of town. The Tuesday night service was also usually a very low attended service, but a little better than if we held it on the Wednesday night before Thanksgiving. These services were, just to be honest with you, not normally very eventful. Because of the holiday week with so many people out of town, even though we normally had mid-week, children's, nursery and youth classes separate from the adult service, we would bring all the children, youth and adults together for this service. We would sing some Thanksgiving-themed songs, I would normally lead the congregation in an exercise designed to get them to write down some things on a paper they were thankful for that year, preach a message about being thankful and then we would take communion. On this year, this small service of maybe 60 to 70 people, including all the kids, did not appear to be anything special.

However, on Tuesday evening of November 25, 2003, it turned out to be a very eventful evening that I will probably remember for the rest of my life. It was one of those nights that looking back on it, you are certain that the tangible presence of Jesus showed up. It was not just a good feeling during the worship songs (which is often the same Holy Spirit that manifests Himself in just as certain of a way), but it was the Holy Spirit manifested that evening as the Great Physician.

I received a call from David Calhoun on the afternoon of November 25. David worked as a roofer and was actively on the roof of a house when he called me. He was hysterical, crying, talking loudly and he was explaining that he and his newlywed wife, Susan, had recently left the OB/GYN doctor's office. David and Susan had just been married a few months and upon getting married, Susan almost immediately had gotten pregnant. As far as they knew, the pregnancy was fine, but on this day, things had drastically changed.

While at the doctor to check on the baby, it was discovered that there was no heartbeat. They checked several times and none could be found. Then as they further investigated, they discovered that the mother had a condition called a bicornuate uterus that was not formed properly, it was deformed in a way that also indicated the baby would probably not be born alive even if there was a heartbeat. The doctor explained that the baby was definitely dead and the couple would need to return on the next day to have a dilation and curettage (a D&C, similar in mechanics to an abortion, but the baby is already dead of natural causes) procedure to remove the dead baby.

While on the phone with David, he received some type of unction (strong, supernatural feeling) from the Holy Spirit that was very encouraging to him, letting him know that things were not going to be what they seemed. David also said some words of faith while we were on the phone. We prayed vigorously in Jesus' name together over the phone. Before we hung up, I had David promise he would be in church that Tuesday night with Susan. They normally attended anyway, but I wanted to make sure they would be there that evening.

When pastoring, it is my habit that on Wednesdays, I only do one thing, I prepare for that Wednesday night service. From about 10 a.m. until about 6 p.m., before the 7 p.m. service, all I do is plan, pray, write the message and do other things to prepare for that evening's service. The only thing that takes me away from those duties is a true emergency. On this particular day, which was like a Wednesday, but was a Tuesday because of Thanksgiving week, after I received that phone call…I could do no more preparation for the service in general. From that moment forward, all I could think of was what should and must be done about this baby. For most of the rest of the day, I prayed, thought, and it has been too many years now to remember clearly, but I believe I fasted as well. I fasted on many Wednesdays until after the church service was over or at least until after 6 p.m. for the 7 p.m. service.

That evening came, our group of 70 or so people showed up and we did our thing, I announced that we would have special prayer at the end of the service. We sang about being thankful, we took up our offering, we played a Charlie Brown Thanksgiving Cartoon clip (which was my weird little custom), we had people write down what they were thankful about, I taught a bit about thankfulness and we took communion. All of those things were good, but all of those things on that night, as most were very forgettable in the long term. Then we called David and Susan to the front of the church building to pray.

They came to the front, as I explained to our group what had happened. They were both crying. If I remember correctly, Susan was profusely crying. It had only been a few months earlier that I had the great privilege of marrying these two. That night differed greatly from this night. That wedding night had been a night of great happiness, but this evening, death was in the air.

As we began to pray for the child, I placed my hands on Susan's stomach. This couple was obviously faith-filled. A lot of people would have sat home as they prepared for the next morning's D&C. This couple had instead, proclaimed some words of faith over the child, come to church (which was a considerable drive for them), and believed for a miracle. As I prayed, words filled my mind that actually kind of scared me. I thought, I cannot say this, I will look like a complete fool if this doesn't happen. As a shy, only child, I had always pridefully (and still sometimes can be) concerned with what others think, so I knew if I said what I thought that maybe the Lord was putting in my mind to say, I would lose lots of credibility and really look foolish if this word failed.

I had been praying in the spirit (in tongues) and building up my most holy faith on and off all afternoon and into the early evening before church. Then in the church service, as I was quietly praying in tongues, those at the altar could hear me even though I do not pray in tongues in the microphone, I could hear the prayers of the saints around me in the altar. There were many times during this season of church growth that a large percentage of the church would occasionally truly be united in reality altering faith. This was one of those nights. I do not claim to know exactly how many were at the front gathered around praying for David and Susan, but I know there must have been at least some 12 to 20 people pushed in and gathered tightly. I had asked for only those with faith for a miracle to come to the front and for others who could not believe for something like this to simply be sure that they said nothing negative. In that tight crowd at the front of the church, I could hear faith. I could sense in that tight-knit group of believers that God was about to do something. There is a certain power, expectation, glory, sense of wonder, electricity, energy, synergy, dynamic, and anointing that only comes when believers who truly believe God can do anything get together.

It is a situation, that may be able to occur over internet connections when several are gathered in the name of Jesus', but it is easier to re-create when people come together in faith in Jesus' name. Faith and fear have one thing in common, they are both contagious. A high level of sincere faith will quickly rub off on people in the near proximity and will spread as fast and easy as the coronavirus of 2020. It does not always happen in Spirit-filled worship services, but sometimes it does...and when it does, ANYTHING is POSSIBLE.

Each person praying in faith played a pivotal role in what was about to happen. If no one would have come forward when I asked, and if no one would have prayed in that gentle, murmuring voice of faith, just under their breathe, then who knows what would have occurred? If doubters who wanted to check our theology or foolishly declare that God no longer heals today would have been the overwhelming crowd in the room, then who knows if the story would go as it did...

Thankfully, just as David had said some good, powerful words on that day, I had one hand on Susan's belly and a microphone in the other, I loudly proclaimed into the microphone, something very similar to these exact words as loudly, powerfully, and authoritatively as I could find the nerve to do so, "We command this child to live. We speak life and say this child will be healed in Jesus' name!" As I prayed, prophesied and declared those words, I cannot explain it fully, but I felt something in my hand as I simultaneously in the Spirit, almost saw this child being energized in the mother's womb. As I prayed this in that powerful environment of faith, it must be recorded that not only were the parents responding with faith, but the majority of the church was at the altar and many were obviously faith-filled. I was only a vessel that was a small part of the Lord's plan to work a miracle on this night. I was prepared for the task earlier that day myself, but I also was charged up, encouraged, energized and filled with the Spirit by the parents and the small crowd gathered around praying at church that evening.

Many may consider those words "unwise, wreck-less, and false-hope filled." Here's the thing about it though, sometimes faith requires at least a little wreck-less-ness. That is surely a controversial statement, but I prefer to ere on the side of faith rather than live with the comfortable, boring, never-see-a-miracle-folks on the side of prudence and "just the facts." No person who studies the facts of an impossible situation for too long has ever done anything great to change those facts.

> *Faith in the almighty power of Jesus, ALWAYS trumps the facts of a desperate situation.*

The next morning, the couple went to another physician. They had explained that the doctor from the previous day was very forceful in his declaration that the baby was dead and nothing could be done. They saw the new doctor and an examination was performed. The new doctor explained there was a heartbeat. In addition, the uterus was formed perfectly fine with no problem whatsoever. There would be no need for a D&C. It was not too long before Robert Daniel Calhoun was born. A perfectly healthy baby boy. At the time of this writing, he is a perfectly healthy teenager with a good heartbeat. Jesus can do anything.

Jack

In the late 2000s, I preached a funeral for a church member's father. As with many funerals, the service gave the opportunity to meet and minister to many new people. One of those people was a man named Jack Wilson. I had briefly met him at the hospital earlier when I was there to pray for the dying man who happened to be his uncle. Later, in the spring of 2008, we had a yard sale. At the yard sale, we bumped into Jack again. This time we invited him to church. He said he would come. The next line is something that most people might be surprised by, but anyone who has ever started a church can appreciate very much…I was shocked when the next Sunday, he actually attended the church service. (People lie to pastors all the time that they will come to church and never actually attend!)

During the next few weeks and months, Jack attended more and more, his wife Linda and his son Tony also got involved and quickly became a vital part of the group. What the church didn't know at this time was that Jack was feeling sicker and sicker as the days and months passed. The whole time he was attending church, he was feeling worse and worse in his body. Although he could not pinpoint it exactly, he was in pain and was having difficulties with his lungs. Though the problems and pain were mild at first, in time, the problem became persistent until he reached the point where he feared something was seriously wrong and almost could not function anymore.

On August 16, 2008, Jack went to the doctor to get checked out, he had been feeling so bad for a while now, but on this day, he knew something had to change. After hours of a lot of pain, he was checked out by a doctor. Jack went to the emergency room at the Baptist Hospital in Pensacola, Florida where he spent most of the night having a litany of tests performed to ascertain his condition and make a diagnosis. He was eventually admitted to the hospital. The physicians were not certain exactly what was wrong with Jack, but the doctors all agreed that it was something extremely dangerous. Jack had been a smoker for over twenty years. He was afraid that God was punishing him for smoking. While the doctors were not positive what Jack's problems were, they knew it was related to his lungs.

The emergency room and hospital team ran a number of tests on Jack, including several scans. The tests showed some type of menacing mass in his lungs. After having been in the hospital for about an hour, a pulmonologist (a physician who specializes in the treatment of lung diseases and conditions) came in and told him, "I have to tell you that something is wrong, and it doesn't look good for you. You either have tuberculosis or cancer, lung or breast cancer." Either way, tuberculosis or cancer are not anything that you want to hear, and for a long-term smoker, these words are even more terrifying.

Shortly after moving Jack to a larger hospital room, which is often to accommodate large amounts of people visiting because the patient is critical, most of his family arrived to hear the news from the doctor, and the news, of course, was not good. The news was so bad in the large hospital room that the mood of family and friends was one of despair and sadness. For two full days, the only reports from the doctors were of doom and gloom with no talk or hope of recovery. Several times he would wake up and the room was filled people murmuring quietly with countenances of sadness all around him. After the news from the physicians, Jack says that it was like his entire family was almost "waiting on me to die."

During this time of darkness, other pastors from the community came and I also visited Jack. While I was there, I spent the time to tell Jack the in-depth story about my son Andrew and how God could do anything even in the darkest of situations. He said that was one of the first times he had felt any hope because of the situation he was facing seemed so desperate. Sometimes hope can change your reality. After two days of this, Jack eventually asked his wife Linda to politely ask the family to leave for a while, as he needed some time alone. Jack said that he told his wife, "It was like they were sitting at a funeral." Eventually, Linda and all the family left.

After everyone left, Jack burst out in tears. Feeling a mixture of emotions of both anger and confusion he turned on the television and surfed through the channels. Eventually, he came across a Christian broadcast of a popular televangelist. The evangelist said into the camera there were some people who needed to tell the devil to get out of their life. The television pastor said that you should "sweep some things out of your life and explain to the devil that you don't own me or control me." The preacher had mentioned that you need to take a broom and sweep the devil out of your life.

At that moment, Jack felt a "surge of power and strength." In that God moment, he proclaimed out loud, "Devil, you don't own me. Get out! Get out of my life! Get out of my room!" Jack took his arms and as if he had a broom, he started "sweeping" the devil out of his room and his life. At that moment, he felt a burden being lifted off of him. He loudly proclaimed, "Devil, you do not belong, because I belong to Jesus!"

After a few days in the big room, the hospital moved Jack to an intensive care unit. While in intensive care for a couple of days, several medical procedures were performed including removing excess fluids from his lungs and heart, and they went through his ribcage to biopsy the lung, he woke up during this procedure. Eventually, Jack was placed back in the big room for several more days. Jack spent seven days in the hospital.

On Saturday, a week after Jack had been admitted to the hospital, he was released from the hospital. He was not released because he was doing so much better, but more there was nothing further for the doctors to do for him at this time. He had several follow up appointments in the days to come to discuss the lung situation and a plan about what the treatment plan going forward would be.

On the Saturday, that Jack was released from the hospital, he went to stay with family who also attended the church. The next day, on Sunday morning, the family and extended family all came to church. Most of the church knew by this point that Jack was very sick. We had prayed for him the previous Sunday morning and Wednesday night midweek service as well. During service, I asked Jack to come to a cross in the middle of the auditorium. While some protestant churches have beautiful ornate cross decorations prominently displayed on the walls and Catholic Churches often have a crucifix statue in the middle of the altar area, we had something much less visually appealing during this time at Harvest Christian Center in Cantonment, Florida. In 2011, the church spent a lot of money on a nice remodel of our auditorium we had built almost a decade earlier. Today the church building looks much more professional and welcoming on the inside, but I regret that I did not incorporate a design element from the previous look of the auditorium.

In 2002, when we were building the auditorium, it was a no-frills operation. At this time, the church was so poor, that I was still working in the meat department and deli of the local Walmart. We cut corners anywhere we could to save funds, so furnishing the auditorium was nothing to impress anyone. On the outside, the building was just a large metal shed kit we put a few bricks on and a small fiberglass cross decoration at the front entrance so it would not be so unappealing to look at. On the inside, there was no dropped or ornate ceiling, just exposed insulation we painted black, white sheetrock walls, the chairs were recycled from another local church that sold them to us for $4 apiece. We painstakingly took those twenty-year-old chairs apart one by one, repainted the frames and cleaned the cushions before reassembling them as "new." The carpet was the least expensive commercial carpet you could buy. For the next several years, we would keep cigarette lighters in the auditorium during cleaning because almost weekly, you would have a run in the carpet. It was that kind of carpet that if a vacuum cleaner snagged it, it would almost immediately pull a fifteen-foot hole in the carpet before you had time to realize that the carpet thread had been caught on the vacuum roller. Your only hope of it not pulling more was to cut the carpet hair where it was sticking out of the floor and burn it with a lighter to singe it closed and melt it into the next carpet loop. By 2011, there were massive runs in the super stained carpet everywhere you looked. Since 2011, the church building is still not extravagant in any way, but it is amazing what an extensive remodel with new chairs, carpet and paint did for the looks of a 350-seat auditorium.

In this almost third-world country finish level of a church building, just as He does in garbage dumps of church buildings, Great Cathedrals and in little old ladies' prayer closets, anywhere that people exercise faith in Jesus, God did amazing things time and again. In the middle of that old, brown, mega cheap carpet, I took a roll of black gaffer's stage tape and made a cross in the floor. This tape is designed to tape down microphone cords, electrical cords, and light cords for theaters and churches. The foot of the cross started about twelve feet down the middle aisle and it was about two feet across. The arms of the cross spread out to the left and right of the altar area which was in front of the first row of chairs and the top of the cross touched the stage. This cross was large enough for several people to stand in. I put that tape down for a very practical reason. Often, as I am a pastor who believes in the "laying on of hands" for the sick, 20-30 people would gather at the church altar area during prayer times. This was a mix of people wanting to receive prayer and others who had come to support them and to pray for them. This is wonderful, but from a pastor's viewpoint, it is confusing on who is wanting prayer and who is wanting to pray for others. So, the cross was installed for a very practical reason, so I could say, "If you need prayer, healing, a miracle, come stand inside of this cross which is outlined in black tape on the floor." It was a cross because that is the symbol of what Jesus did for us on THE cross when He paid the price for our salvation and healing, but as far as the practical purpose it served, it could have just as easily been a star or a plus sign or a square. I realized, though, as the years passed, that the cross on the floor was more than that to many people who stood inside of it. Even though it was just maybe 40 feet of black gaffer tape, to some it was a point of contact with God, it was a place of faith, it was an action they took saying that, "I need God's help and I believe He can help me!"

On this morning, in this cross, the same place that Roberts's parents and so many others would stand over the course of several years and receive miraculous healing...Jack came to stand. I asked him to come stand in the cross. He was very weak and sick and could hardly walk up there. Jack's wife Linda and other family members had to help him come to the cross because he was so weak. Jack recounted that on that day, all he could hear was praying all around him. Much of the church body had joined around him to pray. I didn't even remember saying this before interviewing him for this section of the book, but apparently, I told him something to the effect of, "If he had enough faith that he would get well." I asked him did he have faith? I asked him, do you have enough faith? He said, "Yes, I do." Let me add this, While I do not doubt I said something to this effect. It can sound harsh in a book, but in real pastoral life, I would have only said anything like this to someone who I believe did have faith. It would never be said to someone in a condescending manner. And, as it is stated in this book, I always remind people that even the smallest amount of faith [smaller than mustard seed faith] is all that is needed to receive a miracle. I frequently just ask people, do they believe that it might be possible that they might be healed, as if mustard seed faith can move a mountain, then just the possibility of healing can surely heal a body.

The next few days, he had several doctor appointments. On the Tuesday, after being released from the hospital, he had a day of new scans. On that Thursday, two days later, he went to the pulmonologist for the results of the new scans. After reviewing the new scans, the pulmonologist said, "I don't know what to say, I am baffled. Now, nothing is showing up on your scans. I am just baffled! There is no cancer or mass to be found. We cannot find it."

Linda said to him, I know what happened. Linda knew that God had performed a miracle. Jack hadn't eaten hardly at all for two weeks, but after this appointment, he immediately wanted to eat again.

The next Monday, he had an appointment with a rheumatologist. The rheumatologist said, "I know that you went to the pulmonologist the other day, but have you heard? There is nothing in the scans!" The doctor then added, "What you have had happen to you is like a miracle!" He went to see the hospital doctor who had also treated him while he was in Baptist Hospital. He also confirmed that there was nothing showing that he had cancer or a mass of any kind.

Initially, all three doctors never came up with any options of how he would be healed or a treatment plan of any kind. All three only had to say it just doesn't look good for you at all.

All three doctors agreed that whatever it was, it was there, they did not remove it, but it had vanished.

Today, almost twelve years later, Jack is still alive and well. When God decides you will recover and live, you will recover and live. God is faithful. Jesus is the healer. The Holy Spirit is the Great Physician.

Sally

There was a precious woman who use to attend Harvest Christian Center for several years. She had been known to have painful female issues for several months, if not years. This lady, believed in God with her whole heart and displayed a sweet and gentle spirit. She was what you call an "old soul" at a young age. She was a single parent who attended faithfully with her young children. She never bothered anyone, she often had a bright smile and never caused a problem of any kind. Some church members can be trouble makers, others do fabulously remarkable things and some are faithful, dependable and loving. Sally fell into that faithful, dependable and loving range. She is the kind of person that if you had a lot of them, that you could build a great church with them.

One day, I got the news as her pastor that she would be having surgery to remove a large growth from private areas of the body. The doctor had performed several tests, including imaging tests, which clearly showed a large mass in her female regions. The next day, surgery would be performed to remove the mass. We asked her to come to the front of the church to pray for her in the cross on the floor during one of our church services. Obviously, because of the location of the ailment, I very politely only laid my hand on her shoulder. I also had my incredible wife, Heather, take much of the lead with several other ladies praying for her. As we prayed, what had sometimes become not "familiar" to me, but had become something that I at least recognized, I sensed a healing travel through us from the throne of grace to Sally as we prayed. Much like the account described of the healing of the baby in the womb, the faithful church at Harvest Christian Center, gathered around in faith. Again, much faith was flowing in the room and you could hear it on the lips of the church members. I said in the microphone something to the effect of, "We command for this problem to shrivel and die and that Sally might be fine and live."

The next day, Sally went to the hospital to have the surgery to remove this thing scheduled for early in the morning. When Sally got to the hospital, the doctor said that something just told him or nudged him on the inside that he should run an imaging test one more time. So, before her surgery, he ran the test again. This time the image came back, showing completely healthy female organs. There was no mass whatsoever. The doctor cancelled the operation altogether and sent Sally home.

Ted

There was a man about 50 years old in 2003 who did not attend the church regularly, but visited often. He had no children, but he assisted in some of the children's ministry as an assistant teacher. Ted was very thin. He suffered from Crohn's disease. I had not heard of the disease. This is a painful and life-altering condition of the intestines. Often, portions of the intestines must be removed by physicians to make the situation better. This drastic "solution" speaks to the severity of the condition and people who do not have eating or digestive issues probably cannot imagine the pain and suffering this may cause. As I type these words, I sense the ability to cry when I think of the suffering this man suffered through for years. He had already had portions of his intestines removed.

One day, it was reported that his Crohn's was really flaring up again, giving him a lot of problems. He went to the doctor as he had many times before to see what the course of treatment would be. Unfortunately, he had been having so many problems that the doctors again prescribed surgery to remove another good portion of Ted's intestines. He was in such poor condition there was no other choice about it. We asked him to come to the front of the church for prayer. We all gathered around and asked for the Lord to grant a miracle. I do not recall praying any specific, incredible sounding words, but I know that we specifically prayed for God to grant a miracle. We prayed and believed and the surgery was scheduled for that week.

Due to the severity of the surgery scheduled, I felt like I should be at the hospital. Due to the church being so close to Alabama, some members and attendees lived in and worked in Alabama. This was the case with Ted, so I drove to Mobile Infirmary Hospital, about an hour away, in Mobile, Alabama before the surgery. I believe I prayed with Ted before the surgery, but I cannot be sure at this time because the memory of some details fade after over 15 years. What I remember with extreme clarity is the surgeon who met us in the waiting room that day. The surgery was scheduled to last for several hours. It was planned to be relatively extensive.

Only about ten to fifteen minutes into the surgery, the surgeon came to meet the family and friends in the waiting room and I was there. The surgeon was of Russian descent and spoke with a pronounced accent. His English was good, but it was obviously not his first language, to say the least. His exact words ring as strong in my ears today as they did all those years ago. He was at a loss for words; at least he was at a loss for English words. He explained, "We opened him up, and what is word? What is word? What is word for this? O, yes, word is 'miracle!'." He continued, "When I opened him up, I realized something strange. That is somebody else's intestines in there!" He said, "Those are not the intestines from the testing, those are not the intestines from the imaging. Those intestines do not have Crohn's. There is nothing wrong with those intestines. Those are somebody else's intestines!"

He continued to explain that since those intestines were "miraculously changed" and "somebody else's intestines," he just closed him back up because there was no reason to take out good intestines. The surgery was over in 10-15 minutes, not 3-4 hours. Ted was released from the hospital shortly thereafter.

Jesus can put "somebody else' intestines in you."

Samantha

After a few of these healing stories started being talked about in the community, it would be an exaggeration to say we had large crowds come because of the healings or that we had a full-blown healing revival or anything, but over the course of several years, we had more than one person who attended specifically because they had been told that people were being healed of cancer and other serious illnesses at the church with some degree of frequency. The story of Samantha falls into that category.

Samantha lived in the community where the church was, but had never visited even though she had been told about some miracles happening at the church by some close family members for several years. Samantha was diagnosed with pancreatic cancer, an extremely deadly, fast-moving cancer, which is a death sentence almost always. Not only is this cancer commonly a death sentence, but it is frequently a very, very fast death sentence.

When Samantha was diagnosed with cancer, she was only given a few days or weeks to live at most. Samantha first attended the church, relatively shortly after being diagnosed. This first time that Sam attended the church, she was not very interactive. She seemed a little skittish and standoffish. She attended a few services before coming to the front for prayer. Between the first time she attended and when she came back to receive prayer from the church, she requested that I meet with her and her husband at her home.

This home visit was a little different, but not nearly as different as a phone call that would come a couple years later. At this visit, maybe a week or two after she first attended the church, she wanted to meet with me personally to discuss some things about church and who I was. She did not say this at all, but she wanted to know if she could trust me and if I was sincere or was only sincerely after money, fame, fortune, power or something else that preachers are not supposed to have our sights set on.

After hearing her story, I was not at all offended or hurt by her suspicions. Sam had been out of church for several years, but still believed in God and trusted Jesus for her salvation. She took the time to tell me what had led her and most of her family away from the organized Church. Years earlier, her family was very involved in a large church in Michigan where they lived. While attending the church, a member of the pastoral staff had been involved in betraying the trust of God, the Church, the world and Sam's family when this associate pastor had stolen the innocence of one of Sam's sons. Through a series of manipulations and lies, the associate pastor had eventually been caught preying on the young boy. The scandal eventually made the news, the pastor went to jail for a considerable time and Sam's family had never been the same. Because of this gross abuse of power, perverse unchecked lust of the flesh and the lies and deception of the "minister," Sam and her family were, unfortunately, very understandably leery of churches. So, she wanted to share this with me and explain that she just did not want to be hurt again by a church or minister and some of her family had vowed never to attend a church again. That day, I did not pray for her healing from the cancer, but I prayed for healing from all the hurt.

At Sam's house that day, eventually, the conversation turned to what she was praying for specifically. Sam's son was about to graduate with his master's degree from Auburn University. She just wanted to be alive to see him compete this life milestone. She said that God had been good to her. She was happy with the life she had been given and that if she could just see Billy walk across the stage, then she would be more than happy.

In another week or so, the day came that Sam came to church and then to the front of the church for prayer. She did not want a big deal made over her. Samantha and some of her extended family came to the front for prayer with her. This was a Sunday morning service and we had a similar prayer time as mentioned in some of the other miracles. Once again, there was a certain level of faith that seemed to reside with much of this group for this season and faith rose in the atmosphere. A group of several people helped me pray for Sam and we asked God to perform a miracle. I explained that she had pancreatic cancer, had been given no hope to live for any length of time and that she needed a massive miracle. We then collectively prayed. We believed by faith that God would do something supernatural on this day.

A week passed and Sam was still alive. Two weeks, three weeks passed and she was still with us. Finally, her son Bill, walked across that stage and she was there to cheer him on. During the next month she would show up at church on and off. A few months passed and she was still alive and she would come to church and see us again. Finally, six months turned to a year, Samantha was still alive. She would come to church sporadically and we were glad to see her. Soon, to be honest, she was not very high on my radar screen and I would think about her occasionally as a good shepherd thinks about his sheep.

One day I got a call from Samantha. She wanted to know if I could set a time to talk to her in-depth about her medical situation and pray with her again. I set a time for an afternoon, later that week. As I thought about it, I realized in pancreatic cancer terms, it had been a really long time since we had first prayed for her. The appointment time came, and I made the call.

When she picked up the phone, she was as friendly as she had ever been, she was probably twenty years my senior or better. She had a motherly vibe about her. I was not sure what Sam would tell me or exactly how she would ask me to pray on this day. When I heard what she would say that day, I was very surprised, if not a little shocked. While I imagine a discussion or request like this is made probably several times a day somewhere with some people in the world every day, I had never heard such a request personally, before or since.

Sam explained that she believed that the Lord had worked a miracle or some level of a miracle for her back when she first received prayer at the church. She knew that God had touched her that day and had no doubt He had sustained her. She mentioned that my story about Andrew's healing (which I share frequently with people before I pray with those needing a medical miracle) had helped her faith and she was thankful for the churches' and my help.

Samantha explained that it had been right at two years since Bill had walked the stage and she was overjoyed when he received his masters. He was the first person in the family to do so. She said that was all she had hoped for and that God had miraculously given her that day and she was so thankful. Then she talked about her life since then. She said because of the cancer she could not eat. She had existed with a feeding tube for about two years. She explained that she was grateful that she was not in any pain and had not been in any pain for quite some time. She told me how not only had she generally had a good life, but the last two years had been a special gift and unless you think you are imminently dying, then you probably cannot fully appreciate life. She went into detail about how she had been so thankful for the way her relationship with the Lord had flourished during those two years. She had also grown closer to her husband and family. Except for the feeding tube, life had been very, very good. She explained that she was ready to see Jesus and that she wanted something to eat. Although God had sustained her life, He had not chosen to regrow the parts of her digestive system destroyed by the cancer. Sam explained that even if she could eat, she was ready to see Jesus anyway.

You have to understand when you read this, this woman was not suicidal or depressed sounding. As a matter of fact, she did not seem depressed at all. Rather the opposite, Sam was acting joyful, happy and in a good mood. She explained that she had months and months where she had considered life, eternity, family and so many important things.

Then she asked me if it was a sin to pray to die if you are a Christian. I had never been asked this question and I don't suppose I had ever thought about it either. I took a minute, and then I said that I didn't think it would be. I explained that, of course, taking our life or another's life is a sin, but I could not see biblically where praying for your life to end would be a sin. In fact, on the cross, Jesus prayed, "Father, into your hands, I commit my spirit" in Luke's account of the cross. Sam explained that she in no way was interested in suicide, believed in suicide or had any plans for suicide. I was very glad to hear this.

Samantha explained that she believed that God had touched her at church that day, and just as He had granted her an extension of life two years earlier, she was more than ready to go to heaven anytime now. She asked if I would pray with her that God would take her home in his time. It was very strange, but I prayed with her something like..."Lord, we ask that if it is your will, when you are ready you take Sam home to be with you."

She did not die while I was on the phone with her, nor was I planning on her to die at that time. As a matter of fact, I think that I was planning to possibly hear that God had healed her digestive system and she could miraculously eat again. We prayed, I hung up the phone, turned off my office light, locked the door and drove home to my family for the evening. A few hours after that phone call, I got a call from Sam's family members that Sam had peacefully died. The power of life AND death is in the tongue.

Some names of the persons healed and details in these accounts were changed for privacy, legal and other purposes. Some unimportant details which do not embellish the accounts in any way have been changed due the circumstances surrounding these accounts. These are not "fantasy" accounts, where it is only "based on a true story" and then greatly embellished. The meat of these stories are 100% true and the details changed are equally valid and very similar circumstances. The cancers and/or diseases/illnesses involved are the exact kinds reported. Some accounts have even slightly more spectacular details, but were left out as some could not be recollected perfectly by the author or in more than one case the individuals actually healed which were interviewed during this writing. To make sure no story was exaggerated, any possibly questionable details were left out.

Thoughts and Questions to Discuss:

1. What kind of healing do you need God to do for you?
2. What other kind of miracle are you needing from your Creator?
3. Can God heal a smoker of lung problems and possible cancer?
4. How do you think that works with reaping and sowing?
5. Can God override what we "deserve"?
6. When Jesus died on the cross and we put our faith in Him, do we get what we deserve or something else?
7. According to the Bible, why does God heal?
8. How much difference can a little hope make in a hopeless situation?
9. Do you know anyone who could use some hope today?

10. What truths from God's Word and your own life experience could you share with them?
11. Do you think it made a difference when Jack "swept" the devil out of his life and room?
12. Do you think an action of faith, like stepping into a cross designed of tape on cheap carpet, makes any difference in a sick person's life? Could stepping into a cross be similar to touching the hem of the master's garment?

CHAPTER 13

The Greatest Healing

As we consider praying for people in desperate medical situations, please do not think this book is in any way putting forth the idea that the spiritual is less important than the physical. In any desperate medical situation, we should be stressing the need for salvation. If someone dies, but they did not know Jesus, then this is the most important and serious situation there is. If someone lives, but they do not know Jesus and later dies without knowing Him, then their temporary healing was by no means what mattered. And remember, all physical healing in this life is temporary. It may be a few weeks or months temporary or it may be a few years or decades temporary, but we are all eventually going to die. When we die, where our soul spends all eternity, is FAR more important than whether we were healed of cancer, or some other illness. I try to never pray for anyone in desperate need of healing without first knowing if they have placed their trust in Jesus for salvation. I always stress that the condition of their soul is of much more value than the condition of the body.

Four or five years before I saw the opening scene of the movie, *The Apostle* with Robert Duvall (a great movie by the way), I lived it out in real life. On a bright and sun shiny day in Pensacola, Florida, I was a part of youth car wash at University Church of God, at the corner of Olive Road and Lawton Street. This was a place I knew very well. Olive Road separates two parts of a neighborhood called Ferry Pass, Pensacola, Florida. About a half a mile on the north side of the road was the house my parents owned that I grew up in until I was 18 years old. About a half a mile on the south side of the road was the house that my grandparents owned and I also grew up there much of my life, both of my parents worked, so I was dropped off at my grandparents very early in the morning and I would get on and off the school bus at my grandparents. I also lived with my grandparents in the summertime while my parents were at work until I was about thirteen years old. This church building was literally in the center of my physical and spiritual life. Years earlier, my great uncle had built much of this building. My grandmother and parents had attended for many years. I had been taken there in my mother's womb, where her water broke during a Sunday evening service. I would be baptized in the baptistry. I had attended every Sunday School, Sunday morning, Sunday evening, Wednesday night, revival service and Vacation Bible School for years. I was dedicated to the Lord in this building, preached my first message in this building, taught Royal Rangers in that building, led the children's church puppet team and would marry the love of my life in this building. As bizarre as it seems, through complicated church denominational moves and politics, this building was vacated by the church I grew up in when I was a young teenager. Then the church moved back into this building when I was 17. Then the building was sold again by that church group. And now, three decades later, basically the same group of people bought the building back and have a church in it for the third time. This building on this corner was very important to me, but on this day, it wasn't at all about me.

The church building was on the corner of the most common route we would take between the two houses I grew up in which almost always happened twice a day, and often four or even six times a day. All that travel past this marvelous place and I had never seen one accident happen one that road. Olive Road was not a major highway artery of Pensacola,

Florida, but for a two-lane road, it is one of the most heavily traveled connecting Scenic Highway, Ninth Avenue, Davis Highway and Palafox which are all heavily traveled destinations in Pensacola. Even though Olive Road was and is busy with tens of thousands of cars daily, I had never once seen a traffic accident on this exact corner of Olive Road. On this summer day of either 1992 or 1993, that would change.

About six or seven teenage boys were washing cars with me on this Saturday. We were raising money to purchase puppets for the "Puppet Time" puppet ministry that we put on weekly in children's church. The "Puppet Time" ministry had become very important to us as we told Bible stories and led puppet songs at the church as well as traveled the Southeast to compete in puppet competitions and held Children's Services in the neighborhood and at other churches. The church was an excellent place to wash cars as there was enough traffic you just had a couple of teenagers hold up a car wash sign and people that had no connection to the church would stop and get their car washed at the rate of several an hour. We were right in the middle of washing a car when I heard the brakes of a car locking up just a few feet away. While accidents were common on Olive, just down the road a block or two, it just seemed like people almost always got out of each other's way in time at this particular intersection. On this day, that was not the case as a car t-boned another while one car was most likely traveling at around 50 miles per hour or possibly more. One car careened out of control and landed in a ditch just across from the church. Even though the road was very busy, in the early 1990s, the only other business on the corner was a pool chemical and cleaning store that usually had only one employee inside. The other houses on the corner were occupied by elderly people and they sat back off the road a ways, making it possible that they had not even heard or seen the crash. If someone was going to immediately assist these people, it would be me and the car wash boys.

I ran across the street to see if I could assist in some way. Before I went, I asked one of the more responsible teens with me to go in the church and call 911 as these were the days that only the rich or almost rich had cell phones. When I got to the car, it was very obvious these people were in extremely serious condition. The car was demolished from the side and the driver and passenger were pushed into the dashboard. The occupants of the car were a middle-aged woman and a teenage boy. Without going into extremely graphic detail, let me just say that the mother (I assume) was dead or close to death. The woman was unconscious. The young man on the other hand was seriously injured, but he was still conscious at this point. It was also clear that he would either need a creative miracle or he would probably die as well.

When I got to the car, I did not ask if they were OK, it was painfully obvious that they were not OK and they would not be OK without a massive miracle similar to the sun standing still or the parting of the Red Sea. If they were going to be OK in this life, either a mega miracle was about to happen, or they would be in some form of recovery or another for some weeks or months. The woman was unconscious, but the teenage boy was kind of slipping in and out of consciousness. I had no medical training except for a first aid badge in Royal Rangers and there was no one else there with any training either. The passenger side window was broken out so I spoke to the teenager in what was left of the passenger side of the car. I said something like this to the boy, "You are not in good shape, do you know Jesus? Do you know that if you die, you will go to heaven?" He kind of moaned through tears. I said, "Listen to me, pray with me. Lord Jesus, I believe you died for me on the cross. I believe you came back to life and I ask you to forgive me of my sins and to save me right now." The young man repeated most everything I said. I reassured him that whatever was about to happen to him, if he would continue to trust in Jesus he would be all right. I stayed with him for a couple more minutes until the emergency services arrived, it had not taken too long because the church is only about a mile from the hospital and even closer to the fire department. I prayed and prayed for them, and shortly thereafter, the fire department worked to free them.

If anyone reading this thinks that something more medical should have been attempted first, please note that when the emergency services teams arrived several minutes later, it took several minutes (possibly 15 or more) to use the jaws of life rescue machine to free the victims from the car. By that time, the boy was unconscious.

All these years later, I have no idea if the boy lived or died. If I had to guess, it is almost certain that the woman did not live. I never knew their names, or if either lived, I couldn't tell you if they physically recovered well or if they had lasting injuries that possibly cause them problems even to this day.

The temporary life must always take a back seat to the eternal life.

My point is this, I did not pray for the physical healing of these two on that day. It was not my first instinct to ask God to put body parts back together, to seal up internal bleeding or to stop long term disabilities. After I had prayed with the young man, I spent a minute asking God to help them both live. Whatever I prayed about their physical healing though, here is what I am positive of almost 30 years later…I was not primarily concerned then and I am not primarily concerned now for their physical healing or your physical healing.

Physical healing is always secondary to spiritual healing. The temporary life must always take a back seat to the eternal life. The main thing in desperate medical situations…salvation.

The boy from that story is real, the wreck really happened, it was very similar to what I have written here…since I did not know him personally, I imagine that some of the details are not exact, but this account is accurate and true to the best of my knowledge. I am unclear on what color the car was, what time of day it was, who all exactly was at the car wash and even what year it was 1992 or 1993?- What I am not unclear about is, that if that young man died that day, the greatest miracle of all took place. He was saved from his sins. I am a matter of fact kind of guy, so as sorry as it was, I am telling the truth when I tell you I couldn't tell what his name was because I had not taken the time to ask. I do not know exactly how old he was, I do not know what his goals in life were, I am not certain if the woman probably his mother was his mother or not…I know, that before we die, we need Jesus. I know, that we will all die.

Some might hear a true story like that and think, if he died, that is so terrible to die at a young age, but it is better to die with Jesus at a young age than it is to live to 100 years old and die without Him. The greatest healing of all is when a soul is saved. If we are healed physically often, but we are never healed spiritually once, then we have gained nothing in the long run.

In some ways, knowing we are about to die is also a gift. Regardless of if someone has cancer or some debilitating disease for years or if we are injured in a way we have minutes or hours of consciousness before we die, it is a gift to have time to prepare to die. We are not promised the next moment, and many people die instantly and totally unexpectedly. When this happens, there is not time to repent of our sins and give our lives to Jesus. We are wise to always walk in a relationship with God, not just so we will be ready to meet Him, but it is a bonus we will be ready to meet Him.

When we have a real relationship with Jesus, we will:

- walk in peace and joy because we have been forgiven (Romans 8:1-3)
- know a deep sense of purpose (Psalms 57:2)
- gradually be changed to the image of Christ (2 Corinthians 3:18)
- grow in all of the fruit and gifts of the Spirit (Galatians 5 and 1 Corinthians 12)
- know that we are never alone (Hebrews 13:5)

AND

- know we have eternal life in Christ (John 3:16)

When we love and serve God, yes, we have this great assurance of salvation, but that is not the only reason we follow Jesus, it is just one of the many wonderful reasons.

Make sure if you are praying for people needing a miracle or if you need a miracle yourself that things are right with Jesus first. If things are right with God, then when we die, we will go to heaven, and in heaven, there are no physical problems. In heaven, everybody is whole. There is no cancer, sickness, disease, deformity, sadness, tears or problem of any kind. When someone is spiritually healed, then we can know that the greatest miracle of all has occurred, and in time all problems will be resolved. Make sure that things are right with Jesus before you spend too much time being concerned with the earthly, physical problems of today.

The greatest healing of all is spiritual healing, which comes from a personal relationship with Jesus.

Thoughts and Questions to Discuss:

1. Are you ready to meet Jesus whether or not you receive physical healing in this life?
2. If you are praying with people in dire need of a miracle, have we asked if they are ready to meet their maker, if their life was to end?
3. Have we considered that every person on the planet, regardless of age or health level, may imminently meet the Lord since we are not promised tomorrow?

PART III

GOD SEES YOU COMPLETE

CHAPTER 14

Building Blocks, Patience *and* Trust

Note: If you have not read chapter 6 about "Bam-Bam," it would be best to read that healing account before getting into this chapter.

Even when Andrew was just a baby, he was very inquisitive, playful, and generally liked to "get into things." My mom, says that he was just being a lot like his dad. When I was a baby and a very small boy in the 1970s, I had taken apart things that ended in them breaking. As a toddler, I also was talented at putting food into various electronics. Andrew liked to get into stuff as well.

If you have never heard of "Duplo" blocks, that is understandable, but you have probably heard of their smaller brothers, "Lego" blocks. Duplos are like Legos for babies. According to Lego, they are designed for 18-month-old to five-year-old's. These blocks are larger, the pieces are easier to snap together and they are safer for small children. With Duplo blocks, you cannot make as detailed of structures as with Legos, but the concept is the same.

From when Andrew was just a baby, he liked playing with these and building things. Andrew was good with his hands and could design things.

He was very creative and seemed to build things easily. With time, Andrew grew out of Duplos, but as I am sure it pleased the Lego company greatly, he moved right into Lego. By the time Andrew was about six or seven years old, he was showing a lot of interest in Legos. In second grade, on more than one occasion, I picked up a little $5 set of a Lego truck or something simple for Andrew as a little bonus prize as I walked through a Walmart toy department just because I knew it would delight him, even if it was just for a few minutes. By age 9, he had a lot of Legos blocks and sets. He had built many cars, spaceships, Star Wars sets and other buildings. Some of these he built from his own imagination and some he built relatively complex sets. This love affair with building did not diminish with time, but over the next couple of years he continued to ask for Lego sets as the primary thing he would want and get for his birthdays and Christmas.

By the time he was 11, Andrew REALLY liked Legos. That year for Christmas, all he asked for was Lego sets from his parents and all his grandparents. The "Green Grocer" set was the primary gift he got from his parents that year. We were a little skeptical about buying him this set, because he was far too young for what the set was designed for age-wise. The Green Grocer had the advisory clearly marked on the box that it was designed for ages "16+." Basically, the Green Grocer was designed for what Lego people call AFOLs, A.dult F.ans O.f L.ego. With 2,352 pieces in the box, three instruction manuals required and included since it was a modular set (basically three sets combined into one) and several adults on the internet explaining that they took six to seven hours to complete. The people on the internet, though, explain that while it took six to seven hours to complete, that was with three teenagers or adults assembling the set. So, in man hours, that is 18-21 hours, if only one person was doing the work. People online explain that is takes a considerable amount of time just to find all the varying types of pieces, which most people say the set includes over 300 groups of pieces of same color and type. Due to its popularity, complexity and rarity since it has been retired for many years, when this chapter was written in May of 2020, a new, in box, with all the manuals in complete mint edition was selling for between $1,200 and $1,800 (possibly inflated due to the current coronavirus situation with the popularity of the "Lego Masters" television show, but those are the actual prices today none the less.)

Early on that Christmas day, little Andrew got his big present. It was very obvious which present that year was his favorite. As soon as we gave him permission to do so (others finished opening their presents) Andrew disappeared into his room with the "Green Grocer." Now Andrew had always been rather content to play with Transformers, watch a cartoon or build Legos by himself, but this year was different. For somewhere between the next 10 and 16 hours, we basically did not see Andrew. He would appear from his room to eat and use the restroom; besides that, he was hidden away...building, building, building.

Then finally, sometime late that night, Andrew victoriously emerged from his room. We were invited to see his masterpiece! It is almost a work of art.

For a full-blown adult or if you want to call a 17 or 18-year-old a child, it would be no big deal to see them complete a model kit without stopping, being totally engrossed in the process and finishing it, but to see a kid do this is another thing. Andrew, though, he loved the process. From when he was just a baby, he liked building and tinkering with things like that and as he grew, he enjoyed it more and more.

The finished project is pretty neat. I have even recently watched the Lego Master television show where adults from all over the country compete to build absolutely incredible models that completely dwarf the Green Grocer. For Andrew and for the adults on the Lego Masters show they were in hog heaven, but if you put me in a room with a box of 2,353 Legos and intricately detailed instructions of how you put together all those little pieces to build a three-story corner, city, grocery store, I feel certain I could complete the task, but I would want to pull my hair out!

When I was a kid, my grandmother would often put together jigsaw puzzles and other friends would do the same. Some people love to buy the most complicated puzzles they can find with thousands of pieces and, with many of the same, difficult to tell apart colored pieces. I could often complete those puzzles, but it would be by shoving, pushing and forcing those last few stupid pieces into place! If they didn't fit, that was OK, I could make them fit!

Legos are the same way. You can put a complicated set together your own way, or you can use the instructions to complete the set, the proper way. You may sometimes be able to complete the kit using your ideas and avoiding the instructions, but your finished product will have a high likelihood of not looking like or operating like it was intended to by its creator.

Andrew had an uncanny ability from a young age to both assemble the kits and at the same time enjoy the process. In this way, he was a pretty patient kid. I could assemble the kits, I am sure I still can assemble a complicated kit like that, but I would not naturally enjoy the process. I am more of a big picture person; I would prefer the thing just be built for me. Interestingly enough, with Legos, perhaps 95-99% of the joy of the toy is assembling it. If you have a random box of blocks, you may build and reassemble them any way you want to form anything you want, deconstruct that and build something different time and time again. However, when you purchase a special model kit, whether it be the Green Grocer, the Millennial Falcon, a city airport or a firetruck, the kit is created with a design and an end in mind. With Legos, the joy is in the journey. Once you complete that initial build of a model set, 99% of the joy is finished. You can then show it off to friends, if you are really bored, you could disassemble it and rebuild it, but once it is complete the vast majority of the joy of Legos has been accomplished.

The Green Grocer has many specialized bricks that are just for that kit. You could use them for something else, but if your goal is to complete what the creator of the Green Grocer kit intended for you to build, then it would be unwise for you to use them in other ways. You can take the clear glass pieces that are designed to be the glass, storefront door of the grocery store and make a glass windshield for a Lego car you build, but it will not be its best and highest use for that piece as it will look best and fit perfectly into the story of the Green Grocer.

If a Lego piece is used improperly, not only will it not be its best and highest use, but it could actually become dangerous. Many young parents may think that Lego pieces are designed to be torture devices for young adults. If you are not familiar with this, then just consider when the six-year-old leaves Lego pieces in the hallway, it is nighttime, and in the dark you walk to the bathroom with no shoes on. When a barefoot unexpectedly encounters a Lego piece pointed in just the wrong direction at 3 a.m. in the dark, this can be a special kind of torture. It can also test the holiness level of a young preacher to see what interesting words will proceed from their mouth especially if the Lego manages to pierce the skin. While stepping on a Lego is hopefully more comical than serious, if a Lego piece is swallowed by a child, you could have a much more dangerous situation. If a baby got the wrong piece, in the wrong place of the body, this could cause a very serious situation requiring hospitalization, surgery or God forbid, even worse.

Just as Legos can be a chore or a joy depending on who is building them, their outlook on life and how much time they have on their hands, your life is like a gigantic Lego building set. When I walked into Andrew's bedroom a few minutes after he received his Christmas gift that year, all I could see was a happy kid and about one million little pieces of plastic on the floor. When he looked at the same pile of plastic pieces, he did not see a big pile of work, he saw the coolness of the completed Lego work of art. It's like the old story of two brick masons working on a medieval cathedral. These classic church structures of old were known to often take hundreds of years to complete. So, for the first several generations of cathedral construction workers, there was no possibility that they would ever see the completion of their work. The cathedral architect noticed that two stonemasons working on the same wall of the massive church had two entirely different attitudes, work ethics and productivity rates. He asked the first mason how he was doing at the job. His answer was dull, sad and depressed sounding as he murmured out slowly, "Fine, same as always, shaving the stone, mixing the mortar, building this stupid wall." The architect asked the other mason who answered excitedly, joyfully and with a smile and get enthusiasm, "Today, is an incredible day! I have the opportunity to build a marvelous Cathedral. What a privilege to build a work of art that will serve as the place where many will worship for generations! God will meet man here and this building will be the light of the entire city!"

In life, just like Lego pieces and a single solitary stone that goes into building a gigantically, beautiful church…each piece on its own is not that impressive, but as they come together, they begin to make something beautiful. Andrew did not see the chore before him of tediously putting together piece after piece after piece while straining his eyes looking at sometimes confusing instructions about how these pieces fit properly… Andrew saw the completed project of the Green Grocer. He knew this would mean he was smart enough and talented enough to put something together that you were supposed to be at least five or six years older to complete…it said it right there on the box! If he could do this task, surely, he would enjoy the fruit of his labor for years to come, and little would he be able to imagine that his dad might actually write a book about his accomplishment almost a decade later.

God's picture of you is a lot like the completion of a large, complex Lego set. Of course, our lives are many times more complicated. You can go on YouTube and look at adults who have Lego rooms that hold tens of thousands of dollars' worth of completed Lego sets, which are entire cities with multiple versions of the same sets of Green Grocers and other model kits in the "Creator" line of Legos. These entire towns of bricks are more similar to the masterpiece type of comparison that God desires to make of your life and mine.

Four Things We Can Learn From Legos:

1. **The joy is in the journey.**
2. **The pieces rarely make any sense by themselves.**
3. **The pieces must be assembled in the correct order.**
4. **For those who are patient, the masterpiece at the end will be worth it.**

1) The joy is in the journey. When the build is complete much of the work is done, but much of the joy is complete as well. When going through life, do your best to enjoy the wonderful people, places, events, highs and even the lows you are experiencing day to day. Take the time to laugh sometimes. Love and enjoy your children and grandchildren. Take a minute to not worry about the "bottom line" and instead stop and smell the roses. This life goes very, very quickly, so enjoy it as you live a life pleasing to the Lord. It is in the mundane, the day to day journey, that if we take the time to pause can turn into a life where we can experience growth, learn to love the Lord, Trust Jesus and be a blessing while we enjoy our family and others. Try not to rush life, it comes very, very fast anyway, you will be middle-aged, old and dead before you know it, so instead enjoy every day by making the most of it for the Kingdom of God. Live life to glorify the Lord, leave you with few regrets and bless others in a hurting world. Once the Lego Set is built, much of the enjoyment is complete and the pleasure of building it is finished.

> *A cheerful heart is good medicine, but a crushed spirit dries up the bones.*
>
> Proverbs 17:22 New International Version

> *This is what I have observed to be good: that it is appropriate for a person to eat, to drink and to find satisfaction in their toilsome labor under the sun during the few days of life God has given them—for this is their lot.*
>
> Ecclesiastes 5:18 New International Version

2) The pieces rarely make any sense by themselves. Just as you could look at a few pieces or even a few hundred of the pieces of the Green Grocer individually and you may never be able to guess what Lego set they belong to, the individual pieces, situations, days, weeks, years and messes of our lives also often make no sense without a greater sense of the big picture perspective that only God can see.

Many times, people go through incredible tragic heartache and pain that they would never choose to be a part of if it were up to them, but in time, those events somehow weave together to make a beautiful tapestry of their life. Some victims of sexual abuse (a terrible, in-excusable, injustice) become bitter, hate the people involved and are stunted in emotional, spiritual and mental growth for their whole lives. Some people who experience the untimely loss of a loved one, physically attend the funeral and watch them be buried at the graveyard, but mentally and metaphorically, they end their life with them when they choose not to grieve in a healthy way for a healthy amount of time, but they instead in effect stop their lives completely when the loved one dies. Some people walk through a job loss, divorce, financial disaster, or serious medical set back and cannot seem to move forward because they are stuck looking at this ugly, unappealing, and unwanted piece of their lives.

Other people, though, are blessed with the ability to look beyond the very real, very large, very hurtful and sometimes devastating life circumstance and injustice and move forward. They somehow find the resolve to trust Jesus, get counseling, put one foot in front of the other, find the grace to forgive people who wronged them horribly and find an inner peace that only comes from the infilling power of the Holy Spirit. When their life is dark and bitter on the inside, they move forward, trusting that this dark time will somehow pass, and they discover a loving God who mends the heartache to design a beautiful life from the ashes. They are then able not to be the victim, but to be the overcomer.

If we look only at what may be happening to us today or this week, and if what is happening is clearly negative, then we may very well get depressed or feel a sadness closing in on us. If we concentrate on how we feel emotionally in a crisis, then we can believe the lie that this is how it will always be. We have probably been through a hard time before, and if we will trust God, He will bring us through this difficult season as well.

When you look at that weird little Lego piece, it may be very unattractive by itself, it may be the door hinge, a strange oddly shaped element that connects a lamp to the wall or a tile on the floor, but when you see it all together, later as a whole, it will make sense, fit in and compliment the other pieces. Many of the beautiful pieces of the set would not fit, if it were not for the uglier, less prominent ones that make the structure of the model and tie it all together. In Legos, it takes the ugly pieces and the beautiful ones working together to make a three-story Green Grocer. In the 5,000-piece jigsaw puzzle, it takes 123 oddly shaped blues to complete the sky. In life, it takes the good and the bad, the stuff we welcome and the stuff we wish we could erase to complete the masterpiece of our lives. Don't just look at what may be an undesirable piece of the Lego set of your life today, but remember, in time, it will fit into the bigger picture.

> *And we know that in all things God works for the good of those who love him, who have been called according to his purpose.*
>
> ROMANS 8:28 NEW INTERNATIONAL VERSION

3) The pieces must be assembled in the correct order. The other thing about these pieces is that you cannot assemble the model in whatever order you want to, it must be completed in a timely manner. In a Lego set, you cannot just throw the outside portions of a building together and then build the framework later or it will all fall apart. In 1996 at the church where I was working as the youth pastor, we put on a youth play attended by several thousands of people from the community and other churches' youth groups. The centerpiece of the play's set was a pretty cool mountain that we built in our church's gym. It was almost forty feet tall, had several hidden passageways inside where the actors could pop out of like a life-sized puppet and the top of the mountain had a waterfall that flowed down it. On the outside, you simply saw what looked like rocks, which was some type of painted fabric on top of chicken wire, but on the inside, the entire mountain was a special kind of scaffolding that can be assembled in circular formations. You never saw the scaffolding in the performance, but it took a team of about ten people several days to build it. Once the scaffolding was assembled, then we built walkways, then we built a plastic sheeting system, pump and hoses to run the waterfall, then we covered it in chicken wire that was wired to the scaffolding and finally, we covered it in the painted fabric. You couldn't have just thrown on the painted fabric first, the structure required that the scaffolding be first, then the walkways, then the water, then the chicken wire, then the fabric. The order was essential. Much more recently, I totally rebuilt an older "cheese grater" Mac Pro computer, updating a decade-old machine to run modern software. Similarly, I could not update the operating system first…I had to first change the CPU, RAM, SSD drive and video card to support the modern operating system that goes on top of it all. Many things in life, you must do in the proper order. Similarly, work goes before success. Patience comes before wisdom. Suffering often comes before growth. Pain often precedes humility, and heartache sometimes is required before promotion. No matter how hard we try, we cannot build the decorative outer pieces of the model first, the tedious work of building the structure comes first.

But be sure that everything is done properly and in order.

1 Corinthians 14:40 New Living Translation

4) For those who are patient, the masterpiece at the end will be worth it. The look on little Andrew's face a decade ago when he completed his Lego project was worth a thousand dollars. He was very proud of what he had accomplished and rightly so. He had completed a work project made for young adults, even though he was still a child. In life, if we will remain faithful and patient, God will complete His work in us. You can trust that God is working for your good. Even when life is difficult or really impossible to understand, He is still working for our good. Some things we may never understand in this life, but if we will continue to trust God, many things will come out in the eternal wash. In the light of eternity things that today seem like life stains that serve no purpose, will make much more sense on the other side. Some might say, "Well, I cannot wait till eternity to have these things explained to me!" But, if you will wait and trust God with a good attitude, then you will not regret it. Jesus is entirely good and entirely trustworthy; you can trust Him with your whole life.

I am a terrible artist when it comes to drawing, painting or anything involving creating visual art with my hands. I went to a Christian elementary school. In fourth grade, I signed up for art classes. I took about two months of art classes. The teacher (who got paid based on how many students she had because this was an elective, extra-curricular activity) after many weeks of lessons finally said, "Brian, you are a smart kid, you really are and I like you. You have a lot going for you and will be successful, but you should quit art right now. You simply cannot draw or paint and that is just the truth. You are wasting your time and your parent's money by taking these lessons." This was her response to my attempt at drawing and painting a bowl of fruit. I laugh at it today, and I know she was so right. Even then, I realized that while I was doing OK at several school subjects, I had a little talent singing, I was learning to play the piano a little bit and in several other ways I felt varying levels of confidence, art was NOT one of those areas. It was and is still amazing to me that people can look at and then draw a face that doesn't look like a stickman, or a dog. When I draw a dog, it looks like one of those sad, abused dogs on the Society for the Prevention of Cruelty to Animal commercials even though it was supposed to be a healthy, strong, majestic Golden Retriever. Fortunately, I am not drawing the picture of your life, but God is.

God is no amateur artist. He will not be getting kicked out of the art class by the truthful art teacher. The Great Father makes the art of Michelangelo's Ceiling of the Sistine Chapel's *Creation of Adam*, Handel's *Messiah*, Dali's *Persistence of Memory*, and Eric Weissberg's *Dueling Banjos* all look like my fourth-grade fruit art in comparison. God's handiwork and creativity make Steven Spielberg's movie collection look like home movies shot on a 1980's camcorder and The Vince Guaraldi Trio's *Linus and Lucy* soundtrack to the Charlie Brown Christmas Special sound like a novice piano player playing a detuned toy piano. God has the ability to create a true masterpiece out of our lives!

When we give our lives completely and totally over to God for His direction, care, leading and completion, He makes all things new. The Holy Spirit can take our selfishness and transform it to complete selflessness. He takes our worst habits, teaches us from them and grants us new disciplines to exalt Jesus and assist others. When we say, "Lord, it's not my life, it's all Yours!", at that moment, God begins to lay out a plan for us that is greater than we can imagine ourselves.

While His plan probably will not make us famous or fabulously wealthy, God will make us a blessing to others, an answer to someone's prayers and more truly significant than we could arrange if we tried with all our might. God takes broken pieces and molds them together to create a beautiful end product.

The "Knife Angel" or the United Kingdom's National Monument Against Violence and Aggression was unveiled in 2018. It is a 27-foot-tall angel statue that is made out of 100,000 knives. Many or most of these knives were used in violent crimes, attacks, street gangs and other crimes as England's stabbing incidents reached epic proportions. They were collected at many anonymous sites throughout the country with the promise that if someone dropped off a knife in a bin, there would be no questions asked. Many of the knives that were used to make the sculpture still had human blood on them before they were sanitized, blunted and welded together to create the sculpture. Taking over two years to complete, the statue now serves as a monument to the families of those whose lives were taken by stabbing and a teaching tool for children and adults alike.

Just as the instruments of violence can be used to make something unique and somewhat beautiful, God can take all the terrible things in your life (and some people reading this book have truly, unfortunately, experienced terribly violent and despicable events) and if you give them to Him, forgive those who sinned against you and trust God with the results, He can and will make your life into something wonderful that praises Him and heals others.

Stolen innocence, crushed dreams, lost fortunes, broken promises, missing children, hurtful words, and misplaced trust...can all be redeemed by the Master. Today is a great day to move forward with the best, rest of your life. A 2,353 Green Grocer does not come together in minutes. An entire Lego City Work of Art assembled by Adult Fans of Legos takes years. Most lives that God builds into something beautiful will result from decades of leaning in closer and closer to the Master as He whittles away at all the pieces of you that need to be removed to reveal His Glory in your life that is now dedicated to Him.

> *And I am certain that God, who began the good work within you, will continue his work until it is finally finished on the day when Christ Jesus returns.*
>
> Philippians 1:6 New Living Translation

Thoughts and Questions to Discuss:

1. Have you ever completed a large, life project or milestone and realized that you could have or should have spent more time enjoying the days of the process?
2. Proverbs 17:22 encourages us to have what kind of heart?
3. Has there ever been a time when you could not make any sense of what was happening but later, you were able to clearly see a sense of purpose in the process?
4. Does the Bible say that all things work together for good for everyone in Romans 8:28?

5. In Romans 8:28, what are the two pre-requisites for the Lord to make everything work out for good?
6. Have you ever had problems because you were trying to do things in the wrong order?
7. Do you have a story to tell about God working out difficult situations in your life that He eventually turned into something wonderful?
8. Do you know of any Christian who has experienced great hardship, but whose faith did not waver in the circumstance and they inspired you through their story?
9. Can we trust God with difficult situations?

Andrew Farley, healed at age 20.

CHAPTER 15

If An Angel Appears To You

IF AN ANGEL APPEARS TO YOU...

Remember that question at the front of the book? Remember, if an angel or some other powerful celestial being appeared to you and they had the power to give your child cancer or not. They explained that the doctors could do little to prolong the child's life, almost all other children with this cancer were dead in a matter of six months or less.

Now, an angel or some other powerful celestial being DID NOT appear. Remember, we said that this question and the question review now, were not and are not intended to teach theology about angels or demons... that would take another whole book. Instead, the idea is to get us thinking about, God's Picture of Us.

If you or an angel would have appeared twenty years ago and asked me, if I had the choice, to allow my precious, baby son to contract an "incurable" cancer and all I had to do was to say no, then in about 1/10th of a second, I would have screamed, "Absolutely NOT!" This is what any sane parent would do. Our love for our children makes it incomprehensible to make any other choice. At the same time, God does not see things the way we see things. God sees the end from the beginning. When a corona virus shuts down the world, when cancer comes, when a loved one is taken from us and when just the opposite, incredibly happy things happen- when we receive a promotion, when our children come to the saving knowledge of our Lord Jesus Christ, when we unexpectedly have everything go right for six months in a row, none of it will ever take God by surprise. He sees the end from the beginning. His plan for us is so much greater than the individual pieces of our lives that we see currently.

When our son was diagnosed with cancer, we had no idea why he had this come on him. Immediately, the devil went into overdrive and reminded me of seemingly every sin I had ever committed, all at the same time! Surely, it was my sin that caused this cancer that would take my son's life, I heard whispered in my ear. Then I was literally almost surprised to hear myself tell the doctor that, "The Lord is going to heal my son!" To this day, I do not know all the reasons that my son had cancer, but I know that at that moment, we could not possibly comprehend what was going on!

If an angel had said, "Do you want him to have cancer or not?" Immediately, we would have screamed something like, get behind us, Satan! We would have probably known that there was almost no way that God could use one of the world's rarest cancers for His glory. Cancer seems to be Satan's tool and it is almost unthinkable that God could use cancer for His purposes. Now, don't hear me wrong, I'm not saying that cancer was God's will, God's creation or His judgment, unlike some preachers, I don't claim to have all those answers. I do KNOW that God is good, He is entirely trustworthy (with your whole life) and He can and does do what He wants for His purposes. At the same time, I know that because He is good, he does not create evil and evil is not in His nature. Evil comes from the evil one, the state of a fallen-sin filled world that we are a part of and often, our sinful, human hearts themselves.

Now that we have established that God is entirely good and He sits apart from evil, look again with me at this situation in our lives. We would never have voluntarily accepted cancer for our son, but we also could never have understood how God can transform even the bleakest of situations for His glory. The Lord did more with that cancer than simply heal it or make it go away. He did more than increase my faith. He taught us invaluable lessons that could only be learned from a personal, miraculous experience watching the Great Physician do a work in our son's life. The Lord did not simply teach us He could literally, physically heal our son even today... He also taught us to trust Him. Later, in the story when "something" appeared on the scans of Andrew's lungs two and three years after the initial diagnosis, we learned that God can be trusted in those times as well. Still later, as God piece by piece and bit by bit, miraculously healed all the other conditions that the massive surgery and removal of so many vital parts of a baby's body where removed...God healed Andrew's kidneys, compensated for the missing adrenal gland, healed his endocrine system and regrew parts of kidneys and had no complications from so many other problematic medical conditions, we learned He does even more than we can ask, think or imagine.

> *Now to him who is able to do immeasurably more than all we ask or imagine, according to his power that is at work within us, to him be glory in the church and in Christ Jesus throughout all generations, for ever and ever! Amen.*
>
> EPHESIANS 3:20,21 NEW INTERNATIONAL VERSION

If the story ended there, that would be good, but it would just be a personal testimony. It would have been something among Brian Farley, Heather Farley, Andrew Farley, Aaron Farley (his older brother who watched it all take place), some grandparents and God. It would have been a neat story, and we would all have a stronger faith in God because of it, but God not only never wastes suffering, He takes the negative impact of suffering and turns it into something good.

When I was a kid, my grandmother used to often make bread pudding. Bread pudding is made from taking old, unused bread about to be rotten and cooking it into something good that tastes much better than the original bread ever did.

God took the cancer in Andrew's body and did not just cast the cancer out, he taught me something that would later bless thousands of people. From that true story of Andrew, we learned much of the content of this book. We learned (not just from the Bible [which trumps any personal experiences], not just from parents, grandparents or the Church, not just from Christian teaching, ordination or education) first hand that we are serving a miracle-working God! He is alive, well, GOOD, powerful, loving and can do anything. He still moves for His glory to draw all people to Himself as we lift up Jesus Christ. From this negative experience, God made something good, very good.

During the next few years, several people would come to the church in Cantonment, Florida and get radically healed of cancer. During the next decade, the story would be shared around the country and today, twenty years or more later, it reaches you today via the form of this book. The story would supercharge a young church that would see hundreds of people baptized, many healed and the Good News of Jesus Christ reach a whole community. Without the cancer, this pastor would not know first hand we serve an incredible, miracle-working, personal Savior. Without the cancer, it is hard to know if a church would have flourished and a larger ministry would have been birthed. While I never, ever would have chosen any suffering at all for my son, while I never ever would have chosen to see tubes running in and out of our little baby as he was tied down to his hospital bed for days on end, at the edge of life and death, I can see today, that God can take all that mess and make it into something good. Years later, Andrew sings and plays instruments with a strong voice. He has traveled the country singing the Lord's songs and has played instruments in churches to the glory of God.

If an angel would have appeared twenty years ago and asked the question...I know what my answer would have been, but I could never have known the whole story. Sometimes in this life, we never see the whole story, often God's plans are obscured from our view until eternity. Whether we can see what He is doing or not, whether we can comprehend it today, a year from now, the end of your lifetime or never in this life, we can trust. We can trust He is working it together for our good. If we love Him and remain the called according to His purposes.

> *And we know that in all things God works for the good of those who love him, who have been called according to his purpose.*
>
> ROMANS 8:28 NEW INTERNATIONAL VERSION

> *And we know that all things work together for good to them that love God, to them who are the called according to his purpose.*
>
> ROMANS 8:28. KING JAMES VERSION

> *And we know that God causes everything to work together for the good of those who love God and are called according to his purpose for them.*
>
> ROMANS 8:28 NEW LIVING TRANSLATION

Remember, whatever you are going through right now, if you trust God with it, if you love the Lord and if you are following God's calling in your life- fulfilling His purposes for you as best as you know how...He promises to make every situation work together for your good. This promise is not- everything will work out for good. It is often misquoted in such a manner or some similar wording, but it is a conditional promise that guarantees that if we are loving God and walking out His purposes in our lives, then everything will work together for our good. If we are living evil, wicked, self-serving lives (and truth is, we know if we are doing so) then there is no such promise, but if we are dedicated to the ways of the Lord, then we can take great solace in the fact that things will work out for our good.

The conditions of the promise are two-fold, only that 1) we love God and 2) that we are called according to His purpose. Fulfilling the promise is even more limited in scope. The promise fulfillment is focused to only one category of fulfillment- that it will work out for our good. It does NOT specify: when it will work out, how it will work out, who it will work through or even if we will see that fulfillment in our lifetime. The promise fulfillment is simply that it will work out for our good, but the promise is bigger than us. I am an only child, so my whole life when I am not closely listening to the Holy Spirit, I think possibly even more selfishly than the more common portion of the population with siblings. As an only child, I naturally think of people as objects to be used for my purposes! (I work against this tendency, lol!) After all, I had to entertain myself growing up, but amazingly, this promise is not just for me! This promise is not just for you either! When God makes this promise work out for the good of those that love the Lord and are called according to His purposes, He is speaking of the entire, greater Church of the Lord Jesus Christ. He will make all the stuff, junk, pain, heartache, goodness, emotional highs, valley lows and everything work out for the good of ALL that love God and are called according to His purposes. My life, your life and the life of the entire Church of God are woven together in a tapestry that will work out well for us and for the greater purposes of God in the whole earth and in His eternal framework of bringing His righteous plan to fulfillment. The things we are experiencing now, even if they are difficult, if we are cooperating with God- are being intertwined in the greater story of God's plan for our life.

Whatever you are going through right now take heart, that God will use it for His purposes, according to His will, to bring goodness to His Church. Don't give up. Don't give in. Don't go backwards. Keep moving upward and onward with Jesus. Trust the Lord in all that you say and do and watch what a beautiful tapestry of glory to the Lord your life will one day produce!

QUESTIONS

WHO ACTUALLY DOES THE HEALING?

Lest there be any confusion created by this book about healing- The Triune God of the Bible (God the Father, Son [Jesus Christ] and Holy Spirit) is the One God, who exists in three persons who both does the actually healing and provides the ability for the healing by Jesus' death on the cross. People do not spiritually heal. Angels do not spiritually heal. All supernatural healing power comes from the Kingdom of God or the kingdom of darkness. While spiritual forces heal, there are only two sources for spiritual healing, God or Satan. Any person who claims to have spiritual healing power besides the God of the Bible, if they are actually healing people, they are using the satanic powers regardless of what they may call their healings. All healings recorded in this book are ultimately due to the power, grace and mercy of Jesus. Brian Farley and the people involved in the stories and the church people involved are not special or sinless in any way. God uses our faith. God desires that we exercise faith, to ultimately build our faith in Him, but it is always God and God alone who ultimately does any Christian healing. It is always and only God and God alone who deserves any credit and praise for healing. Anyone who claims glory for themselves or angels concerning a Christian-based healing, is walking on dangerous ground and should not be listened to about healing or spiritual power as they are certain to mislead many people.

WHAT IF I DON'T GET HEALED?

Ultimately, in this life, there will come a time that all of us will "not be healed" physically. The aging and dying process is coming for all of us. When we die, if we know Jesus, we will all be healed. (See Chapter 13- The Greatest Healing). Biblically speaking, the only exception to not eventually physically dying a normal earthly death will be the rapture discussed in 1 Thessalonians 4:13-18. The rapture will be a worldwide, simultaneous event, so anyone claiming that they or a small group will be the only ones to experience the rapture are not teaching scripture. We will all die, no special revelation will stop us from dying and any teacher who says that they or their followers are teaching that they will not die is misleading people.

HOW CAN I PRAY, PRACTICALLY SPEAKING, FOR HEALING?

There is no special formula in praying for healing. Here are some thoughts that may assist, though. When praying, for healing or anything else, it is powerful to pray "In Jesus Name." Speaking of the power of the name of Jesus, the Bible says...

> *Wherefore God also hath highly exalted him, and given him a name which is above every name: That at the name of Jesus every knee should bow, of things in heaven, and things in earth, and things under the earth; And that every tongue should confess that Jesus Christ is Lord, to the glory of God the Father.*
>
> PHILIPPIANS 2:9-11 KING JAMES VERSION

According to the scriptures, the name of Jesus is ABOVE every other name. So, that name is above cancer, lupus, diabetes, every illness of every kind, every sickness and disease and every foul and evil spirit. At the name of Jesus blind eyes open, the deaf hear, and dead men come back to life.

So, when you pray actually, physically say, "In the name of Jesus, we ask for healing of..."

There is power released into the atmosphere when the name of Jesus is spoken audibly. When the name of Jesus is thought, there is also power, but when spoken audibly, things literally change in the atmosphere. Have you ever noticed that when the name of Jesus is spoken even quietly on a crowded train, bus or plane it seems like all the other noise around quiets down? Jesus can quickly clear a room. He is the greatest power in the universe, so great that even the whisper of His name brings immediate change.

When you pray, literally, speak, "***In the name of Jesus.***" Another thing I do that I encourage others to do in prayer is "Pleading the Blood of Jesus." Here is just a very small sample about what the Bible says about the Blood of Jesus...

> *Having predestinated us unto the adoption of children by Jesus Christ to himself, according to the good pleasure of his will, To the praise of the glory of his grace, wherein he hath made us accepted in the beloved. In whom we have redemption through his blood, the forgiveness of sins, according to the riches of his grace;*
>
> EPHESIANS 1:5-7 KING JAMES VERSION

The Word tells us you can "overcome" by the Blood of the Lamb (Jesus)...

> *And they overcame him by the blood of the Lamb, and by the word of their testimony; and they loved not their lives unto the death.*
>
> REVELATION 12:11 KING JAMES VERSION

And Jesus said in His own words as He instituted communion that His blood was the New Covenant, which remits sins (remission means cancellation of debt). In other words, His Blood removes the debt caused by sin...

> *For this is my blood of the new testament, which is shed for many for the remission of sins.*
>
> MATTHEW 26:28 KING JAMES VERSION

When we "***plead the Blood***" of Jesus, it is similar to how one can "plead the fifth amendment" in an American court of law. To plead the fifth means, we are appealing to our right to not self-incriminate ourselves. To plead the Blood means we stand on our legal spiritual right for salvation and healing based on the Blood of Jesus.

So if you are trusting Jesus for your salvation and healing, you can say out loud about whatever sickness you may be praying for that you "Plead the Blood of Jesus over..." and then insert the situation, person or name of the illness there. Jesus' blood is more powerful than any force we may face in the universe.

Also, practically speaking about praying for healing, ***pray specifically***. For example, instead of saying, "Lord, please heal this body." You may find it helpful to pray, "Lord, we are asking you to reach in my body, touch the back nerve that is hurting, regrow it properly and cause anything around it that is growing improperly to cease. We ask that you totally heal this area of the body and perform a life-giving miracle." Or maybe the prayer concerning cancer sounds something like this, "Jesus, please reach inside, curse this cancer and every cell that is growing improperly, and reprogram the DNA to regrow this area properly and quickly. Heal anything that has been damaged, restore anything that needs restoration."

While praying, we will find it beneficial to ***quote healing scriptures*** scriptures as well. *(For partial list see Chapter 10 at the end of the section "Garbage In/Garbage Out")* We can stand on the promises of God about healing found in His Word. Like the name of Jesus, when we say the Words of God (scriptures) out loud, there is a profound effect on the environment and physical bodies we are praying for.

This may sound very specific, and it may not be the best way to pray, but it is how I pray often. I believe it is better to pray specifically than generically. Also, as we pray for healing, keep our eyes, minds and mouths on healing- see chapters 10 and 11.

Is it wrong to use medical treatments and seek the advice and help of physicians?

It is absolutely not wrong to use modern medical treatments and seek the advice of physicians. Medicine and physicians are a gift from God. We should first pray and ask God to heal us, but it is unwise to shun medical treatments, medications and the assistance of physicians when we need healing. Like anything else, otherwise, good medical drugs can be misused and cause damage to our health (the abuse of prescription pain killers), but we should not be opposed to medical assistance and medicines. There is no scriptural mandate for shunning medical help or medications.

What of those who have tragically and unexpectedly lost loved ones?

I hope it has been adequately stated in the book that those who have tragically lost a loved one to disease, illness, cancer, accidental death or whatever the case may be that there is certainly no judgment of the family members in these situations. We do not always understand why people die. We all wish this type of pain did not exist in the world. If one has lost a family member tragically and unexpectedly (especially the loss of a child), know that you are in the prayer of the author. It often takes time and effort for one to overcome such sad circumstances, but we mourn with you. We also know that we do not grieve like those who have no hope.

Brothers and sisters, we do not want you to be uninformed about those who sleep in death, so that you do not grieve like the rest of mankind, who have no hope.

1 Thessalonians 4:13 New International Version

We recognize that in the face of seemingly unsurmountable pain, there is always hope for those who know Jesus. This life is not all there is and one day, if they knew Christ, we will be reunited with those loved ones again, who will never experience pain, heartache, cancer, disease of any kind again and Jesus will eventually wipe away every tear from our eyes.

Don't give up, you are loved by God and if you have breath in your body, He is still painting your masterpiece.

WHAT TO DO IF THIS BOOK WAS A BLESSING TO YOU?

Please get in a good, Bible-believing church, spend time in prayer and Bible study every day, and believe for a miracle!

If you found the book helpful, it would be greatly appreciated if you would- tell someone, positively review it on Amazon or anywhere that you can review it online, share about it on social media, form a small group Bible study using the book at your church, share it with a friend, purchase a copy as a gift and tell someone about the book today. Thank you sooooo much for reading *God's Picture of You*! Remember, masterpieces take time to complete. -Brian

IS ANDREW'S STORY DOCUMENTED?

Andrew's story was documented by the Nemours Foundation. He was one of the main stories in the Nemours. "The People of Nemours: 2001 Annual Report" on pages 14 and 15. Inside the report he is called "Michael: Michael's Case Study, but "Michael's" parents are named "Brian and Heather". His name was changed due to the Health Insurance Portability and Accountability Act (HIPAA Law), but be assured- this is Andrew's true story. If you would like more information, the Nemours Foundation still exists and can be found on the web at www.nemours.org.

RESOURCES

CORRESPONDING VIDEOS FOR THE BOOK

There are matching videos to be used in small group studies. These videos can be found on Youtube.com. On Youtube.com search for "Encourage Church of NYC". Once you find the Encourage Church of NYC channel, search for "God's Picture of You". These videos contain bonus material connected to the book that you may enjoy personally even if you do not do a group study.

DOCUMENTATION FROM ANDREW'S TIME IN THE HOSPITAL

The following is a page from the 2001 Nemours Children's Clinic Annual Report of Andrew's documented story. Just as some people's names had to be changed in some of the true accounts of healing in this book, Andrew's name was changed by the hospital to "Michael." If you notice carefully under the large words, "Michael Case Study" there is a quote credited to "Heather and Brian, Michael's Parents"- our first names were not changed.

Special Note: The pictures in this book were not taken with a Polaroid Instant Camera, and they took some time to develop. Andrew's middle name is "Micah" which means, "Who is like Jehovah?". Before he was born, he was named prophetically. Jehovah God showed Himself to be more powerful than a rare cancer.

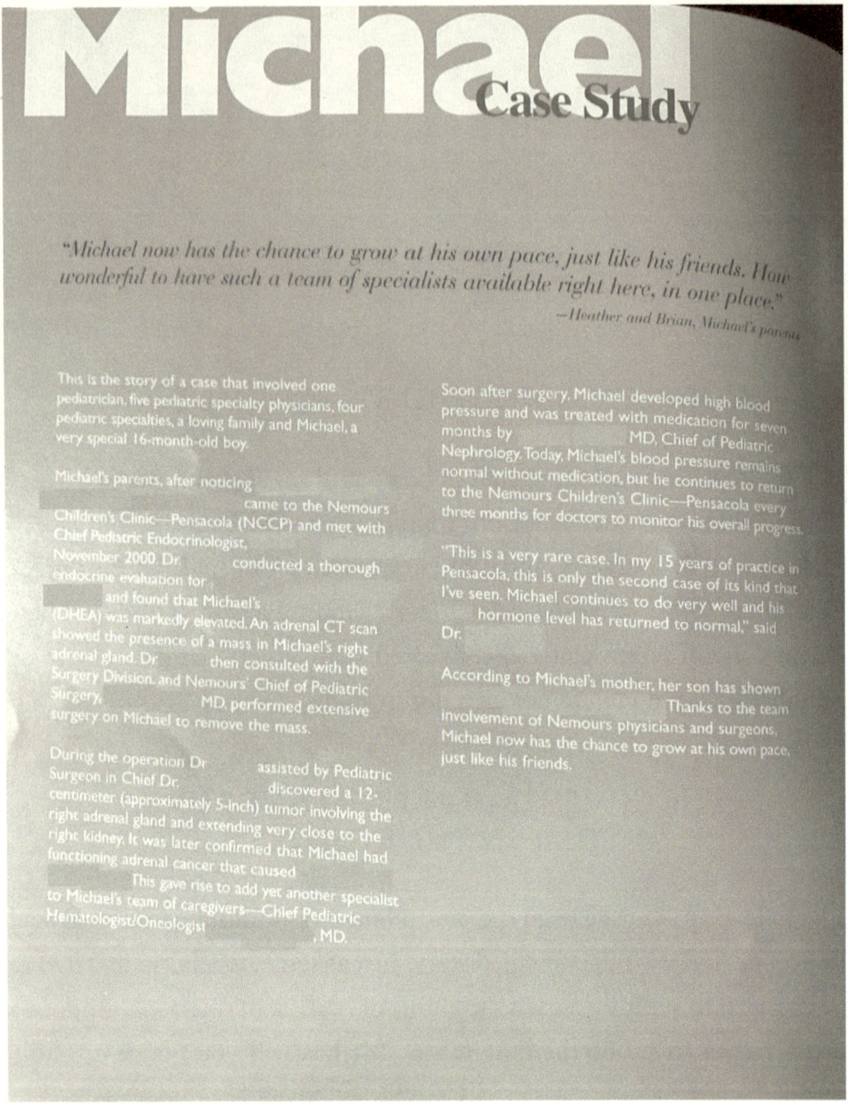

Michael

Case Study

"Michael now has the chance to grow at his own pace, just like his friends. How wonderful to have such a team of specialists available right here, in one place."

—Heather and Brian, Michael's parents

This is the story of a case that involved one pediatrician, five pediatric specialty physicians, four pediatric specialties, a loving family and Michael, a very special 16-month-old boy.

Michael's parents, after noticing came to the Nemours Children's Clinic—Pensacola (NCCP) and met with Chief Pediatric Endocrinologist, November 2000. Dr. conducted a thorough endocrine evaluation for and found that Michael's (DHEA) was markedly elevated. An adrenal CT scan showed the presence of a mass in Michael's right adrenal gland. Dr then consulted with the Surgery Division. and Nemours' Chief of Pediatric Surgery, MD, performed extensive surgery on Michael to remove the mass.

During the operation Dr assisted by Pediatric Surgeon in Chief Dr. discovered a 12-centimeter (approximately 5-inch) tumor involving the right adrenal gland and extending very close to the right kidney. It was later confirmed that Michael had functioning adrenal cancer that caused This gave rise to add yet another specialist to Michael's team of caregivers—Chief Pediatric Hematologist/Oncologist , MD.

Soon after surgery, Michael developed high blood pressure and was treated with medication for seven months by MD, Chief of Pediatric Nephrology. Today, Michael's blood pressure remains normal without medication, but he continues to return to the Nemours Children's Clinic—Pensacola every three months for doctors to monitor his overall progress.

"This is a very rare case. In my 15 years of practice in Pensacola, this is only the second case of its kind that I've seen. Michael continues to do very well and his hormone level has returned to normal," said Dr.

According to Michael's mother, her son has shown Thanks to the team involvement of Nemours physicians and surgeons, Michael now has the chance to grow at his own pace, just like his friends.

Andrew's Case Study in the report. Because of privacy laws, Andrew's name was changed to Michael. Some information was redacted due to privacy.

Other books by Dr. Brian D. and Heather Farley that you may like are available on amazon.com...

Church Planting in the 2020s: Starting Churches in a Rapidly Changing Culture by Dr. Brian D. Farley. -a contemporary study of and practical methods of church planting today

Why Weight? Change Now! *by Heather Farley* -Heather shares secrets of her 100+ pound weight loss and her journey of becoming a certified personal trainer

Al Argo's Latest Book A dear friend, Pastor Al Argo, has written several great books. Have you ever wondered what it would be like to survive a skydiving accident? In his latest book, ***Blessed Beyond Stress,*** he deals with overcoming adversity, reducing stress and living a resilient life. Al is a powerful man of God, leader of leaders and inspirational speaker. In his new book, he reveals a life long personal struggle with visual impairment that he has kept secret for many years. In ***Blessed Beyond Stress***, Pastor Al Argo reveals how stress is not the enemy, but it is how we react to stress that is important. If you enjoy a good read that will encourage you, challenge you, stretch you and possibly change your life, check out ***Blessed Beyond Stress*** by ***Al Argo*** today on amazon.com. You will not be disappointed with this book. (***Blessed Beyond Stress*** launches in late 2020 or early 2021.)

Booking for Healing Services/ Speaking Engagements:

Please send requests and correspondence to life@encourage.church or Brian@NYCJesus.com and someone will get back with you as soon as possible.

www.ingramcontent.com/pod-product-compliance
Lightning Source LLC
LaVergne TN
LVHW091040080826
845145LV00002B/564

* 9 7 8 1 9 5 0 9 4 8 5 2 9 *